3

Wittgenstein was I think wrong when he said that about that which we do not know, we should not speak. He closed by fiat a great amusement park, there.
—Donald Barthelme

For the only way we can speak of nothing is to speak of it as though it were something. . . .
—Samuel Beckett

Personally, I like words to sound wrong.
—Wallace Stevens

The Comedy of Language

Studies in Modern Comic Literature

Fred Miller Robinson

The University of Massachusetts Press

Amherst, 1980

Acknowledgment is made to the following publishers for permission to reprint selections from copyrighted material:

From the book *Comedy,* copyright © 1956 by Wylie Sypher, which contains "Laughter" by Henri Bergson. Reprinted by permission of Doubleday and Company, Inc.

From Henri Bergson, *An Introduction to Metaphysics,* translated by T. E. Hulme, copyright © 1949, 1955 by The Liberal Arts Press, Inc., and reprinted by permission of The Bobbs-Merrill Company, Inc.

From J. P. Lebel, *Buster Keaton,* translated by P. D. Stovin, reprinted by permission of The Tantivy Press, London.

From Samuel Beckett, *Watt, Stories and Texts for Nothing,* and *Three Novels* reprinted by permission of Grove Press, Inc.

From James Joyce, *Ulysses* (published by Modern Library, copyright © 1942, 1946 by Nora Joseph Joyce); from Wallace Stevens, *The Collected Poems of Wallace Stevens* (published by Alfred A. Knopf, copyright © 1954 by Wallace Stevens) and *Opus Posthumous,* edited by Samuel French Morse (published by Alfred A. Knopf, copyright © 1957 by Elsie Stevens and Holly Stevens); and from William Faulkner, *As I Lay Dying* (published by Vintage, copyright © 1957 by William Faulkner), reprinted by permission of Alfred A. Knopf, Inc.

To my mother,
Florence Carmon Robinson

Contents

Preface

My intention in writing this book is to make a contribution both to the theory of comedy and to a specific practice of it in the twentieth century. My subject is the comedy engendered by the contradictions between the nature of reality and the nature of language, the subject and the medium of the comic writer. The twentieth century did not invent these contradictions, and it is possible that earlier comedies—for example, *As You Like It* or *Don Quixote* or *Le Bourgeois Gentilhomme* or *Tristram Shandy*—can be profitably analyzed as comedies of language. It is my opinion that they can be, although that is the subject of another study. Certainly the twentieth century is the century *obsessed* by these contradictions. As I will argue in my first chapter, it is a century peculiarly concerned with (1) reality as metaphysical flux, and (2) language as a symbol-making process. Because of these deep and pervasive concerns, the comedy of language can be said to be a period style of modern comic literature, if not of modern literature in general.

There are many kinds of twentieth-century comedy not touched on in this book. This study is not meant to be a comprehensive review, a compendium, a display of range and variety. My argument is that comedies of language are our *essential* texts in the study of modern comedy. They are major texts by some of our greatest writers. They have the range and complexity to touch on our most profound and representatively modern problems. *The Comedy of Language,* then, is a study, or a series of studies, in depth. I am assuming that detailed analyses of major works will have their own peculiar resonance for readers, that the essential experience of this comedy will be illuminated in ways that a more summary treatment could not provide.

I have another reason for the length of my analyses. I wish to demonstrate that a theory of comedy—as outlined in my first chapter—can produce a working method of close analysis. If a work is fundamentally comic, then a comic theory should illuminate it whole, provide us with a comprehensive understanding of its intimate workings, its life as a text. The works studied here have been analyzed at length by others, but not strictly as comedies—and this is precisely because the study of comedy is so often a method of categorization rather than analysis. I hope, in these chapters, to bridge the gap between comic theory and practice, and in the process to solve some of the difficulties these works have offered readers. My principal interest is not in literary history or genre distinctions, though I hope this book will make its natural contributions to these subjects. My principal interest is in the discovery of the comic in the heart of great modern works, in the tangle of their most fundamental ideas.

Of course I have not exhausted the field. I think that works like Faulkner's "Old Man," Stevens' "Notes Toward a Supreme Fiction," Beckett's Trilogy and *Waiting for Godot,* Chekhov's *The Cherry Orchard* and "The Duel," Kafka's *The Castle,* Nabokov's *Lolita* and *Pale Fire,* Cary's *The Horse's Mouth,* Pinter's *The Birthday Party,* Albee's *A Delicate Balance,* Barth's *The Floating Opera,* Bellow's *Henderson the Rain King,* Naipaul's *A House for Mr Biswas,* and Barthelme's short stories, to mention an idiosyncratic few, can be illuminated by the theory and method offered here.

The Comedy of Language

1. Introduction

So much of the energy and accomplishment of modern literature is realized in comedy that comedy can be said to constitute a period style. The most striking thing about the best of modern comic literature (James Joyce and after) is its discovery and display of the comic potential in the relationship between reality and language. The following passages, selected at random, are characteristic:

> Which example did he adduce to induce Stephen to deduce that originality, though producing its own reward, does not invariably conduce to success?[1]

> And the rattle, what about the rattle? Perhaps it is not de rigueur after all. To have vagitated and not to be bloody well able to rattle. How life dulls the power to protest to be sure. I wonder what my last words will be, written, the others do not endure, but vanish, into thin air. I shall never know. I shall not finish this inventory either, a little bird tells me so, the paraclete perhaps, psittaceously named.[2]

> Chieftan Iffucan of Azcan in caftan
> Of tan with henna hackles, halt![3]

> "My mother was a royal virgin," Peterson said, "and my father a shower of gold. My childhood was pastoral and energetic and rich in experience which developed my character. As a young man I was noble in reason, infinite in faculty, in form express and admirable, and in apprehension. . . ."[4]

Quine the Swine. Guilty of killing Quilty. Oh, my Lolita, I have only words to play with![5]

In all of these passages two major things happen: (1) the language is never transparent, but calls attention to itself, and (2) it calls attention to itself *comically*. This book is an investigation of the shape and resonance that the comedy confers on the subject of language. Why and how are these passages funny? This most difficult of questions is at once profound and immediate, because comedy is both a specific and affective strategy of style, and a vision of the world. To answer it we need to understand the mechanics of the comedy, and the reason for those mechanics.

There is, on the one hand, a body of comic theory that describes comedy as a genre of vision, and because of its generalizing tendency it loses a *sense* of the comic. For example, we might suppose, reading Northrop Frye, that the fifth-act reconciliations in Shakespeare's comedies are the most comic scenes. There is, on the other hand, a body of work on what specifically occurs when something strikes us as comical; and this work characteristically suffers from a failure to discover any vision in comedy, from an assumption that comedy is merely a series of isolated effects. Precisely because modern comic literature is obsessively concerned with language as both medium and subject, a study of it gives us the opportunity to bridge the gap between the general and the specific. Such a study allows us to analyze how a comic style shapes a comic conception. The authors quoted above are not simply playing with words, they are deeply interested in the nature of the act of playing with words. And so they bring into high relief what occurs in all significant comic works but is so seldom studied: the continuous interaction of comic effects and comic ideas.

In the passages quoted above, the comic effects have little or nothing to do with characters in a social context, and everything to do with how we, as individuals, create our sense of the world through language. By punning on paraclete/parakeet, Samuel Beckett's Malone reduces the Holy Spirit to a chatterbox, a voice interceding not with aid and comfort but with words squawked from memory. So the passage is a burlesque of the highest order, its comedy deriving from the jarring association of a Spirit that bears the Word of God and a domesticated bird filled with words it does not comprehend. The parakeet is an image for Beckett of ourselves, or the spirit within us that recites to us our banal *pensum* of language. Wallace Stevens' Chieftain is a character virtually created out of words, someone inflated with his self-created world. So he is described in words that verge on opacity, in an almost pure effusion of sound. The comedy derives from the clash between our experience of Stevens' language (as a linguistic game, like nonsense) and our customary experience of language, as something more or less transparent, as an evocation of a reality rather the stuff of its own reality. Without the clash there would be no comedy; we would merely find Stevens' lines aesthetically pleasing. In the fourth passage, from Donald Bartheleme, the comedy derives from our double sense that Peterson is lying (in using the borrowed language of myth) and yet telling truly how he feels about himself. Like Gayev's absurd little speech in praise of his bookcase in *The Cherry Orchard*, Peterson's speech is both comically rhetorical and emotionally true. It brings us to a sense of the complex relationship between what we mean to say and how we say it.

Clearly, in each of these representatively modern passages, the comedy does not reflect on the characters in relation to their societies. Although in Barthelme's story, there is an important and immediate social context—the deadly television program, with its audience lusting for the humiliation of the contestants—against which Peterson's speech becomes emotionally clear, even so the comic effect yields a comic idea that transcends the social, and describes the necessity of our self-created orders in the face of their absurdity. Peterson's speech could, without risking its essential comedy, take place outside the society that Barthelme satirically sketches, could occur in a story in which Peterson, like Malone, is the sole character making an inventory of himself.

We need to enlarge present comic theory to understand modern comedy. Most theory assumes or concludes that comedy depicts people as social animals, that the comic is only present when characters are depicted in their dealings with one another. This is no doubt due to the fact that most comic theory is based on, or circumscribed by, comic drama —and drama is almost always, by its nature, concerned with the relations between people. Generic theories of comedy can be descriptive, but they should not be considered all-inclusive. It is our generic predisposition in regard to comedy that has for so long prevented us from analyzing —indeed, appreciating—the comedy of *Don Quixote* or of *The Cherry Orchard*, not to mention *Ulysses* or *The Castle* or *Waiting for Godot*, except as a passing and pleasurable and puzzling diversion.

In this chapter I have two interconnected objectives: (1) to describe the limitations of social theories of comedy and, working from this critique, (2) to develop a theory of comedy that transcends the social, and that I will call, for purposes of convenience, metaphysical. By "metaphysical" comedy I mean all comedy that has reference beyond the physical and the social, comedy that has epistemological, ontological, theological, or philosophical dimensions. Metaphysical comedy did not begin with, say, *Ulysses,* although it cannot be considered representative before *Ulysses.* It has simply been the case that the metaphysical implications of comedies have been ignored, or the metaphysics of the text has not been thought of as comic. This has been true of discussions of, for example, Shakespeare's comedies, *The Misanthrope, Don Quixote, Tristram Shandy,* and much of Chekhov. The implications of this "period" study for comedies in general, past and present, can unfortunately only be touched on; they require another book, with analyses of other texts.

2. Comic Theory: Social

It is appropriate to begin with a commentary on Henri Bergson because Bergson was a metaphysician who wrote what remains the best and most influential social theory of comedy. In *Laughter* (1900), Bergson confined himself, as Wylie Sypher points out, "within the narrow range of the comedy of manners,"[6] yet he needn't have done so had he realized the implicit connection between his social theory and his own metaphysics.

One of Bergson's problems in this regard is indicated by his title. His commitment to laughter leads him to a view of comedy as social in nature (or vice versa) because, as he points out, the "natural environment" of laughter is society. And because society is its natural environment, laughter "must have a social signification."[7] Bergson asks, "What does laughter mean?" and proceeds to an analysis that draws heavily on comic drama. Yet what makes a play comic and what makes an audience laugh are two distinct areas of study. And the latter area is beset by problems of relativity. Some find a joke or a play funny and some don't. Even when amused, some laugh and some don't. When Freud says that "the hearer of the joke laughs with the quota of psychical energy which has become free through the lifting of the inhibitory cathexis,"[8] he seems to assume— perhaps he has to assume, for his purposes—that anyone who gets and appreciates a joke will laugh at it. That is to say, a physiological process can be argued from the logic with which the technique and purpose of jokes are analyzed. Perhaps neither Freud nor Bergson wished to bring up the problem of the relativity of laughter for fear he would become mired in it. Bergson's lucid analysis of the comic could have been written without reference to laughter; indeed, *what creates laughter* becomes, for him, simply another way of saying *what is comic.* Nevertheless, his title allows him to place his theory strictly within the realm of the social, and from this he then proposes a theory of "The Comic in General."

This theory can be summarized as follows: according to Bergson the comic occurs when "*something mechanical*" is "*encrusted on the living*" (84), and by "the living" he means the "living energy" that inheres in everything. This energy is adaptable to circumstance (a banana peel in one's way), it flows in creative and useful channels. But when a person, despite this energy within him, behaves mechanically, according to some more or less rigid pattern or attitude (his mind is absent, his head is in the clouds), then the comic occurs (he slips on the banana peel).

> The comic is that side of a person which reveals his likeness to a thing, that aspect of human events which, through its peculiar inelasticity, conveys the impression of pure mechanism, of automatism, of movement without life. Consequently it expresses an individual or collective imperfection which calls for an immediate corrective. This corrective is laughter, a social gesture that singles out and represses a special kind of absentmindedness in men and in events. (117)

Laughter, then, humiliates the abnormal or "mechanical" person in order to restore him to the fold of the normative. Bergson would agree with Baudelaire's familiar opinion that laughter is intellectual and not emotional. For Bergson laughter is accompanied by an "*absence of feeling*," its "appeal is to intelligence, pure and simple" (63–4).

Given his terms, Bergson needn't have concluded so; he *did* so conclude because of his assumptions. The idea that the comic occurs when the mechanical is encrusted on "the living pliableness of a human being" need not be confined to the realm of the social. It has a metaphysical dimension that Bergson did not explore. His concept of "the living" is closely related to his metaphysical concept of the *élan vital,* which he elaborated in later works. Early in *Laughter* he stated,

> . . . whatever be the doctrine to which our reason assents, our imagination has a very clear-cut philosophy of its own: in every human form it sees the effort of a soul which is shaping matter, a soul which is infinitely supple and perpetually in motion, subject to no law of gravitation, for it is not the earth that attracts it. This soul imparts a portion of its winged lightness to the body it animates: the immateriality which thus passes into matter is what is called gracefulness. Matter, however, is obstinate and resists. It draws to itself the ever-alert activity of this higher principle, would fain convert it to its own inertia and cause it to revert to mere automatism. (78)

Bergson brings this subject up, of course, in a social context. The point he is trying to make involves the difference between the rigid and the comic in the social perception of human physiognomy; facial rigidity is comic because it can be imitated, and so it reminds us how our own personalities can be absorbed in an unnaturally immobile preoccupation. But this passage, among others from *Laughter*, has metaphysical and theological implications as well, implications suggested by the language that comes naturally to a metaphysician: form, soul, matter, infinity, motion, immateriality. When we (the presumed normal perceivers) observe the conversion of grace to somatic automatism, are we not observing principles that transcend our social relations to the rigid individual? One cannot question Bergson's premise that the comic "does not exist outside the pale of what is strictly *human*" (62). But does the *human* presume the *social*? There are forces at play in Bergson's argument that suggest a link between human action and the metaphysical world, the reality of Being rather than a link between human beings. If we can analyze the metaphysics of comedy, might we not be understanding *human* in both its strictest and broadest sense?

The section from which the above passage is taken is entitled "The Comic Element in Forms and Movements," and those very words take us beyond the limits of the social. As Bergson stated elsewhere, "Everything is always in movement, and that which we call *immobility* or rest is the state which springs from the coexistence of two movements under certain peculiar conditions . . . we ourselves move in the same direction as a moving object."[9] So what is immobile is a metaphysical illusion, not simply a human attitude, and *forms* are not simply social but are aspects of the entire presentational universe.

Using the sort of visual example that Bergson so appreciated (he who later discussed the cinematograph as a symbol for the illusory vision we have of reality), let us regard Buster Keaton running south on a northbound train—as he does in *Sherlock, Jr.* Since Keaton runs as fast as the train moves (it's just pulling out from a station), and since the camera is stationary, the highly comic effect is of Keaton running in place. Why do we find this action comic? Clearly the comedy has to do with a clash between motion and stasis, but who or what is immobile? Well, the camera is, and so we the observers are. Yet this stasis from which we see Keaton does not in any way reflect on us; it is simply a condition. We have a conjunction of conditions here, then, that has nothing at all to do with Keaton or ourselves as social animals. When we try to analyze the comedy of the scene, we discover that notions about Keaton's mechanical foolishness over and against our normality are irrelevant. We identify completely with Keaton in a bizarre situation in which any ideas we might have had about the normal and the abnormal are suspended. Instead, we discover that an analysis will involve terms that concern the general relation of the human being to the physical conditions of the world, to reality. The comical contradiction in the scene is, of course, between Keaton's frantic but purposeful motion and the exactly opposing motion of the train. The result is an image of hilariously poised futility, the futility of a human endeavor in a reality that, simply and blindly, goes its own way.

But there is more to the image of Keaton than futility, which can be a grave or painful thing to behold. We know that Keaton is successfully accomplishing his purpose, which is to keep from being borne off by the train. So that we *at once* behold his success in remaining at the station, and his futile attempt to run south. Keaton's behavior is mechanical in the sense that he persists in his obsession. But do we wish to correct this, we who identify with his desire to remain at the station and who are impressed by his success (even if it is hard-earned, since, when Keaton runs out of train, he must suffer a fall)? No, he is only doing what he must do to achieve his end, and we would be forced to do the same. And are we emotionally removed from the scene? No, we feel as he does, and are excited and disturbed by his futility and success, precisely as we find them comic. We are, in sum, laughing (if we laugh) at a profoundly human image that has nothing to do with society, and everything to do with, in its largest sense, reality. The forms and movements at play are both physical and metaphysical. Bergson's metaphysics of mobility and immobility can provide us with a better understanding of them than *Laughter* can.

Three years after *Laughter* appeared, Bergson published *An Introduction to Metaphysics,* and in this brief monograph, which never addresses the idea of the comic, he outlined a metaphysic that has profound implications for comedy, implications that were present only nascently in *Laughter.* In it he argues that philosophy should be based more on "intuition" than on intellect. Our intellects accept immobility as anterior to mobility, and so perceive change as the *dissolution* of form into a series of pseudo-"parts," the whole of which is immobility.

> We place ourselves as a rule in immobility, in which we find a point of support for practical purposes, and with this immobility we try to reconstruct motion. We only obtain in this way a clumsy imitation, a counterfeit of real movement, but this imitation is much more useful in life than the intuition of the thing itself would be. . . .
> The difficulties to which the problem of movement has given rise from the earliest antiquity have originated in this way. They result

always from the fact that we insist on passing from space to movement, from the trajectory to the flight, from immobile positions to
mobility, and on passing from one to the other by way of addition.
But it is movement which is anterior to immobility, and the relation
between positions and a displacement is not that of parts to a whole,
but that of the diversity of possible points of view to the real indivis-
ibility of the object.[10]

Intuition, on the other hand, perceives that movement is anterior to immobility, and in proceeding from the moving to the fixed *"installs itself in
that which is moving and adopts the very life of things."*[11] It thus comes
closer to a perception of reality, which in essence is mobility. With intuition we "transcend ourselves" and are brought into contact with an essential "continuity" of motion, the "inward life of things."[12]

In his summary Bergson states that I) *"There is a reality that is external
and yet given immediately to the mind,"* and that II) "This reality is
mobility," flux, process. And yet III) "Our mind, which seeks for solid
points of support, has for its main function in the ordinary course of life
that of representing *states* and *things*. It takes, at long intervals, almost
instantaneous views of the undivided mobility of the real. It thus obtains
sensations and *ideas*. In this way it substitutes for the continuous the dis-
continuous, for motion stability, for tendency in process of change, fixed
points marking a direction of change and tendency. This substitution is
necessary to common sense, to language, to practical life. . . ." But the
mind, in so substituting, misrepresents reality, because IV) "With stoppages, however numerous they may be, we shall never make mobility";
fixed concepts can be extracted from mobile reality, but not vice versa;
V) philosophical dogmas, in attempting to reconstruct reality from fixed
concepts, must fail. And yet, VI) "the truth is that our intelligence can follow the opposite method. It can place itself within the mobile reality, and
adopt its ceaselessly changing direction; in short, can grasp it by means of
that *intellectual sympathy* which we call intuition."[13]

The thesis of *Laughter,* then, can be restated in Bergson's metaphysical
terminology. The human condition itself can be seen as comic, above and
beyond the exigencies and impulses of society. What is "encrusted" on
us, the living, is our intellect, which perceives in fixed products a reality
that is in constant process. The natural, the adaptable, the pliable, the
creative, are not strictly social ideals, but the very life of things. So that
when we discover the comic, we are not always *correcting* mechanical
behavior, we can be observing an aspect of human behavior that is beyond correction, that is universal. In this sense the comic has a broader

range and a deeper resonance than the satirical thrusts of comedies of manners (viz. Bergson) or the overcoming of social inhibitions (viz. Freud). The discovery of the comic can involve, not only the perception of the falsity of forms, any forms, but the intuition of what makes these forms seem false—that is, the reality of "the inward life of things." This intuition of life invincible and indivisible is entirely sympathetic, positive, pleasurable. We can see Keaton's running on the train as both an absurd (because "futile") behavior and a pleasurable (because "successful") behavior. By exposing us to how much we all move against the general motion of things, Keaton brings us to a realization of that general motion and how we can achieve, however momentarily, some hectic rapport with it. Like Chaplin, Keaton is a figure inviting our sympathy as much as, if not more than, our superiority, without our losing for a moment the sense of the comic. Bergson is quoted above as calling intuition an *"intellectual sympathy,"* and this is a fine phrase for describing our experience of the comic at its most resonant. In its doubleness the phrase suggests the paradox of distance and involvement that comedy, and particularly modern comedy, demands of us.

The complexity of intellectual sympathy resists the schematic, *schema* being characteristic products of the intellect. In his influential theory of comedy, *The Dark Voyage and the Golden Mean,* Albert Cook argues schematically in order to confine comedy to its traditional—that is, social —areas of operation. Cook sets up what he calls *antinomic symbols,* "two basic ways of regarding life": the probable and the wonderful.[14] It turns out that the way of comedy is the probable—that is, social, reasonable, Aristotelian, predictable, etc.; and the way of tragedy is the way of the wonderful—that is, individual, imaginative, Christian, non-predictable, etc. There are degrees, of course, but these are the basic antinomies. Cook assumes that the subjects of "all forms of comedy" are "family, the difference between generations, types, the problems of sex, manners, and social action" (26). His reasoning is best suited to Aristophanes, Moliére, and W. S. Gilbert; his longest chapters are on comic drama. But in regard to *Don Quixote* Cook says, "To comedy, where social man lives as best he can in the mechanical struggle for survival, all idealism is folly, all individualism the unpardonable social sin. To the comic writer all men . . . are Don Quixotes" (146). The problem with this is that it implicitly identifies Cervantes with Sancho Panza's point of view. To Panza, at least for most of the adventures, "idealism is folly." But the comedy of *Don Quixote* resides, not simply in the character and point of view of Sancho Panza, but in the interplay between Panza and Don Quixote. Cook notes that, at the end of his journey, Don Quixote "casts aside the folly of his

ideals, and honestly faces his own delusion" (146)—that is, he returns to
the social and "probable" fold, to the realm of the Golden Mean. Bergson, as we have seen, would agree with this notion of comedy as socially
restorative. But the comedy of *Don Quixote* is not in the Don's return to
being just Alonso Quixano. The last chapters of Cervantes' book, which
would seem to clinch Cook's argument, are not at the heart of the comedy except when the Don concludes by saying that "my sole object has
been to arouse man's contempt for all fabulous and absurd stories of
knight errantry."[15] And the comedy does not lie in our nodding at the
wisdom of this recanting, but rather in our acknowledging that such fabulous and absurd errantry is the very stuff of comedy, and in our realizing that the Don has now become a dull and humorless fool, comic only
in his misapprehension of the effect of his travels. Indeed, he *sustains* his
character by regarding himself as a realistic knight jousting the windmills
of romance; the hoax of the ending is that he continues in his self-aggran-
dizement. The fictive imaginings of Don Quixote are a joy to us, and we
recognize them in ourselves. As Borges said, "In his intimate being, Cervantes loved the supernatural."[16] We perceive the joy *and* the absurdity
of the literary world in which the Don attempts to dwell, and towards
which so many other characters in the adventures are drawn. Without
the joy of recognition and pleasure, the absurdity would be insufficient,
and vice versa. The world of the Don and the world of Panza are one, or
have become one in the course of the adventures.

In Cook's discussion of *Finnegans Wake* it becomes even more clear
that not only is his view of comedy as "probable," limited and reductive,
but that it need not be so. He begins his book by stating that, "However
man may will or desire otherwise, his life falls into patterns of probability; and even the turning of the sun in night and day, the cycle of the seasons, the biological course of human life are only the scene of his probable actions" (3). But these patterns are not just the scene of such actions.
Such a statement neatly divides the metaphysical and the social. "Man"
partakes of this changeless change, and is but another form among
forms. Cook assumes that in comedy these patterns, these closed systems,
are merely accepted; the Void is not confronted. But it is possible that
even if, in comedy, the human participation in the pattern is assured, still
a sense that this pattern is an entrapment and an illusion can and often
does enrich the comedy. Such a sense is metaphysical in nature; it bears
on manners and mores, families and sex, social ills and joys, but it is not
limited to them and often transcends them. (Even the "probable" can be
viewed as a metaphysical concept, and not a comforting one. Morris
Kline points out in his *Mathematics and Western Culture* that probabil-

ity as a concept has developed from its use as a handmaiden to determinism to its causing "the orderly structure of nature to crumble about our heads."[17] Kline points out that Pascal began by applying the theory of probability to gambling and ended by applying it to God.) When Cook gets to *Finnegans Wake,* he says that it "presents in probable focus the recurrence of individual-social life according to probable pattern," and concludes that "the ultimate meaning of life is the pure action of sexual and social life course, birth through death" (155–6). But *social* seems interpolated here; surely these conclusions about Joyce's novel need not be considered bounded by the social. Later on Cook says that "the themes that pervade *Finnegans Wake*—sex, politics, law, and war—are recurrent subjects for comedy and other probable thought" (159). And so, in the course of his argument, the broad scene of man's actions has disappeared; the cycles of birth and death, the "riverrun" of being, of change, are ignored. Cook might argue that *Ulysses* is only a more or less naturalistic exposition of a day in the life of some Dubliners—hunger, politics, sex, and so on—and that it is not the simultaneous mythification of such a day, which transcends the social and which is such a vital aspect of the novel's comedy.

Neither Cook nor Bergson need have made his traditional assumptions, assumptions which are still being made and which confine our response to modern comedy. In Robert Corrigan's collection of essays on comedy,[18] for instance, most of the essays seem determined to describe comedy as a sort of felicitous and even superficial guardian of the social status quo. Corrigan himself sounds the keynote in his introduction by stating that "the constant in comedy is the comic view of life or the comic spirit: the sense that no matter how many times a man is knocked down he somehow manages to pull himself up and keep going. Thus, while tragedy is a celebration of man's capacity to aspire and suffer, comedy celebrates his capacity to endure."[19] Corrigan's prose belies any sense he may have of the implications of what he says: to endure means, to him, to get up after slipping on the banana peel. Later he says, "in comedy death is never taken seriously or even considered as a serious threat."[20] What, then, of *Don Quixote* or *Catch-22* or *Molloy*? Are these books to be regarded as not-comic because their protagonists endure in the face of death and decline?

It is not far from Corrigan, and it is not far from Bergson, to Benjamin Lehmann's assertion that "the vision of comedy fixes its eye on separateness, on diversity, even on oppositions, but it insists at last on togetherness for lovers and on the restored social fabric, on solidarity for the group";[21] or to L. J. Potts' statement that the "business" of comedy "is to satisfy a healthy human desire; the desire to understand the behaviour of men and women towards one another in social life."[22] Comedy, then, is a kind of balm. From here it is easy to proceed to Harold Watts' assertion that "no comedy is true to nature as we seriously know it . . . it has nothing to say of that nature when it is really most human; that is, private, retired, tragic. It is the trick of comedy to confirm all our superficial judgments; it must make us ignore those which we regard as profound and eternal."[23] Watts clearly doesn't regard comedy as highly as do Cook and Bergson, but his conclusions logically develop from their more respectful theories. If comedy deals only with manners and mores it is bound to seem superficial next to confrontations with Eternity, God, the Void. It is not enough for us merely to deflate these common attitudes, but to demonstrate how they are related to the more serious and considered theories of Bergson and Cook, and of Northrop Frye, who contends that "the theme of the comedy is the integration of society."[24] Restricting comedy to the subject of people in society limits our perception of past comedies, such as *Don Quixote, The Tempest,* or Dante's *Commedia,* and does little to illuminate our best modern comic writers. Indeed, it can be argued that comedy is most profoundly *comical* when it has reference beyond the social.

William F. Lynch, S.J., realizes the depth of comedy as clearly as does any contemporary writer on the subject. He states flatly that any theory of comedy, "if pitched below the theological level, would make stupid sense indeed."[25] Father Lynch's theological persuasion has enabled him to see through the superficial masks of the comic to its ontological essence: "for the most part we cling to the surfaces and the forms of things, away from their true being which is also an incredible non-being" (93). He is well aware of the destructive nature of the comic as it pierces through the illusion of forms; for him comedy "goes below all the categories within which the most of life is spent. . . . In this descent it discovers a kind of rock-bottom reality in man, the terrain of Falstaff and Sancho Panza, which is profoundly and funnily unbreakable, which has no needs above itself. It seems to be the most inherently confident rung of the finite. It is ugly *and* strong" (91). The true sound of comedy, then, is "this song of indestructibility . . . of the human thing, of the finite with the vulgar interstices and smells, which lies below all categories" (100). This is clearly not the song of Bergson's mechanical man, but a song of Bergson's *élan vital*—or, as Lynch puts it, using a metaphor that Bergson would find too stationary, of "rock-bottom being" (100), something indestructible and true and impossible to fix or conceptualize.

> The comic is par excellence the great enemy of the univocal mind. I
> call univocal that kind of mind which, having won through to all the
> legitimate unities and orderings of the logical and rational intel-
> ligence, insists, thereafter, on descending through the diversities,
> densities and maelstroms of reality in such a way as to give absolute
> shape to it through these unities and orderings . . . it cannot abide the
> intractable differences, zigzags and surprises of the actual. (107)

It would seem to Father Lynch that the movement of the comic is toward
some formless essence of "being" *beyond* man (and indeed he sometimes
confuses the ontological and the instinctual or psychological; "being,"
after all, suggests more than a "rock-bottom reality in man")—or at least
toward the anarchic vision of what Lynch calls the "equivocal" mind, "a
mentality which believes that in the whole world of reality and being no
two beings *are* in the same sense; everything is completely diverse from
everything else" (130). But such is not the case, for "on the surface,
comedy, with its antipathy to the order of things, seems anarchic. . . . But
it is not at all anarchic; it is only the defender of another and more human
order. . . . Metaphysically it is a defender of being against the pure concept of category" (107). The frame of mind which seeks for a new order
while maintaining intact the diversity and freedom of reality is what
Father Lynch terms the *analogical*. The analogical imagination is rooted
in paradox, in "keeping the same and the different, the idea and the detail, tightly interlocked in the one imaginative act" (133). This imagination is "the home of the comic" (108), involving the destruction of
orders and the creation of order as two contraries brought together and
held in suspension as one.

This paradox is in force in Friedrich Duerrenmatt's pithy statement
that "the comical exists in forming what is formless, in creating order out
of chaos."[26] It is also central to Arthur Koestler's analysis of the comic in
The Act of Creation.[27] In his attempt to establish analogies between the
creation of laughter, science and art, Koestler centers his argument on the
bisociative act: "When two independent matrices of perception or reasoning interact with each other the result . . . is either a *collision* ending in
laughter, or their *fusion* in a new intellectual synthesis, or their *confrontation* in an aesthetic experience . . . the same pair of matrices can produce comic, tragic, or intellectually challenging effects" (45). After analyzing several jokes, Koestler concludes that "the pattern underlying all
varieties of humour is 'bisociative'—perceiving a situation or event in
two habitually incompatible associative contexts" (95). And the two
contexts are not resolved, nor does a catharsis result from their confron-

tation (as in tragedy). Rather, and this is a key phrase for our purposes, "comic discovery is paradox *stated*" (95, my emphasis).

Koestler is more interested in the phenomenon of laughter, particularly as a response to oral jokes, than he is in comic literature, and his relevance to our concerns is limited by that. But his bisociative act can help us to understand the artist in his role as comedian. When Koestler states that "the creative act . . . is an act of liberation—the defeat of habit by originality" (96), he can be said to be talking about comedy, though not necessarily about laughter.

Comedy, in the sense in which we are using the word, is an "aesthetic experience" of a "paradox stated," the paradox of form dissolved and form created, words denied and words affirmed. R. W. B. Lewis touches on this paradox when he says, "the really significant development in the comic mode, both at home and abroad, over the past century or so has been the development of comedy as a way of registering artistic and human defeat, and the use of the clown figure as a means of living with despair. And yet a note of something more than sheer endurance . . . a note even of positive joy, these too are inherent in the comic tradition."[28] Defeat and joy: the paradox stated. Lewis would agree with Father Lynch that comedy explores "the lowest of the low to find and expose elements of the highest of the high, to dig in the human debris for intimations of mythic grandeur or of sanctity."[29] If modern literature, which is Lewis' subject, is obsessed with the darker elements of human life, comedy might be a way of keeping balance in the process of expressing that darkness. Father Lynch says that "things are funny, precisely because they can recall the relationship between God and themselves" (109). Whether or not we wish to restrict ourselves to such a theological view, the point is to keep the two terms of the paradox *in suspension,* to experience them simultaneously. In Lewis' exegesis of Hart Crane's poem, "Chaplinesque," he speaks of Crane's ashcan becoming a grail, but Lewis must also keep in mind that the grail can be seen, comically, as an ashcan. Hart Crane himself needs to see this if he's going to talk about Chaplin. An essential aspect of Chaplin's physical comedy is that he seems clumsy and human at the same time that he seems graceful and spiritual. The act of transformation is a *comic* act of transformation. When Father Lynch concludes that "comedy stands, with full, cognitive confrontation and remembrance, in the presence of man, down to the last inch of the little beastie. And seeing what can come of it, seeing how safe and strong a way it is . . . it laughs indeed" (110), he is in danger of adhering too closely to his paradigm of the crucifixion and resurrection of Christ. We are led too easily into the leap of faith and redemption. The paradox of defeat and

joy, destruction and creation, death and rebirth, must remain an unre-
solved paradox or we will lose the sense of the comic.

Albert Camus is especially lucid about the dangers of the nostalgic leap
into faith, the leaving behind of one term of a paradox in order that the
other may triumph. *The Myth of Sisyphus,* while not about the comic,
can be profitably discussed as a theoretical analysis of the nature of the
modern comic spirit. Camus centers his argument for not committing su-
icide in a meaningless universe on "a constant awareness, ever revived,
ever alert," of the contradictions between his mind and the world, between his "nostalgia for unity" and the fragmented world that confronts
him. "Faced with this inextricable contradiction of the mind, we shall
fully grasp the divorce separating us from our creations. So long as the
mind keeps silent in the motionless world of its hopes, everything is reflected and arranged in the unity of its nostalgia. But with its first move
this world cracks and tumbles: an infinite number of shimmering frag-
ments is offered to the understanding."[30] The world moves and we desire
it to be "motionless," we hope to fix it. Neither the world nor the mind is
absurd; the "feeling of absurdity" comes from the divorce between them,
from "the confrontation of this irrational and wild longing for clarity
whose call echoes in the human heart" (17). Camus concludes his first
chapter in these words: "My reasoning wants to be faithful to the evidence that aroused it. That evidence is the absurd. It is that divorce between the mind that desires and the world that disappoints, my nostalgia
for unity, this fragmented world, and the contradiction that binds them
together" (37). This "contradiction" is Koestler's "paradox stated." It
binds mind and world, imagination and reality "together," while keeping them distinct, keeping the divorce between them clear.

Camus cannot accept the nostalgic desire of the mind to stamp the universe with the seal of the human. He severely criticizes what Father Lynch
would call the "univocal" imagination. He recognizes its attempts as futile. But he knows that this nostalgia exists, powerfully. He accepts it as a
given, as much a given as the world that eludes its unities. The mind is
able to leave "the arid, dried-up path of lucid effort" (38), but it must not
resolve itself to bitter defeat, for as Camus demonstrates in his critique of
Jaspers, Heidegger, Kierkegaard and Chestov, it is when faced with the
defeat of utter meaninglessness that the mind makes the leap into faith.
Rather, the sense of the absurd must return "to a man's life and find its
home there," where "all problems recover their sharp edge," none of
them settled, all of them transfigured (38–9). If one adapts one's life to
the contradictory rhythms of despair and hope, then these very rhythms
are transcended in their being suspended in the clarity of the paradox.

Camus' absurd man faces his universe much as Einstein's observer faces his: each takes himself, his desire and his point of vantage, into account.

In his short essay on Sisyphus, Camus suggests that the vision of the absurd man may be comic.[31] Sisyphus is the "absurd hero" because his "whole being is exerted toward accomplishing nothing." There are essentially two aspects of Sisyphus' mind, held in suspension. On the one hand, Sisyphus "knows the whole extent of his wretched condition: it is what he thinks of during his descent." To this extent his myth is "tragic." But it is this very "lucidity" that enables him to surmount his fate. The rock that he carries is the image of his tragedy, of his futile and bitter suffering, but Sisyphus "is stronger than his rock" because he knows and accepts that his effort will be unceasing. And so on the other hand, his descent takes place "in joy." He sees, in an intense focus, on the way down the hill, that his fate is tragic, but he also sees that *it has a rhythm,* that he will walk down and push up over and over again. He no longer exists in an eternal present, but can prefigure a pattern, a series extending into infinity. He realizes change and he realizes the formal quality of this change. The rock is his consciousness of his task, and he is the master of it. In this form there is a meaning to the meaninglessness of his fate—this is the paradox stated. As Camus says, "happiness and the absurd are two sons of the same earth. They are inseparable." This statement is more final than his mention of the tragic. Camus concludes: "one must imagine Sisyphus happy." The paradigm of modern comedy could be a solitary person and his consciousness alert in a vast and seemingly indifferent but strangely formal universe. It is a metaphysical comedy.

3. Comic Theory: Metaphysical

Using Bergson's metaphysics, we have developed the terminology of comic theory to establish that the human condition can be depicted comically, not only in the light of social reality but in the light of metaphysical reality. We have seen that the nature of metaphysical comedy can be expressed in the paradoxical relationship between form and formlessness, immobility and flux, what the intellect perceives about reality and what the intuition can evoke about reality. And we have seen that our response to these comic paradoxes can be at once distant and sympathetic, intellectual and emotional, corrective and pleasurable. All this is a necessary background for a theory of modern comedy that will allow us to understand fully the comic life of some of the best—and most difficult—of this century's literature.

Bergson's metaphysics provides us with an essential distinction between the illusory life of forms and the reality of flux. The idea that reality cannot be grasped by the concepts that we construct to describe it is basic to modern consciousness. It is an idea directly related to a philosophical and scientific conception of reality as pure energy existing in ceaseless change, random and fragmentary beyond any concept of fragment. The main tendencies of modern science have justified Bergson's *élan vital* as an imaginative model. Loren Eiseley, who understood so well the implications of modern science for the life of the imagination, said that in the nineteenth century "the cell was discovered, and the single machine in its turn was found to be the product of millions of infinitesimal machines—the cell. Now, finally, the cell itself dissolves away into an abstract chemical machine—and that into some intangible, inexpressible flow of energy."[32] It has become increasingly clear that ontological descriptions are merely interesting but problematical constructions, and that reality cannot be expressed. Discussing the collapse of laws (cause and effect among them) that govern the behavior of matter, Allen Wheelis declares that "our holy mission to get it all straight has yielded an ever proliferating brood of erratically behaving elementary particles, each of which is composed of elementary particles," and then goes on to quote from Heisenberg's book on modern physics: " 'the conception of objective reality . . . has thus evaporated . . . into the transparent clarity of a mathematics that represents no longer the behavior of particles *but rather our knowledge of this behavior.*' "[33] One legacy of Einstein's is that we are inextricably a part of what we observe and describe. It is possible, then, to find ourselves, in attempting to describe reality, involved in the vicious circle of Epimenides the Cretan, who affirmed that all Cretans were liars. That is, we express the idea that reality cannot be expressed, and so, like Epimenides, we speak falsely if we speak true, and speak true if we speak falsely.

The problem of how to describe a reality beyond description, how to make expressible Eiseley's "inexpressible flow of energy," is at the heart of our concern with literary comedy. We need to focus Bergson's metaphysics of form and formlessness on the problem of *language*. Language is, fundamentally, a system of forms, a naming and hence an abstracting of the world. Given a conception of reality as chaotic energy, a major modern concern is with how language frames our perception of this reality, and how that perception is an illusion of reality, divorced from how things really are. Susanne Langer writes, "the Kantian challenge: 'What can I know?' is . . . dependent on the prior question: 'What can I ask?' And the answer . . . is clear and direct. I can ask whatever language will express."[34] Langer's ideas on the symbolizing function of the mind accord with one of Bergson's conclusions (quoted in the second section of this chapter) that language depends on the substitution of fixedness for change. Langer says that our experience of reality is inevitably transformed symbolically into *ideas about reality,* and that "the readiest active termination" of this process of symbolization is verbal language.[35]

Bergson himself developed the relationship of language to his metaphysics in *Creative Evolution* (1911). In parts of this masterwork he describes the paradoxical nature of the operations of language, its simultaneously liberating and confining functions. He makes his most significant remarks in this regard when discussing his idea that the intellect, which needs to fabricate fixed things, nevertheless must always be "*decomposing*" and "*recomposing*" its systems.[36] The intellect sets itself in motion in the very process of seeking static forms. "So a language is required which makes it possible to be always passing from what is known to what is yet to be known. . . . This tendency of the sign to transfer itself from one object to another [and from "things to ideas"] is characteristic of human language." It is this very "mobility of words" that has made language contribute to the "liberation" of the intellect from its reliance on material objects. The intellect "profits by the fact that the world is an external thing, which the intelligence can catch hold of and cling to, and at the same time an immaterial thing, by means of which the intelligence can penetrate even to the inwardness of its own work." And yet language "is made to designate things, and nought but things. . . . Forms are all that it is capable of expressing." So that words, which helped to release the energy of the intellect in motion, must by their nature deny the reality of motion, and so become only the useful agents of the intellect after all:

> it is only because the word is mobile, because it flies from one thing to another, that the intellect was sure to take it, sooner or later, on the wing, while it was not yet settled on anything, and apply it to an object which is not a thing and which, concealed till then, awaited the coming of the word to pass from darkness to light. But the word, by covering up this object, again converts it into a thing. So intelligence, even when it no longer operates on its own object, follows habits it has contracted in that operation. . . .

In the very process of realizing its strength to reveal, by its very energy and malleability, language can only extend the creation of forms, and so deny the reality it wants to express.

The comedy of the following passage from Beckett derives from the interplay between the mind's (the character Molloy's) awareness of its own mechanical nature, and its awareness that there must necessarily exist a reality beyond its mechanical nature, which it tries to express but can only express mechanically.

> And when I say I said, etc., all I mean is that I knew confusedly things were so, without knowing exactly what it was all about. And every time I say, I said this, or I said that, or speak of a voice saying, far away inside me, Molloy, and then a fine phrase more or less clear and simple, or find myself compelled to attribute to others intelligible words, or hear my own voice muttering to others more or less articulate sounds, I am merely complying with the convention that demands you either lie or hold your peace. For what really happened was quite different. . . . And then sometimes there arose within me, confusedly, a kind of consciousness, which I express by saying, I said, etc., or Don't do it, Molloy, or . . . by means of other figures quite as deceitful, as for example, It seemed to me that, etc., or, I had the impression that, etc., for it seemed to me nothing at all, and I had no impression of any kind. . . .[37]

To continue using Bergson's terms from *Laughter*, there is clearly in this passage the spectacle of something "living" struggling in a linguistic mechanism to express its life, and failing, and yet in the very process of failing expressing its life. Molloy expresses his predicament by undermining the medium of his expression. The comedy lies in the interplay of life and automatism, reality and language, not simply in the correction of one by the other.

The modern comic writer recognizes that the more intent he is upon conveying reality in language (as Molloy tries to express "what it was all about"), the more clear becomes the distinction between reality and language. It is, after all, our mental processes that tell us that there *is* a reality of which our mental processes do not give us true information. And it is language that expresses that there is a reality which it cannot express. So while the writer is aware that language creates an illusion of reality, he recognizes that it is a *necessary* illusion, an unavoidable illusion, indeed—and here the paradox unfolds its comic bloom—that language is all the reality we can know *at the same time that* we sense a reality beyond language. The awareness of the necessity of language results in a pleasure in seeing language fulfill its function, extend its field of operations. The awareness of language as an illusion, a lie, results in an ironic voice. As these two awarenesses are inextricable, so too are the pleasure and irony in the voice inextricable. Another character of Beckett's describes the circularity of the paradox when he says, apropos of Watt's feelings as he attempts to construct mentally the reality of

Mr. Knott: "but he had hardly felt the absurdity of those things, on the one hand, and the necessity of those things, on the other (for it is rare that the feeling of absurdity is not followed by the feeling of necessity), when he felt the absurdity of those things of which he had just felt the necessity (for it is rare that the feeling of necessity is not followed by the feeling of absurdity)."[38] While it may be imprecise to say that Watt feels "pleasure" in the necessity of his constructions (Beckett's "necessity" is more or less an urge that gives pain), he certainly achieves by them a "semantic succour,"[39] creates for himself "a pillow of old words, for a head."[40]

The pleasure that language affords the writer (and the reader) in the expression of its power is, then, inextricably related to the writer's (and the reader's) ironic awareness that language is impotent to describe reality. This is one of the essential points of Heidegger's two essays on the poet Friedrich Holderlin. While Holderlin was not a comic poet, and Heidegger's concern is not the comic, still the essays describe as "joy" the very pleasure that we have argued as one major tone of the modern comic voice—and they link it to irony, the other major tone. Since Heidegger's sense of the word "joy" is important to this book, and particularly to the chapter on James Joyce, it is worth analyzing in some detail. "Joy," with its suggestions of pleasure and exultation, is a word that seldom appears in theories of comedy, and is worth abstracting from Heidegger's context for that purpose alone.

Heidegger's argument, in "Remembrance of the Poet," is that "the vocation of the poet is homecoming, by which the homeland is first made ready as the land of proximity to the source. To guard the mystery of the reserving proximity to the Most Joyous, and in the process of guarding it to unfold it—that is the care of homecoming."[41] The source is that which makes the poet feel at home, at one with the universe. It is a mystery and the poet can only come into proximity to it and guard its mystery, and in guarding it reveal it in joyousness. "The Joyous is that which has been made into poetry" (246). For Heidegger, the poet is an angel, acting for men as God with the power of the Word. "To name poetically means: to cause the High One himself to appear in words" (263). Werner Brock's note on this last sentence is as follows: "the power of the Father (the High One) has departed from the gods and from men and alone remains existent in the Word. The patriarchal power absent from reality comes for the last time to exist *as language*" (363). Thus the poet creates in joy. But what he creates is not the mystery itself. He creates his home in proximity to the mystery. The "innermost essence of the homeland . . . is reserved" (260). The poet is God and is not God. His creation is language, and not the real; cr reality has *become* language.

To say that something is near and at the same time it remains at a distance—this is tantamount either to violating the fundamental law of ordinary thought, the principle of contradiction, or on the other hand to playing with empty words, or merely to making a presumptuous suggestion. That is why the poet, almost as soon as he has spoken the line about the mystery of the reserving proximity, has to descend to the phrase:

"Foolish is my speech."

But nevertheless he is speaking. The poet must speak, for

"It is joy." (260)

Words are empty and foolish at the same time that they are powerful and joyous.[42] Heidegger elaborates this paradox more darkly in "Holderlin and the Essence of Poetry," in which he says, "it is language which first creates the manifest conditions for menace and confusion to existence" because it must "make itself ordinary" (275), is trapped in its own creations. "Poetry is the establishing of being by means of the word," but that being is not Being, not the mystery, which is "never an existent" (281). The poet creates joy out of his failure, and failure is implicit in his joy. "Foolish is my speech" and yet "It is joy." The poet retains the mystery of Being by acknowledging that in his approximation of it is both his joy and his sense of his own emptiness. The universe is not ordered, and he must convey this disorder in the necessary order of his words. "That which keeps things apart in opposition and thus at the same time binds them together, is called by Holderlin 'intimacy.' The affirmation of belonging to this intimacy occurs through the creation of a world and its ascent, and likewise through the destruction of a world and its decline" (274). The poet simultaneously creates and destroys the world of his language in order that we may see this world in its joyful necessity and its absurd illusion. "The pure and the ordinary are both equally something said" (275–6).

Joy, then, comes from the experience of creating forms that will bring us into intimacy with a reality that, nevertheless, eludes us because the intimacy is, by its very nature, a formal one. The world of forms, the world of the poet's language, is necessary because it is the *given* world. It cannot be made to dissolve by our raising the specter of a Reality Beyond, because we would necessarily be raising that specter in words. That is the writer's predicament.

It is the complexity of this predicament that Susanne Langer does not take into account in her otherwise fine essay, "The Great Dramatic Forms: The Comic Rhythm."[43] Langer has a valuable respect for the abstract reach of comedy. Basing her discussion on biological evidence, she argues that "the underlying feeling of comedy" is "the pure sense of life," a "rhythm of sheer vitality," the "basic biological pattern which all living things share: the round of conditioned and conditioning organic processes that produces the life rhythm." This is another way of expressing what we have been calling reality. But what is especially interesting in Langer's essay is that this pure sense of life is one of "the fundamental *forms* of consciousness" (my emphasis); it is a *human* concept of what belongs to all life, of what is not distinctively human. There is, then, nothing really *pure* about this sense of life. A pure sense of life could not be realized in forms. But nevertheless we feel that this vitality *is* reality to us. Its infinitely complex cellular (and beyond cellular) flux is a *rhythm,* a pattern, a symbolic structure.

Langer's preoccupation with language, as expressed in her *Philosophy in a New Key,* should have had more effect on her essay on the comic rhythm. We have already noted her argument that symbolization is the essential act of the mind. "The fact that the human brain is constantly carrying on a process of symbolic transformation of the experiential data that comes to it causes it to be a veritable fountain of more or less spontaneous ideas. As all registered experience tends to terminate in action, it is only natural that a typically human function should require a typically human form of overt activity, and that is just what we find in *the sheer expression of ideas. . . .*"[44] This earlier passage of hers would suggest that the "human life-feeling" that is the essence of comedy is not the experiential data of reality, but the transformation of that data into a form of consciousness, the most common form being language. Because, like Bergson, Langer does not make this connection between her broader philosophy and her theory of comedy, she does not see how intimately the human element becomes involved in—indeed, disrupts—the purity of her biological vision. And so she can use this vision to support existing theories of comedy as social in nature. The pure sense of life becomes human life—feeling becomes fertility rites and festival games[45]—and the ontological basis of her argument never suggests a metaphysical comedy.

Another comment which Werner Brock made on Heidegger's "Holderlin and the Essence of Poetry" can help us to develop Langer's ideas on comedy beyond the social, and beyond drama. Brock is trying to connect Heidegger's fundamental notion of "Time" to his comments on "conversation" (the essence of language): "Something 'that remains and is constant' must have been experienced by man, before conversation was possible and could come into its own. And this, Heidegger suggests, took place in that very moment that 'Time' opened itself up for man in its dimensions of present, past, and future. Up to that moment the life of the race, like that of other species, went on in a flux where no consciousness could fix on anything."[46] The flux of pure time could only be realized as an orderly progression, something man could *fix* on. Frank Kermode addresses the same paradox when he says that "we can perceive a duration only when it is organized."[47] What is constant in both Langer and Heidegger is (1) the flux of life lived in an eternal present, and (2) the dimension of human consciousness which fixes the present in a spectrum of time, a series of "presents," and issues in language.

The forming of what is formless: it is from this that comedy, and language, springs. The comedy is not simply in the forming, but in the realization that one is forming what is formless. The sense of formlessness, of life in its undifferentiated motion, is basic and ever-present in comedy, but this sense in itself is not what is comic, as Langer would have it. Comedy, as Friedrich Duerrenmatt says, "supposes an unformed world,"[48] but it develops from that. The formlessness is just a supposition. In comedies of language, this sense of formlessness underlies and undercuts the creation of all forms, especially words, rendering them absurd. The creation of forms from chaos is necessary and joyous. The realization that forms are an illusion *because* their essence is formlessness, is ironic. In comedies of language, and this is our conclusion, these two perceptions (of form and formlessness), and these two feelings (of joy and irony) are interdependent and simultaneous. They result in a dual voice expressing an essential paradox.

This voice is profoundly *comic* because it keeps its paradoxical vision exquisitely posed, and so is able to exploit at once the joy that gives comedy its element of positive pleasure, and the irony that gives comedy its bracingly critical edge. Without joy, comedy tends toward the satiric, the corrosive. Without sufficient irony, comedy tends toward romantic affirmation. In either case the comic spirit and the comic range diminish. Examples of the former are Nathanael West's *Miss Lonelyhearts* and Evelyn Waugh's *Vile Bodies,* works in which the characters are not given enough positive strength, enough expressive life. Examples of the latter are Joyce's *A Portrait of the Artist as a Young Man* and Iris Murdoch's *Under the Net,* works in which ironic deflation is not as vigorous as it could be. All of these novels can be regarded as comedies, and fine ones, but they lack comic depth. It is also worth noting that none of them could accurately be called a "comedy of language." It is when a modern author derives his comedy from a preoccupation with language, with the very medium of his expression, that he is most able to engage metaphysical issues with immediate effects—or, putting it another way, to derive metaphysical issues from immediate effects. Joyce was able to make Stephen Dedalus a more comic and a more touching figure in *Ulysses,* in which Joyce's irony is given more play. And Waugh was able to write the richer comedy of, say, *A Handful of Dust* when he created a protagonist whose strength could survive irony without diminishing its impact. It can be said, then, that comedies of language are the best, and most difficult, of modern comic literature.

In the following chapters we will examine major works by using the comic theory outlined in this chapter as a method of analysis. To examine these works as comedies of language will enable us to discover and describe the broadest reach of their comedy. As we have noted before, literature of this depth and difficulty is not often regarded as comic, and we shall assume that this is because a common predisposition is toward comedy as limited in range. It is my hope that what we assume now we can demonstrate clearly through the detailed analyses that follow. It is time to put theory into practice.

Joyce: *Ulysses*

1. Introduction

Ezra Pound reported that *Ulysses* "was in its author's own mind a mine of rich comedy, not a crucifix set in a chapel or a bag of saint's bones to be worshipped ... it may as well go on record that in the storm of abuse in the 1920's Joyce emitted only one mild complaint, thus verbatim: If only someone had said among all those critics, that the book is really damn *funny!*"[1] Frank Budgen, a close friend of Joyce's and still one of the best commentators on his work, said that "the prevailing mood" of *Ulysses* is "humour," and goes on to compare Joyce's laughter at the foibles of mankind with Chaucer's.[2] Many critics have remarked that the novel is comic. But, as is normally the case in discussions of specific comedies (Chaucer's included), the fact of their being comic is only noted (when it *is* noted) in passing, with an appreciative wink or a flight of rhetoric. Even if *the comic* is declared to be at the heart of the matter, it is not regarded as a way of grasping the meaning or vision of the comic work.[3] It is, rather, simply a term that accounts for tone, spirit, a vague feeling of affirmation—if, indeed, it is regarded at all as having to do with more than reflections on local or social life.

But Joyce, in his often-ignored comments on comedy, certainly thought of it in the most inclusive terms. In his Paris Notebook of 1903 he wrote the following:

> And now of comedy. An improper art aims at exciting in the way of comedy the feeling of desire but the feeling which is proper to comic art is the feeling of joy. Desire, as I have said, is the feeling which urges us to go to something but joy is the feeling which the possession of some good excites in us ... desire urges us from rest that we may possess something but joy holds us in rest so long as we possess something ... a comedy (a work of comic art) which does not urge us to seek anything beyond itself excites in us the feeling of joy.[4]

Joyce does not go on to describe *joy*, but it is clear at what level of representation he thinks we can discover the comic. For him comedy is a profound sense of and response to the nature of things. *Joy* carries with it all the resonance of an abstraction. Like pity and terror in tragic art, joy arrests us ("holds us in rest") so that we may apprehend the beautiful. If the apprehension of beauty is joyful, then the work is a comedy. Comedy is a genre of the highest art. Joyce goes on to say that if tragedy excites in us the feeling of joy it can be said "to participate in the nature of comic art," and that in this sense comedy is the "perfect" and tragedy the "imperfect manner" in art.[5] It seems clear that if Joyce were to write a comic novel, it would be more than a comedy of manners; it would aspire to the highest art. *Ulysses* is certainly not a comedy because Joyce wrote these comments on comedy, or because he thought the book was funny. But I will argue, here and in the chapters that follow, that if a work of art strikes us, again and again, as comic in strategy and spirit, then its author is up to something more than merely diverting us from, or making variations on, his deeper and graver concerns. He is, rather, describing the nature of these concerns *as comic*. Comedy informs and shapes the work: this is the burden of Joyce's remarks on comic joy. The question that I will attempt to answer here is: does *Ulysses*—since we assume that Joyce intended it as a work of art—bring us to a static apprehension that is joyful? I must discover the answer in a specific analysis of its comic development. Such an analysis will help us to understand what the comic joy entails, what *joy* means.

2. The Comic Interaction of Style and Subject

Discussions of *Ulysses* have centered around the dual nature of Joyce's narrative. There is on the one hand the subject matter, the outer and inner lives of some people in Dublin in 1904, rendered with astonishing detail. On the other hand there are Joyce's styles, the intricate system of strategies with which he attempts to shape his material. Critics have used various terms for these two aspects of the narrative: naturalism and symbolism, particularization and mythification, content and form, the existential and the metaphysical, the phenomenal and the noumenal, kinesis and stasis, action and language, vitality and artifice, among others. Every critic who addresses the subject of Joyce's narrative agrees that these aspects are at odds with each other, as the above terminology makes clear. The problem, the source of the differences between the critics, is the nature of the interplay between these aspects, and the meaning shaped by that interplay.

On one extreme, Harry Levin says that the "paradox of the book is that it imposes a static ideal upon kinetic material," that Joyce's "underlying purpose is to call a halt . . . to set up an immovable object against the irresistible forces of the city."[6] Once Levin has decided that Joyce's artistic ideal of stasis can only be an *imposition* on the perpetual movement of the subject matter, it seems natural for him to conclude that the achievement of stasis involves a kind of despair. And so he argues, using darker and darker rhetoric, that as the novel aspires to the "permanence of myth" it fixes its characters in their "incurable loneliness." The "statuesque coldness" of Joyce's creations overtakes "the doomed inhabitants" of Dublin and petrifies them "in the insensate agonies of paralysis." Bloomsday becomes "doomsday"; stasis is death.

At the other extreme is Frank Budgen, who senses very little contradiction between Joyce's material and technique: "Joyce, in *Ulysses*, takes life as it is and represents it in its own material."[7] The narrative flows as reality does. "We see the city as a whole, in a wide sweep, so that the individual destiny is merged in the mass of experience. Death and decay are robbed of their sting, for they are never isolated, but a part of the texture of life, continuing always." This sanguine view allows Budgen to argue that "the prevailing mood is humour," but it is not his purpose to analyze the novel as a comedy. He is content to say that it is affirmative in spirit, and generally ignores the ironies that Joyce's styles engender, the ironies that Levin finds "pathetic."

Because neither Levin nor Budgen sees active interplay between subject and style, the former doesn't acknowledge the comic at all, and the latter can only suggest the comic as a positive mood and vantage, an unequivocal "yes" to life in all its variety. But as I have argued in my first chapter, comedy is a complex action, a contradictory interplay of ideas the reflections of which illuminate a vision. We must keep the constant *activity* of its comedy in mind if we wish to argue, rather than merely declare, that *Ulysses* is a comedy. L. A. Murillo and A. Walton Litz, among many other critics, argue for a close interaction between subject and style, but conclude that the contradictions are resolved. Murillo speaks of "the particularization of the myth of Ulysses" (Ulysses as Bloom) and its opposite, "the mythification of the particular lives represented" (Bloom as Ulysses), and concludes that Joyce establishes a "coincidence" between them.[8] He wisely points out, in reference to Levin's comment that Joyce's style is "two-edged," that "what Levin does not seem to consider is that we do not have two effects, one following and contingent on the other, but that Joyce may have attempted to produce a highly radical *single* effect." He calls this single effect Joyce's "irony" and regards it as "a 'balance,' or *stasis,* of tensions . . . a resolution of these tensions." This idea of resolution is echoed in Litz's claim that "the greatness of *Ulysses* resides in the novel's synthesis of scrupulous naturalism and complex symbolism."[9] Like Murillo, Litz finds "these two modes" to be equal and simultaneous.

The problem is that once they have agreed that there is a synthesis or a resolution of the opposition between style and subject, mythical symbolism and naturalistic detail, the purpose of the tension between them seems to be to cancel itself out. It is difficult to say what this "unity" expresses. Litz begins by saying the *Ulysses* "is essentially a comic work," but his notion of "synthesis" only leads him to conclude, weakly, that "it was part of Joyce's purpose to present Bloom as simultaneously ridiculous and magnificent, comic and heroic. Bloom is comic in that his actions are often cramped and mean when compared with the wide-ranging experience of Ulysses. . . ."[10] So comedy becomes *not* something essential, but the result of one direction of the correspondence: Ulysses as Bloom. Comedy is contained in the narrow confines of irony.

In the following analysis I will argue that Joyce's novel is essentially a comedy because its comedy derives from the complex and developing interplay between the material and the way Joyce talks about it, and so involves a vision of the novel as a whole. Joyce recognizes from the very start that how we talk about things can be funny because things have a deeper and more forceful life than language can express. The gap between the reality of "the stream of life" that flows through the novel and the attempt of Joyce's language to arrest it widens as the novel proceeds, and achieves its most ironic comedy in the "Ithaca" chapter. Then the gap narrows but persists in "Penelope," so that we can experience the power of a reality that has only been suggested by the various failures of language in the preceding chapters. That power is finally realized by Molly (and by us) as joyful because it seeks a form of expression in language. The comic interplay modulates, sometimes radically (as in the shift from "Ithaca" to "Penelope") but it never ceases, is never resolved. A day in the life of Dublin is an enormous, multitudinous, changing force. Joyce writes a novel about it, a work of art in language, and for him the achievement of art is stasis, a final forming, a *possession.* So he must fail because he wants to be faithful to both reality and art, and they are fundamentally opposed. But if their opposition is conceived and developed in comic terms, then both can be expressed, without either one ceasing to be what it is. And so the feeling of joy that *Ulysses* evokes is not the joy of changing reality, because reality is not expressive, does not declare itself. Neither is it the joy of language, because language falsifies the very power of reality. It is the joy of possessing the contradiction. It is *comic* joy.

How does Joyce conceive and develop the interaction between subject and style in comic terms? It is difficult to trace comic strategies in a novel that has a different style for every chapter. But if an analysis of the kinds of comedy in *Ulysses* would be bewildering, perhaps pointless, an overall development can be discerned that will allow me to argue that *Ulysses* is a comedy and not just an encyclopedia of comic effects. The novel becomes gradually more comic as Joyce's style (or styles) asserts itself *qua* style— that is, as the very act of relating *Ulysses* becomes more involved in and inextricable from the subject of *Ulysses*. As Arnold Goldman points out, "there is a deliberately played-upon gap between the narrative styles and the material which is their subject."[11] Any reader experiences this as he feels himself drawn into the vortex of Joyce's narration. If I can show, now, how this gap is comic, I can trace a comic meaning that circulates to the heart of the novel.

In the first chapter the comic nature of Buck Mulligan is played off against Stephen's grumpy irritation with him. Mulligan's mock-religious antics derive their obvious comedy from the discrepancy between, for example, the actuality of shaving bowls and the ceremonies of the mass. His comedy conveys to us that there are no words that can order or transform this world, which is immediate and sensual.

> —For this, O dearly beloved, is the genuine Christine: body and soul and blood and ouns. Slow music, please. Shut your eyes, gents. One moment. A little trouble about those white corpuscles. Silence, all.
>
> He peered sideways up and gave a long low whistle of call, then paused awhile in rapt attention, his even white teeth glistening here and there with gold points. Chrysostomos. Two strong shrill whistles answered through the calm.[12]

Mulligan would not be comic to us if we thought his lather was or could be transubstantiated. His comedy springs from the gap between the power that the Catholic references evoke and the power of actuality, which resists transformation, between the body and blood of Christ and white corpuscles. Somber Stephen is Mulligan's foil because Stephen wants to *wed* words with a world that to him is charged with a fearful mortality, the very flux of which threatens him. He cannot bear to have Mulligan call his mother "beastly dead." So, hearing Mulligan drone the lines from Yeats—

And no more turn aside and brood
Upon love's bitter mystery
For Fergus rules the brazen cars.

—Stephen has this vision:

> Woodshadows floated silently by through the morning peace
> from the stairhead seaward where he gazed. Inshore and farther out
> the mirror of water whitened, spurned by lightshod hurrying feet.
> White breast of the dim sea. The twining tresses, two by two. A hand
> plucking the heartstrings merging their twining chords. Wavewhite
> wedded words shimmering on the dim tide. (9)

This is most definitely not a comic passage because in it, momentarily,
Stephen is able to achieve Fergus' mythic power and transform the sea
into his instrument. The poem and the sea are "wedded," and the passage is a lyric celebration of the wedding. Then, as "a cloud began to
cover the sun slowly, shadowing the bay in deeper green" so that "it lay
behind him, a bowl of bitter waters," we come to realize that the sea reminds him of his dying mother, and that he had sung "Fergus' song" to
her as she lay dying. To no avail. Words had failed, and Stephen, of
course, can only find this painful. It is worth noting that both Mulligan's
and Stephen's voices, in the above passages, are subsumed in Joyce's; it is
Joyce who adds "Chrysostomos" to Mulligan's comedy and whose
words carry the lyricism of Stephen's vision. So that Joyce's play and
problems with words subsume his characters'.

In his first chapter Joyce is describing, among other things, a comic gap
between the power of language and the power of reality, as well as a possibility for that gap to be bridged. Mulligan's kidding is simple burlesque
and Stephen's ruminations are non-comically poetic. There can be, here,
only the dramatization of the hostility between them.

When Stephen is able to be alone, on Sandymount in the third chapter,
he can again experiment with wedding his poetry to the spectacle of
change that the beach offers him.[13] In Bergson's terms, he can adapt his
mind to the nature of things, to the eternal flux of reality. Joyce's narrative is a mingling of the first and third persons, so that Stephen's thoughts
become his, and his Stephen's. The finest poetry of the chapter comes in
the last sentence: "He turned his face over a shoulder, rere regardant.
Moving through the air high spars of a threemaster, her sails brailed up
on the crosstrees, homing, upstream, silently moving, a silent ship" (51).
Here Stephen/Joyce is able to arrest, through words, a vision of motion.
Movement is all: there is no finite verb in the sentence, and the subject,

the thing that is moving, is delayed until it serves as a punctuation, never ceasing to move but coming to rest in the act of being apprehended. Words either fail Stephen dismally, or he makes them triumph, momentarily. He cannot appreciate the comic. In the scheme of Joyce's comedy he establishes, early on, a lyric undercurrent that will run through Bloom's comic ruminations and emerge in Molly's thoughts: a sense of poetic possibility that can only be realized, finally and by others, in the comic.

As Joyce's language gathers allusions (heroic, religious, literary, and so forth) in his description of Bloom's journey through Dublin, it becomes increasingly parodic in Mulligan's style. But with these differences: Joyce can do more with his irony than Mulligan can, and the butt of it is not the morose Stephen but Leopold Bloom, who cannot and would not resist it, but who modulates its effects with his peculiar humanity. Mulligan has no interest in the failure of language to express reality. His irony is merely a mocking device, a strategy of reduction. It is the source of his cynicism that the reality that his irony reveals is not important to him: its force is simply there, available, resistant, water that won't become wine, bones that fail to fly. But the action of irony in Bloom's chapters, which Joyce controls more and more as the narrative becomes increasingly and self-consciously his own, is not just a mocking revelation of failure. Because Bloom is closer to Joyce. When we first see Bloom, beginning his day, he is contentedly sunk in reality. He can regard his cat with empathy. He can "relish" the very beastliness of reality ("the inner organs of beasts and fowls") that Stephen dreads. When Bloom imagines, while walking out into Dublin's warmth, what it might be like to travel, in one day, around the world "in front of the sun," passing turbaned faces and hearing dark language, he can acknowledge to himself that what he fancies is "probably not a bit like it really. Kind of stuff you read . . . " (57). His restless mind is constantly attempting to formulate ideas about a reality that he is content to have evade the ideas. The ideas give him pleasure, and so does the actual world. This is the source of the "equanimity" that he will achieve after a day that harrows his spirit. So the comic irony of his chapters is never only destructive, nor reality ever only beastly.

In the later chapters, as Joyce's increasingly insistent styles distance us from Bloom, the gap between language and reality widens. It is as if the mannered language were an index of Bloom's troubled mind as he approaches the necessary return to his adulterous wife. In the "Sirens" chapter, the gay music in the Ormond and the music of Joyce's style, in which language is manipulated as sound, are played off against Bloom's lonely suffering. The irony is mostly sad, precisely because the music and

Bloom's thoughts are juxtaposed but not allowed much interplay. When Dollard cries *"bless me, father,"* Bloom is "unblessed" (285). But Joyce can make the irony comic. Bloom sees, under a "sandwichbell," "one last, one lonely, last sardine of summer. Bloom alone" (289). Here his thoughts mingle the song he has just heard, "The last rose of summer," with a headless sardine, an image of Bloom. The comic result is that, briefly, the song becomes Bloom's own, and the sardine is elevated into music, the connection between song and sardine being a sense of loss, romantic and real. In this way the musical language is made to seem absurd, and Bloom's sorry vision of himself is made musical, part of a rich phrase. It is not a simply parodic comedy, like Mulligan's introit.

In the famous ending to the "Cyclops" episode, Joyce produces one of his most hilarious comic moments:

> When, lo, there came about them all a great brightness and they beheld the chariot wherein He stood ascend to heaven. And they beheld Him in the chariot, clothed upon in the glory of the brightness, having raiment as of the sun, fair as the moon and terrible that for awe they durst not look upon Him. And there came a voice out of heaven, calling: *Elijah! Elijah!* And he answered with a main cry: *Abba! Adonai!* And they beheld Him even Him, ben Bloom Elijah, amid clouds of angels ascend to the glory of the brightness at an angle of fortyfive degrees over Donohoe's in Little Green Street like a shot off a shovel. (345)

If we imagine these words coming from the nameless Dubliner who narrates this chapter, the comedy strikes us as merely ironic, a nastier version of Mulligan's parodies. Bloom, who has just shouted to the enraged Irish "citizen" that "your God was a jew. Christ was a jew like me," is seen being driven away while standing up in Martin Cunningham's car. The description of his hasty departure as Elijah's ascension, then, completes the picture that the narrator draws of Bloom as a ridiculous and feeble fool "with his dunducketymudcoloured mug on him. . . . " He ascends like a shot off a shovel, a burlesque Elijah. But of course the comedy of the passage is more complex than that because Bloom has already displayed, in Barney Kiernan's pub, a kind of heroism that makes the comparison with Elijah not entirely inappropriate. If Bloom does not ascend in glory, he has been superior to his circumstances. He has defended, however rhetorically and ineptly, justice, love and his race in the teeth of narrow-minded hostility. So that, in the above passage, we hear Joyce's voice over the narrator's; indeed, the language is not the narrator's familiar dialect (with the possible exception of the last six words);

one does not imagine him parodying II Kings. Joyce celebrates Bloom's moral victory even as he undercuts him. The Biblical language both elevates and mocks Bloom. The comedy results both from the ironic disparity and from the uplifting correspondence between Bloom and Elijah. The paradox is that the reality of the situation is best revealed in a language inappropriate to it.

Bloom is too weak and foolishly human to achieve Biblical glory and too courageously human to be something shot off a shovel. He moves, he exists, in a reality that both resists and requires elevation in order to be fully expressive. Joyce's increasingly comic language enables him to maintain and enlarge Bloom's love of abstract thought (his formulations, his fantasies) and at the same time his love of reality by allowing them to contradict each other without cancelling each other out, by allowing a full and dynamic interaction that is both skeptical and gay. This language fulfills its comic potential in "Ithaca," Bloom's last and funniest and climactic chapter.

3. "Ithaca"

"Ithaca" is the most influential of Joyce's chapters, a watershed of modern comic literature. If the permutations and philosophical slapstick of Beckett, the "scientific" comedies of Thomas Pynchon and Don DeLillo, and the detached tone and nonsense lists of Donald Barthelme can be said to have a common ancestor, it is this strange catechism. When Joyce told Frank Budgen that "Ithaca" was his favorite chapter, he said, "It is the ugly duckling of the book."[14] This suggests to me that what Joyce and many others have described as its cold and unemotional quality conceals the opposite, that "Ithaca" involves a transformation of its abstract style into something unexpectedly affecting and immediate, the discovery of the beautiful in the guise of the ugly. Analyzing its comedy helps us to realize this.

In this chapter, Joyce's style achieves its greatest distance from its subject matter at the very moment when the most significant action occurs: the return of Bloom and Stephen to Bloom's apartment.

> Of what did the duumvirate deliberate during their itinerary?
> Music, literature, Ireland, Dublin, Paris, friendship, woman, prostitution, diet, the influence of gaslight or the light of arc and glow-lamps on the growth of adjoining paraheliotropic trees, exposed corporation emergency dustbuckets, the Roman catholic church, ecclesiastical celibacy, the Irish nation, jesuit education,

careers, the study of medicine, the past day, the maleficent influence
of the presabbath, Stephen's collapse. (666)

Here, as in all the questions and answers in the chapter, the comedy derives from the contrast between the efficient objectivity of the style and
the human material that is its substance. Or, in this specific passage, the
contrast between the brisk and impersonal marshalling of topics and
what must have been the natural flow of a lively conversation. It demonstrates with a vengeance Bergson's idea of the mechanical encrusted on
the living, only its reference is beyond the social interaction taking place.
Here the mechanism is the imposed style, the hectically categorical narrative, with its mad orderings of human experience and exchange. And
what most characterizes this mechanism is its love of words. Here, it
seems, is where we've been headed with all the words so far in this book:
a comical height from which all the flux and chaos of human life can be
arranged and ticked off in a series, without regard to value or emphasis or
importance. This style, this vision of the two men, would be deadening
were it not for the aesthetic pleasure we derive from the sounds and the
rhythms of all these words. The above list is mechanical and impersonal,
but in its strange beauty it also conveys Bloom's and Stephen's savoring
of language. At this crucial moment in the action of the novel, Joyce slyly
turns our attention to the appreciation of language at its most abstract:
how inappropriate it is, and yet how pleasing.

When we read "the influence of gaslight or the light of arc and glow-
lamps on the growth of adjoining paraheliotropic trees," we react at once
to the discrepancy between the scientific precision of the telling and the
simple aesthetic pleasure of the subject. But is the comic message received
the wholly ironic one of how *wrong* this language is? Most critics have
either regarded Joyce's detachment in "Ithaca" as expressing a bleak and
"ironic indifference,"[15] or a cold, self-contained repose.[16] But if we miss
how funny this language is, we miss what the detachment is played off
against, we miss the interplay that allows us a comic pleasure. We feel
this comic pleasure—akin, no doubt, to Bloom's appreciation of science
as providing a perspective on rather than an escape from human affairs—
in the sounds of the words, from the way they *can* be precise and musical,
even when concerned with things for which their precision is hilariously
unnecessary. William B. Warner, who argues, as I am doing, that the
"movements of language" are "the central 'events' of the novel," finds
that "the strange peace" of "Ithaca" comes from Joyce's "exploration of
the otherness of language."[17] But language can never be wholly "other,"
can never be, as Warner says elsewhere, "autonomous." It *refers* us to re-

ality, however inappropriately. "Ithaca" is more comically active than peaceful. In a fine phrase Stanley Sultan calls the charm of Joyce's style "the charm of harmonious unfailing wrongness,"[18] and it is the clash between harmony and wrongness that is the source of its comic life.

The form of "Ithaca" is the question-and-answer of a catechism, and the business of catechism is to instruct. This in itself is comic, since the material at hand, ranging from a catalogue of books to ideas about "the critical turningpoint of human existence," hardly lends itself to an authoritative exposition of doctrinal teaching. How can a catechism, with its zest for elementary and condensed principles, instruct us about the chaotic multiplicity of modern life, of modern knowledge?[19] Joyce exploits every aspect of this comic irony, from asking simple questions that require insanely elaborate answers, to inventing turgid questions that elicit simple responses ("For what creature was the door of egress a door of ingress? For a cat"). The art of the chapter is "science." Joyce shows us that the modern passion for scientific analysis is a botched way that we have of trying to understand the fundamental principles of the world. Science replaces religion, and the result takes us back to the derivation of "catechize" from a Greek word meaning "to sound amiss, to din in." To get inside his locked apartment, Bloom lowers himself down from the railings and "allows his body to move freely in space" for two feet, ten inches.

> Did he fall?
> By his body's known weight of eleven stone and four pounds in avoirdupois measure, as certified by the graduated machine for periodical selfweighing in the premises of Francis Froedman, pharmaceutical chemist of 19 Frederick street, north, on the last feast of the Ascension, to wit, the twelfth day of May of the bissextile year one thousand nine hundred and four of the christian era (jewish era five thousand six hundred and sixtyfour, mohammedan era one thousand three hundred and twentytwo), golden number 5, epact 13, solar cycle 9, dominical letters C B, Roman indication 2, Julian period 6617, MXMIV. (668–9)

What dins in our ears here, and in almost every exchange in the chapter, is the invasion of simple and fundamental reality by a consciousness determined to seek a basic order (and hence an impossible instruction) in the nature of things, to penetrate to the mechanisms of the universe through analysis. The result is, of course, not a revelation of the workings of reality but a machine of language fed by a profusion of facts, a machine that necessarily sounds amiss. In Bergson's metaphysical terms, this machine can only account for a simple, natural, continuous, fluid motion (falling) in terms of stoppages in sequence, like a cinematograph. The comedy of this resides, as it always does, in our awareness of a contradiction, and so we are forced, as the chapter proceeds, to consider what it is that this machine is doing wrong, what it is that contradicts and evades its analytical activity.

Joyce liked the "reassuring ghostliness"[20] of "Ithaca." Its ghostly or superhuman style is reassuring because it doesn't work, because through the failure of its comic mechanisms we can glimpse the reality of Stephen's and Bloom's quiet communion. We experience the interpenetration of the subdued and minor human circumstance and the noisy, inflated, impersonal language that attempts to describe it.

As the language tries to shape the reality we come to see the scene in Bloom's apartment as ironical. We think: what a pathetic and unfulfilling climax to the novel's action. The two men sip cocoa, disagreeing more than they agree; Stephen refuses Bloom's offer of accommodation for the night, and probably will never take up Bloom's offer of having him give Molly Italian lessons. Nothing is resolved, nothing is satisfying. The language puts us at a vast remove from whatever might affect us. At times we are so buoyed up by the swelling air of scientific and scholarly speculation that we view this interaction as an almost interpolated thing, something slipped in and only fitfully glimpsed in the context of astrological coordinates and geological eons. At other times we view the data of the interaction so minutely that the context of the duumvirate's conversation seems to swell away *from* us, in absurdly burgeoning detail. Is "Ithaca," then, the ironic result of Joyce's double technique of particularization and mythification: the disappearance of human character in the obsession with style?

Not entirely. Precisely because the mechanisms of Joyce's language are *comic*, they create for us whatever joys the reality can contain, whatever emotions the language cannot, except in its ineffectuality, order for us. This is the more difficult aspect of the comedy to describe. What sort of communion does take place, and what vision emerges from it, in a joy that the irony cannot circumscribe?

Bloom's scientific temperament leads him to imagine a rather comprehensive chaos.

Why would a recurrent frustration the more depress him?
Because at the critical turningpoint of human existence he desired to amend many social conditions, the product of inequality and avarice and international animosity.

He believed then that human life was infinitely perfectible, elimi-
nating these conditions?

There remained the generic conditions imposed by natural, as distinct from human law, as integral parts of the human whole: the
necessity of destruction to procure alimentary sustenance: the painful character of the ultimate functions of separate existence, the
agonies of birth and death . . . the fact of vital growth, through con-
vulsions of metamorphosis from infancy through maturity to decay.
(696–7)

In the face of this knowledge, Bloom has ceased speculating about the
amelioration of the conditions of mankind, feeling dejectedly that "it was
a task for a superior intelligence to substitute other more acceptable
phenomena in place of the less acceptable phenomena to be removed"
(697). He has felt, at various times during his day, impotent to deal with
the flux of things that his mind characteristically apprehends or conjures.
Just before the carriage bearing Bloom and the others to Dignam's fu-
neral stops at the cemetery, they see "the high railings of Prospects
rippl[ing] past their gaze. Dark poplars, rare white forms. Forms more
frequent, white shapes thronged amid the trees, white forms and frag-
ments streaming by mutely, sustaining vain gestures on the air" (100).
We assume this is Bloom's vision. It certainly speaks to him of the vanity
of human forms in the mortal motion of the world. Later, the style of the
"Lestrygonians" chapter makes us experience Bloom's unblinking vision
of the "stream of life" (153). And his thoughts in "Ithaca" take him to
the stream of the universe, the chaos of the constellations of heavenly
bodies. His "logical conclusion" about the multitudinous features of
the constellations is "that it was a Utopia, there being no known method
from the known to the unknown: an infinity, renderable equally finite by
the suppositious probable apposition of one or more bodies equally of
the same and of different magnitudes: a mobility of illusory forms im-
mobilised in space, remobilised in air . . ." (701). Bloom's vision is that
we have no clear relation to what is Out There, above or around us. It recalls the modern scientific vision sketched in my first chapter.

In the face of this vision Stephen, whose temperament is declared to be
"artistic," "affirms his significance as a conscious rational animal proceeding syllogistically from the known to the unknown and a conscious
rational reagent between a micro- and a macrocosm ineluctably constructed upon the incertitude of the void" (697). He does not participate
in Bloom's "dejection." Rather, he seeks a rational (what Father Lynch
would call a "univocal") order. One way of describing Stephen's condi-

tion is through his desire to become precisely the "superior intelligence" that Bloom despairs of becoming, to substitute more acceptable for less acceptable phenomena. Stephen distrusts "aquacities of thought and language," which he finds incompatible with "the erratic originality of genius" (673). Of the stream of impressions that come to him at Sandymount, he tries painfully to make a poem, to discover the genius of phenomena and declare it. So although, in "Ithaca," the phrase that describes the spectacle of the constellations, "the heaventree of stars hung with nightblue fruit" (698), seems to come from Joyce as a description of what *both* men confront as they emerge from the house, it surely expresses Stephen's artistic vision. Bloom rejects it; in the passage on the constellations quoted earlier, he is declaring that what they saw "was not a heaventree, not a heavengrot, not a heavenbeast, not a heavenman" (701). For him to describe the constellations poetically is to make, "in the delirium of the frenzy of attachment" (701), a nostalgic connection between the human and the not-human, between the known and the unknown, between form (tree) and formlessness (heaven). In doing so, one creates a new word, "heaventree," but one has not described reality.

Yet the comedy of Bloom's language is not a function of what Father Lynch would call his "equivocal" vision, but of the interaction between the exaggerated formality of his language and the immensity of the micro- and macrocosmic reality to which it is applied. In the thick of Joyce's / Bloom's words there is a constant sense of form, of mathematical play with dividends, divisors, series, succinctness—of an infinity rendered finite by the veritable process of the human mind. In passages such as these—

> . . . the parallax of parallactic drift of socalled fixed stars, in reality evermoving from immeasurably remote eons to infinitely remote futures in comparison with which the years, threescore and ten, of allotted human life formed a parenthesis of infinitesimal brevity. (698)

> . . . of the universe of human serum constellated with red and white bodies, themselves universes of void space constellated with other bodies, each, in continuity, its universe of divisible component bodies of which each was again divisible in divisions of redivisible component bodies, dividends and divisors ever diminishing without actual division till, if the progress were carried far enough, nought nowhere was never reached. (699)

—language becomes a comically frantic machine, attempting in sheer profusion to capture a reality that is, finally, a "nought," never to be reached. In the latter passage, words are elaborated with increasingly anxious precision and confidence, only to be followed by a stutter of negatives. The language *increasingly evokes chaos* as it attempts to dispel it, and so fails as it succeeds, and vice versa. Something immense and impossible to comprehend is being rendered in terms of precision, and this paradox is the source of the comedy. In his way Bloom, too, is an artist, a comic artist, a failed artist. His vision is shot through with the humanity of his aspiration and incompetence.

If, then, we study the complexity of the comedy of Joyce's language, we can see that the distinction between it and the reality it wants to describe results *at once* in an ironic clash and an evocation. The humanity of Bloom and Stephen is not cancelled in Joyce's method. Rather, the technique of the dual narrative achieves its climax in "Ithaca" in the extremity of its presentation: the situations and thoughts of the two men are severely diminished (in the context of the enormity of the universe) *and* elevated (by the context of the enormity of the universe). The irony of the former and the affirmation of the latter are realized, gradually, in what Father Lynch would call the "analogical" vision of equanimity.

Equanimity, the key word in "Ithaca," first appears in the discussion of Mrs. Riordan, a common acquaintance of both men. Bloom used to wheel her in her bathchair to where she could observe, through his "one-lensed binocular fieldglasses" the progression of citizens passing "from the city to Phoenix Park and *vice versa*." The question is then asked, "Why could he then support that his vigil with the greater equanimity?" —and the answer is as follows: "Because in middle youth he had often sat observing through a rondel of bossed glass of a multicoloured pane the spectacle offered with continual changes of the thoroughfare without, pedestrians, quadrupeds, velocipedes, vehicles, passing slowly, quickly, evenly, round and round and round the rim of a round precipitous globe" (681). Equanimity, then, seems to be achieved through seeing the continual changes of the world—"the stream of life"—in the context of its neverchangingness. The citizens move to and fro in their passage through the single lens of the fieldglasses, strangely formal in their variety. And through the distortion of the rondel, the young Bloom could see the spectacle of change in the context of the reality of its occurring on a "round precipitous globe," on which there is no movement that does not take place on the arc of a single shape. The lens of vision here imposes its own order, and equanimity is the result of the balance of change and changelessness, of apprehending that balance.

It is this equanimity of Bloom's which balances the artistic and scientific visions, and which results from the communion of Stephen and

Bloom. Bloom wishes Stephen to see that we are as brief nothings in an immense series, extending infinitely outward to the constellations and inward to the atomic makeup of matter. He sees himself as having "proceeded energetically from the unknown to the known through the incertitude of the void" (697). He has, during his day, spiralled inward to home and Molly *through* this void. Stephen, on the other hand, has proceeded from the known to the unknown and so has been spiralling outward, and will step from Bloom's home *into* what seems a void of uncertainty. The two of them have, in small but important ways, affected each other, though not in terms of any plot action. The brief coming together of their visions has affected how each sees himself in the vast spectrum of time. Hearing Bloom chant his anthem, Stephen "heard in a profound ancient male unfamiliar melody the accumulation of the past," and Bloom, chanting, "saw in a quick young male familiar form the predestination of a future" (689). It is here, at home, Ithaca, the present, that they truly meet. Later, under Molly's window, each contemplates "the other in both mirrors of the reciprocal flesh of theirhisnothis fellowfaces" (702). What they see in each other and in themselves simultaneously is that although they are surrounded by the void, they can view that immensity by their place together in the present, in their present reality. This present is the order from which disorder can be apprehended.

As they part, we are not allowed to know what Stephen feels. Bloom, alone, feels the "cold of interstellar space" and is reminded of the deaths of his companions (704–5). But then, seeing dawn approach, the formality of the world again asserting itself ("this disparition of three final stars, the diffusion of daybreak, the apparition of a new solar disk"), he returns with "deep inspiration . . . retraversing the garden, reentering the passage, reclosing the door" (705). No longer dejected, he continues his immemorial ways. Seeing several volumes "improperly arranged" on his bookshelves, he reflects on "*The necessity of order*, a place for everything and everything in its place" (709, my stress). However absurd the order, whether of volumes on a shelf or of the completed familiar shape of a trying day, it is affirmed with an equanimity gained from necessity.

As Bloom prepares to climb into bed, the following questions occur:

> What did his limbs, when gradually extended, encounter?
> New clean bedlinen, additional odours, the presence of a human form, female, hers, the imprint of a human form, male, not his, some crumbs, some flakes of potted meat, recooked, which he removed.
>
> If he had smiled why would he have smiled?
> To reflect that each one who enters imagines himself to be the first

to enter whereas he is always the last term of a preceding series even
if the first term of a succeeding one, each imagining himself to be
first, last, only and alone, whereas he is neither first nor last nor only
nor alone in a series originating in and repeated to infinity. (731)

The ironic joke here is that Bloom's abstract train of thought leads us to
imagine an infinity of "suitors." But this very abstraction helps Bloom to
locate himself. He realizes that we *are* a small unit of an immeasurable
series, and yet that that series is gauged in terms of the present, Molly's
"endless" suitors gauged in terms of Bloom (which we will later realize,
in Molly's monologue, is true). The preceding series ends with Bloom and
the succeeding one begins with him. Camus' Sisyphus has the same vision, and it is important to note that, just as Camus imagined Sisyphus
happy, so Joyce imagines that Bloom might have smiled. Joyce may have
made the smile conditional to indicate simply that it is not in Bloom's nature to smile; the passages that follow derive directly from his imagination of series, and are not expressed conditionally. In any case it is this
vision, and the smile it might have induced, that banishes the suitors by
overcoming their destructive effect upon him. It is both a painful joke and
an heroic act.

Bloom's "subsequent reflections" are affected by the sentiments of
envy, jealousy, abnegation and, finally and most conclusively, equanimity (732). Why equanimity? Because Molly adulterously copulating is
"as natural as any and every natural act. . . . As not as calamitous as a cat-
aclysmic annihilation of the planet in consequence of collision with a
dark sun," and as "irreparable" as the past (733). And so, in the terms
that Father Lynch used to describe the analogical imagination, Bloom
comes to grasp "the human reality . . . according to the measure of its
every dimension, according to the measure of all its definiteness, according to the measure of its time phases. . . ."[21] It is a comic equanimity because it derives from a contradiction between the immediate, painful
facts and the way these facts may be ordered in abstract ways, seen in a
larger context. Bloom's equanimity is painfully ironic because the contradiction reveals only a cuckold's futile rationalizing, a mechanical
ordering shored up against the ruins of a marriage. But it is also joyful because it reveals to us the order, or the necessity for an order, that enables
him to go on, to accept the irreparable. The tendency of Bloom's mind to
the abstract, which has dominated "Ithaca," achieves its transcendence of the base and the self-defeating and the self-consuming (envy,
jealousy), at the same time that it reveals itself as its own reality-creating
machine, a machine of language.

In "Ithaca," then. *Ulysses* arrives at the sheer *wordness* towards which it had been tending. At the very end of the chapter, as Bloom is falling asleep and the catechism continues to murmur questions like some sort of lullaby, and the reality of the day in Dublin fades, Bloom's /Joyce's words beget words.

> Womb? Weary?
> He rests. He has travelled.
>
> With?
> Sinbad the Sailor and Tinbad the Tailor and Jinbad the Jailer and Whinbad the Whaler and Ninbad the Nailer and Finbad the Failer and Binbad the Bailer and Pinbad the Pailer and Minbad the Mailer and Hinbad the Hailer and Rinbad the Railer and Dinbad the Kailer and Vinbad the Quailer and Linbad the Yailer and Xinbad the Phthailer.
>
> When?
> Going to a dark bed there was a square round Sinbad the Sailor roc's auk's egg in the night of the bed of all the auks of the rocs of Darkinbad the Brightdayler.
>
> Where?
> ● (737)

Noting that Joyce merely mentions Sinbad as an example of a great traveller who gets home, and doesn't develop the image beyond that, Robert Martin Adams concludes as follows:

> The going-to-bed litany is a piece of inspired stupidity . . . containing layer after layer of meaninglessness—an unfathomable depth of mental void. Relaxing its hold on external reality, and on its own thought processes, the mind is shown drifting off into a mechanical word-cuddling, and so into complete darkness. The more we project conscious intellectual meaning into the process, the less it serves its overt purpose. Like a Rorschach-blot, the passage will absorb anything we want to put into it. . . .[22]

But there is more to be noted about a nonsense passage than its resistance to intellectual analysis. In creating all his versions of Sinbad the Sailor, Bloom is playing with language as a child plays with it, creating new words through logical analogies. Children (and adults) find it comical to do this because they are engaged in the difficult process of learning lan-

guage, and in such nonsense talk they can make free with a logical process. The comedy of nonsense, as Elizabeth Sewell has argued, derives
from the play of order and disorder; nonsense enables us to conjure an
anarchic dream world of unlike things while controlling things in a system of order.[23] Bloom's inventions are combinations of the meaningless
(Tinbad, Jinbad, etc.) and the meaningful (Tailor, Jailer, Hailer, etc.). At
the same time that this passage shows language to be arbitrary, a mere
game of sounds, it also shows us how language creates our reality for us
by naming it, how inexorably logical it is in its symbol-making function.
In the "Eumaeus" chapter that precedes "Ithaca," Stephen, barely listening to Bloom's loquacious prattle, "could hear, of course, all kinds of
words changing colour like those crabs about Ringsend in the morning,
burrowing quickly into all colours of different sorts of the same sand
where they had a home somewhere beneath or seemed to" (644). It is
amazing how many of Bloom's words in the Sinbad passage have a home
(is a "Kailer" one who makes a scotch broth?) and how many seem to
("Dinbad" *sounds* like a word, a Jabberwocky word, part of a system
we're familiar with).

In the "Darkinbad the Brightdayler" passage we can see how Bloom's
scientific and Stephen's artistic temperaments can come together in a
game of words. Here the analytical style of Bloom's consciousness makes
a comedy of Stephen's "Heaventree" poetry. Both men are trying to put
words together to better understand their reality. Bloom helps us realize
the failure of this endeavor, and Stephen helps us realize the necessity for
it. In this final arrangement (we are drawn to the self-conscious shape of
the sentence), we glimpse language poised between not making sense and
revealing some hidden truth.

Finally, in the controversial dot or spot that, in the original edition and
in some later editions, served as a mute answer to "where?"—we see the
language of the novel fade into its pure material, printer's ink, just as
Bloom fades into sleep. He has travelled through hundreds of pages of
printed language, not through a veritable Dublin. As language has tri-
umphed in the course of the novel, lifting us from an easily perceived quotidian reality into its (language's) sphere of influence, just so has it failed.
In its very beauty, in the creation and shapely arrangment of sounds and
meanings, language has revealed its mechanisms, its separation from
what it has so brilliantly evoked. But Joyce does not, of course, end his
novel with this large, silent punctuation. In Molly's monologue the joy
that the manner of "Ithaca" so comically failed to quench, comes flowing
forth, almost without punctuation.

4. "Penelope"

Molly Bloom's soliloquy is Joyce's spirit of comic joy released. The ordering consciousness of "Ithaca," its attempt to shape experience into
question-and-response, gives way suddenly to a stream of thought, "like
a river winding through a plain, finding its true course by the compelling
logic of its own fluidity and weight,"[24] to use Budgen's lovely description. As everyone who has read the novel knows, this is a startling
change. R. M. Adams declares that the "*clou* of the book is that turn by
which the perversely 'rational' mind in 'Ithaca' . . . gives way to the dark
rhapsody of 'Penelope.' "[25] Molly's thoughts seem to have the chaotic
"stream of life" quality that Bloom often apprehends in reality, if only
momentarily. During "Lotus Eaters" Bloom is standing under the railway arch when he has this fleeting vision: "An incoming train clanked
heavily above his head, coach after coach. Barrels bumped in his head:
dull porter slopped and churned inside. The bungholes sprang open and a
huge dull flood leaked out, flowing together, winding through mudflats
all over the level land, a lazy pooling swirl of liquor bearing along wide-
leaved flowers of its froth" (79). This vision of flood, so like the various
descriptions of "Penelope" one encounters (except that Molly's flood is
anything but dull), occurs to Bloom just after he has been thinking about
a million-pound check that Lord Iveagh of porter fame was said to have
cashed: "A million pounds, wait a moment. Twopence a pint, fourpence
a quart, eightpence a gallon of porter, no, one and fourpence a gallon of
porter. One and four into twenty: fifteen about. Yes, exactly. Fifteen millions of barrels of porter. What am I saying barrels? Gallons. About a
million barrels all the same" (79). Bloom's mathematical bent leads him
directly to his fantasy of the porter's having burst from its containers to
cover the land. It's a comic yielding: the multiplicity of forms conjures the
very formlessness that had made order so necessary. Just so, the odd,
compulsive orderings of "Ithaca" subside into an unconsciousness that
then seems to find release, for the reader who turns the page, in Molly's
flood of remembrance, which celebrates the *élan vital* that Bloom knows
is inextricable from—indeed, is the coursing life of—his world of forms.
That is one way of describing why he returns to Molly, to that necessary
part of himself. But Molly too, as we shall see, celebrates her husband as a
necessary focus for her thoughts, a way of ordering her experience. Nothing could better illustrate the intricacy and depth of their relationship
than the drama of his consciousness seeming to yield to hers, as her consciousness begins to imagine him at the moment when they lie together in
bed. It is a moment when language, having in its comical failure dwindled

to a mere period, is suddenly revived in joy. But we must realize that that joy, too, is comical. For if Bloom's rational formulations have given way to Molly's relatively intuitive consciousness, so Molly's *élan,* being a stream of language, will increasingly express itself in form. There is no avoiding the contradictory interplay of language and change in this novel.

The uniqueness of Molly's chapter seems to provide us with a dramatic example of Langer's "life invincible" or Bergson's "intuition." Seen this way, it becomes a happy ending to *Ulysses,* but not necessarily a comic one. To say yes to life in all its pain and pleasure, loss and gain, is not, in and of itself, a comic act. Rather than strictly oppose Molly's fluidity to the mechanisms of Bloom's chapters, her "reality" to his language, we should understand that the comical contradictions remain the same, except that in "Penelope" they are more heavily weighted to joy (the expression and celebration of formlessness) than to irony (the dissolution of form). It is not enough to say that "Penelope" is a river, or a "teeming chaos" (Goldberg) or "the motion of life itself" (Adams). It is not the motion of life itself because her thoughts are composed of words. Molly's language, like all language, seeks to fix itself in form, and so the comedy of contradiction continues in a different key. As Bloom sought, in bed, the Molly in himself, so Molly seeks the "Poldy" in herself. Her river of words is not, like Wallace Stevens' "River of Rivers in Connecticut," a river of Being, flowing "nowhere, like a sea"; it has a direction. As Warner says so well, in "Penelope" we experience "language as it begins to shape itself into fictional projections ... language informed by its human origin."[26]

This is a typical comic passage from "Penelope"; Molly is referring to Bloom's body beside her: "O move over your big carcass out of that for the love of Mike listen to him the winds that waft my sighs to thee so well he may sleep and sigh the great Suggester Don Poldo de la Flora if he knew how he came out on the cards this morning hed have something to sigh for ..."(778). The comedy here derives from the clash between what is naturalistically observed (Bloom's bedtime noise) and what is romantically evoked ("the winds that waft my sighs to thee"). Bloom's noise reminds her of his very real presence as an aging man with strange habits, an annoyance. His noise immediately makes her remember the conventional and rhetorical loveletters he wrote to her long ago, which in turn reminds her of the Spanish nobleman, Don Miguel de la Flora, she invented as a fiancé to make her first lover jealous (759). Then she returns to her real and considerably less romantic domestic situation. The irony, of course, works against Bloom, who is no romantic figure at the moment and hasn't been since the death of their son. And yet it is Poldy's romantic nature that she evokes, in the love-language that she is so fond of and that drew her to Bloom. So there is an affection and a regret in this passage, and others like it, that points to something more than irony, something that is the force, the current in the stream of her thoughts.

Molly's comedy is an interplay between the natural and the poetic. Much of this involves Joyce's exploitation of the familiar conventions of comedies of manners, especially the way in which the forms of social life are exposed as foolish and unstable in comparison with the insistences of lust that underlie them. For Molly what is natural is what is vivid—the desires, and especially the sexual desires, that put her in touch with the ongoing energies of the world. There is a direct and traditional connection between her describing her own sexuality as "only natural" and her celebration, toward the end, of nature: "that would do your heart good to see rivers and lakes and flowers all sorts of shapes and smells and colours springing even out of the ditches primroses and violets nature it is . . ." (781–2). It is from her feeling of what is natural that she is able to make comedy out of male hypocrisy and indirection, all that men use to cover their lust. When one of her lovers, Bartell d'Arcy, "said wasnt it terrible to do that there in a place like that," Molly's reply is "I dont see anything so terrible about it Ill tell him about that some day not now and surprise him ay and I'll take him there and show him the very place too we did it so now there you are like it or lump it . . ." (745). There it is, she will point out: desire, as natural on the choir stairs as anywhere else. Soon after this she describes Bloom's begging her to let him feel her drawers in public: "theyre so savage for it if anyone was passing so I lifted them a bit and touched his trousers outside . . . he was shaking like a jelly all over" (746). Soon afterward, "he wrote me that letter with all those words in it how could he have the face to any woman after his company manners making it so awkward after when we met asking me have I offended you with my eyelids down of course he saw I wasn't . . . of course I had to say no for form sake dont understand you I said and wasnt it natural so it is of course . . ." (746–7). That letter "with all those words," she says. Language is the most common social *form* that she undercuts with her exuberance. When, during confession, Father Corrigan rather too eagerly asks where a man touched her, "on the leg behind high up was it yes rather high up was it where you sit down," Molly replies "yes O Lord couldn't he say bottom right out and have done with it," then adds (though not to Father Corrigan) how much she really liked being touched there (741). Later on she remembers Dr. Collins' asking her if she had "frequent omissions," and thinks, "where do those old fellows get all the

words they have omissions" (770). The doctor's use of such circumlocu-
tions ("could you pass it easily pass what I thought he was talking about
the rock of Gibraltar the way he puts it") makes her distrust him. Yet
she likes to play with such words and get her own comic effects out of
them, as when, near the end, describing how she'd clean Bloom's spunk
off her rump, she returns to the doctor's words: "Ill wipe him off me just
like a business his omission . . ." (781).

But the words Molly most enjoys are the poetic ones of conventional
romance, and it is her interest in them that enables Joyce to bring the
chapter to its comic climax. Molly constantly expresses her love for a
poetry that, Rosalind-like, she is always undercutting in the manner described above. While rambling on about letters she'd received, she says,

> I wish somebody would write me a loveletter his wasnt much and I
> told him he could write what he liked yours ever Hugh Boylan in Old
> Madrid silly women believe love is sighing I am dying still if he wrote
> it I suppose thered be some truth in it true or no it fills up your whole
> day and life always something to think about every moment and see
> it all around you like a new world I could write the answer in bed to
> let him imagine me short just a few words. . . . (758)

She wants love to fill her life, for her to imagine and be imagined by her
lovers when the acts of love are over, to have love be *continuous*. In this
her vision is as romantic (and as deluded) as Miranda's first glimpse of
her brave new world. Molly knows that words are just words, possibly
true, probably not. Her inability to get the crass Boylan to be romantic
leads her to think of the "silly women" in her youth falling for the stale
rhetoric of romance. Such language is a lie, comically exposed. When she
thinks later of the letter she caught Bloom writing, she says, "he thinks I
dont know deceitful men all their 20 pockets arent enough for their lies
then why should we tell them even if its the truth they dont believe
you . . ." (772). And yet there is for Molly something in the language of
loveletters and lovesongs that speaks the "truth," something that gets
expressed despite the intentions of the author ("thered be some truth"
even in Boylan's letter). So that the comedy develops a complexity, as
"false" and "true" come to have a more than simple relationship to one
another, the easy formula of "true" feelings undercutting "false"
language.

The passage quoted above about loveletters leads Molly to think of her
first lover, Lieutenant Mulvey. She fell for him when he wrote her a love-
letter. She wonders if she should wear a white rose for him, like the
"silly" Andalusian women she mentioned earlier. Then, in a crucial pas-

sage, she says, "what did I tell him I was engaged for fun to the son of a
Spanish nobleman named Don Miguel de la Flora and he believed that I
was to be married to him in 3 years time theres many a true word spoken
in jest there is a flower that bloometh a few things I told him true about
myself just for him to be imagining . . ." (759). Don Miguel de la Flora is
both an invention, designed to deceive, and something that reveals a
truth about Molly's nature: her love of romance revealed as the love of
the sound of words. The flower of Molly blooms in the creation of her invented flower finacé. She gives a conventional phrase, "theres many a
true word spoken in jest," a twist. The narrator of "Cyclops" used the
phrase more conventionally. When the citizen asks, Who does Bloom
suspect as the father of his children? the narrator replies, "Gob, there's
many a true word spoken in jest" (338), meaning that the citizen has hit
on the scandalous truth of Molly's promiscuity that they all knew about.
When Molly uses it, she means that the jest is harmless and the truth can
shine through it. For her language, however false, can express a truth
deeper than the fact of her promiscuity, a truth that is the source of her
promiscuity: her desire to heighten and make beautiful the life that she
lives from the life that she feels within her. This desire is the current in her
soliloquy, and her thoughts of Bloom the letterwriter, the language-
lover, are its channel.

Molly's recounting of her chaste affair with Mulvey is told with a
typically comic mixture of romanticism (white rose, flirtation, blushing
innocence) and sexual candor ("I pulled him off into my handkerchief
pretending not to be excited"). This same comedy informs her thoughts
about Bloom, to whom she constantly returns. With "his mad crazy letters my Precious one everything connected with your glorious Body
everything underlined that comes from it is a thing of beauty and of joy
for ever something he got out of some nonsensical book . . ." (771)—that
is, with his combination of rhetoric and lust—he is the perfect match for
Molly. She finds his letters "nonsensical" but is "excited" by them. Later
she says she "thought he was a poet like Byron," though it turned out he
wasn't: "they all write about some woman in their poetry well I suppose
he wont find many like me where softly sighs of love the light guitar
where poetry is in the air the blue sea and the moon shining so beautifully
coming back on the nightboat from Tarifa the lighthouse at Europa point
the guitar that fellow played was so expressive will I never go back there
again all new faces two glancing eyes a lattice hid Ill sing that for him
theyre my eyes if hes anything of a poet two eyes as darkly bright as loves
own star . . . " (775). In this extraordinary passage, Molly moves smooth-
ly from the trite poetry of love to the poetry of reality that no doubt once

inspired it. She remembers her youth as a poem, and its beauty is still in her eyes, and if Bloom is a poet he'll write about *that* reality; even if his words were silly, they would be beautiful, as they once were. In the lie of language is its *expressive* truth, because it can catch in its form, however false that form may be to reality, the truth that the very flux of reality bears away from us.

Near the end of *Ulysses* Molly gathers her energies to celebrate the moment when Bloom asked for her hand. It was the moment in her life when romance became real; it is the moment, in the narrative, when the truth and falsity of language become one: "yes 16 years ago my God after that long kiss I near lost my breath yes he said I was a flower of the mountain yes so we are flowers all a womans body yes that was one true thing he said in his life and the sun shines for you today yes that was why I liked him because I saw he understood or felt what a woman is and I knew I could always get round him and I gave him all the pleasure I could . . ." (782). It is here, in her own use of Bloom's love-language ("I near lost my breath") that she can speak the true thing as she remembered Bloom speaking it. It is a truth beyond the gross turmoils and changes of the body, the sexual naturalism that so marks her soliloquy: if the flower bloometh and fadeth it is still a flower. It is a truth that can only be expressed in a language that is necessarily false, that denies or ignores so much in the power of its nostalgia, that fixes a moment of lost youth. In Joyce's last words, Molly confuses Mulvey and Bloom in her desire to relate her youth and her marriage: "and Gibraltar as a girl where I was a flower of the mountain yes when I put the rose in my hair like the Andalusian girls used or shall I wear a red yes and how he kissed me under the Moorish wall and I thought well as well him as another and then I asked him with my eyes to ask again yes and then he asked me would I yes to say yes my mountain flower and first I put my arms around him yes and drew him down to me so he could feel my breasts all perfume yes and his heart was going like mad and yes I said yes I will Yes" (783). Here the flow of Molly's thoughts gather into a deep pool in which we can see, finally and clearly, an image of herself and Bloom that is her poem. Despite what Joyce wrote to Harriet Weaver, the stream of "Penelope" is not endless, does not imply endlessness.[27] It culminates in this vision of romance, in which Bloom, the letterwriter, actually *becomes* Mulvey, and his proposal of marriage becomes the realization of the dreams of her youth. In a sense it is an absurd moment of pure nostalgia: here is Molly dreaming of lost days while her husband, who hasn't approached her sexually since the death of their son, lies snoring in the imprint left by her latest lover. Because the image expresses her desire to deny the tendency of things, the particularly dreary stream of her life, it is as false as the love-prattle she has made fun of. And her refrain of "yes" is an expression of her *will* to affirm and accept the truth of her illusions: a yes spoken against an implied no. All this is true, and yet this climactic image is also a moment of comic joy. To return to Joyce's remarks on comedy in his Paris Notebook, joy, "the feeling which is proper to comic art . . . is the feeling which the possession of some good excites in us." Joy holds us in rest so that we may apprehend the beautiful. Just so, Molly's final vision allows her to possess something beautiful that is *still* true about her and Bloom, despite all. Her refrain of "yes" is an affirmation and endorsement of the truth of this. It culminates in the final, capitalized "Yes" that seems to affirm the entire chapter, all the life she has led, Life itself, the energy of which she can now comprehend joyfully in poetic form. It is at once the falsity and the joy of language that it can hold in rest a reality that must, by its nature, move on irremeably. It is fitting that Molly, who so mistrusts words, should be the most successful poet in this comedy of language.

Molly does not resolve the tensions between the multitudinous and changing reality in *Ulysses* and the various strategies of language that attempt to contain it. It is precisely the comic nature of the novel that makes the stasis she achieves (and Bloom achieves in his equanimity) a suspension of opposing forces rather than a resolution. The same is true in the last acts of Shakespearean or Restoration comedies, in which the anxieties and ironies that make up the comic life of the bodies of the plays are not so much resolved or transcended as they are gathered and embraced —*possessed,* to use the language of Joyce's comic theory. What Molly and her husband come to possess, in their respective last chapters, is the force of their lives, a force that dissolves all their efforts to comprehend or compose it. They can apprehend irony and joy at the same time because they come to realize the comedy that makes each one an aspect of the other. Their failure is comic because it reveals the nature of what it cannot contain; their joy is comic because it can only be expressed in the various forms it denies. In the same way Joyce is able, in irony and joy, to express the life of Dublin, the life of the world, in language. The "Yes" is Joyce's final word, too, the affirming of his novel's bringing to "rest" what cannot be arrested.

Faulkner: *As I Lay Dying*

1. Introduction

In his great novels of the late twenties and thirties, William Faulkner displays a more anarchical imagination than does Joyce in *Ulysses*. If Joyce can dissolve truth and falsehood in Molly's gathering yesses, bringing his novel to a joyful peroration, Faulkner's attempts to affirm the strength and endurance of the human result in a kind of clumsy and subdued folk comedy (as in the scenes between Byron Bunch and Lena Grove in *Light in August*), or excessively rhetorical set pieces (like the mule passage in *Sartoris,* or some of the passages celebrating Dilsey in *The Sound and the Fury*). Faulkner's most intense energies are expended in the realizing of characters like Benjy and Quentin Compson, Joe Christmas and Thomas Sutpen, characters in whose minds swirl the dark waters of dissolution and doom, the protagonists of tragic novels. Jason Compson, in *The Sound and the Fury,* is a major comic character, but his hilariously inept adventures carry no joy, no lyric undercurrent; what survives in his chapter survives in opposition or indifference to his manic greed. The irony that Faulkner employs in skewering Jason is a comic variation on tragic themes of dissolution, like the comic scenes in Shakespeare's tragedies. Jason functions more as a Polonius than as a Falstaff.

Beginning with "Spotted Horses" (1931) and other stories that found their way into *The Hamlet* (1940), however, Faulkner developed his easygoing later comic style, which derived more from the sense of the indefatigable intrinsic to folk material than from his metaphysical preoccupations. V. K. Ratliff has none of the anarchic about him. That is his charm and strength. His philosophical stance is strictly humanist. He is

the first and best of Faulkner's later comic characters. I would argue that
Faulkner's fiction declined as he settled into either comically (as in *The
Reivers*) or melodramatically (as in *Intruder in the Dust*) affirming the
values he outlined in his Nobel Prize Address. As Alfred Kazin says, "he
became a Wisdom Figure rather more entertaining than anything else."[1]
His comedy after *The Hamlet* became more and more conventional, less
and less intense, as it restricted itself to the moral and the social.

Three comic works, however, emerge from his most productive period: *As I Lay Dying,* "Spotted Horses," and "Old Man." These are his
greatest and most modern comic works, precisely because they involve
his most intense concerns with language and metaphysics, the relationship of reality to the forms that people make of it—concerns that more
often had a tragic dimension for him. In these works a balance is struck
between doom and endurance, despair and tenacity, that reveals Faulkner's deepest speculations as powerfully as do his tragic novels. In *The
Sound and the Fury* and *Light in August*, Faulkner separated his comic
from his more powerful tragic characters, and the comic characters bear
no weight. Dilsey, who bears the weight of what Langer calls "life invincible," is not comic. In his greatest tragic novel, *Absalom, Absalom!,* he
creates no significant comedy to speak of. But in *As I Lay Dying,* his most
considerable and full-length comedy from this period (1929–1936), he
creates a whole raft of comic characters who float—the image is apt, as
we shall see—on the floodtide of his metaphysics and the exuberance of
his best prose, in the very waters in which Quentin and Joe Christmas and
the Sutpens sink.

As I Lay Dying has been problematical for critics—perhaps more so
than any other Faulkner novel—because it is both improbably humorous
and intensely metaphysical. The critics are almost weirdly divided on its
substance and tone. Some, regarding it from the perspective of Faulkner's
later work, discover it to be a ringing affirmation of the human spirit, a
celebration of pride and endurance over terrible circumstance.[2] These
critics tend to ignore the metaphysics of the novel and confine their remarks to the social realm, whence the humanist values that they cherish
—pride, duty, community—can be safely drawn. The characters of Addie and Darl and Vardaman and Dewey Dell Bundren, whose visions,
either in part or in whole, seem destructive of these values, are discussed
as either tragically deluded or insane; whereas poor, dogged Cash Bundren is tricked out as the hero, the bearer of light from the dark mental re-
cesses of the rest of the family. Needless to say, these critics do not discuss
the novel as comic; they perceive that it celebrates something, that it is

not tragic, and so turn that something into the values Faulkner affirmed
in his later years.

The critics who respond more to Faulkner's comedy (these are considerably fewer), regard *As I Lay Dying* as "an absurdist joke," a masochis-
tic exercise in cosmic pessimism.[3] They find its comic irony utterly destructive, a negation of human activity as futile and meaningless. For
them, Addie and Darl are the heroes, but they, like tragic protagonists,
are doomed. In this way, the comedy of the novel becomes a kind of rictal
grin affixed to a tragic mask. The difference between these critics and the
others, while striking, is superficial. All of them separate the elements of
irony and celebration in the novel rather than try to come to terms with
their relationship. One group negates what the other affirms, and vice
versa. If these critics think of the comic at all, they think of it merely as an
adjective modifying their other concerns. But, as I hope to demonstrate,
to see Faulkner's central and pervasive concerns as comic—or to imagine
the comic as having its proper range—is to see the novel whole. So I will
try to cover as much of it as I can.

Whether Faulkner is writing the hilarious folk humor that led Irving
Howe to call *As I Lay Dying* his "warmest . . . kindliest and most affectionate" novel,[4] or whether he is writing passages of a dark and surreal
lyricism, his comedy is animated by the same obsessions. He is constantly
observing "forms" of all kinds dissolved: objective forms like trees and
bridges, and forms constructed by the mind, whether promises made,
duties imagined, or words shaped, the forms that mental and verbal life
take. Like Joyce—one of his literary mentors—Faulkner loves to express
this dissolution as comic irony, showing how etiolated forms are when
compared to the exuberant, chaotic reality that bears them away. The
irony is comic, as I have said in reference to *Ulysses,* because the emotional investment is made in the formless reality, not in the forms that
cannot withstand its pull. Hence dissolution holds no tragic terror. And
yet, again like Joyce, Faulkner loves to create forms, to celebrate imagining them, to see them exfoliate in a landscape dangerous to them. The re-
sulting complexity is the life of the comedy, and the source of its range.
Let us analyze the comedy of two passages that are quite different in tone
even as they are similar in substance.

> We picked on down the row, the woods getting closer and closer
> and the secret shade, picking on into the secret shade with my sack
> and Lafe's sack. Because I said will I or wont I when the sack was
> half full because I said if the sack is full when we get to the woods it
> wont be me. I said if it dont mean for me to do it the sack will not be

full and I will turn up the next row but if the sack is full, I cannot help
it. It will be that I had to do it all the time and I cannot help it. And we
picked on toward the secret shade and our eyes would drown together touching on his hands and my hands and I didn't say anything. I said "What are you doing?" and he said "I am picking into
your sack." And so it was full when we came to the end of the row
and I could not help it.[5]

Here Dewey Dell (there is no more comically sexual name in fiction)
relates how she got pregnant by Lafe. As in Cora Tull's monologues, and
the preacher Whitfield's, and Anse Bundren's—where a folk humor prevails, immediate and straightforward in its effects—the comedy here lies
in our awareness that Dewey Dell's words and "doing" are "far apart"
(to use her mother Addie's words from another context). What she says
and what the real situation is, are two very different things. The irony
works to expose the rationalizing of her impulses. The "it" that she invents to abstract the situation and make her actions seem fated and inexorable, beyond her responsibility, is only her desire: "I could not help it."
Her reasoning is funny because it is so obviously fragile and makeshift
compared to her sexual drive. The comedy, like most folk comedy, is benign, the irony not vicious, because our lot is cast with her desire, which is
strong and real to us, however much it is exaggerated. We have to understand her desire in order to understand the comedy of her language. And
so her desire, too, is expressed, at the same time that her reasoning is revealed as a rationalization. Our sense of what subverts the form of her
reasoning is as necessary and vital an aspect of the comedy as the reasoning itself. And yet this "it"—the reality of her desire—is not dwelt on, nor
celebrated, nor affirmed—except by implication. We may or may not
consciously acknowledge it as we appreciate the immediacy of the comic
irony: she couldn't help *what*? But it is there, as pregnant with meaning
as poor Dewey Dell is with child (as she relates this), and Faulkner finds
other occasions to express and extend the reality of which it is a part, as in
this passage:

When I used to sleep with Vardaman I had a nightmare once I
thought I was awake but I couldn't see and couldn't feel I couldn't
feel the bed under me and I couldn't think what I was I couldn't
think of my name I couldn't even think I am a girl I couldn't even
think I nor even think I want to wake up nor remember what was
opposite to awake so I could do that I knew that something was
passing but I couldn't even think of time then all of a sudden I knew

that something was it was wind blowing over me it was like the wind came and blew me back from where it was I was not blowing the room and Vardaman asleep and all of them back under me again and going on like a piece of cool silk dragging across my naked legs. (115–6, italicized in text)

Here "something" is evoked that is beyond the struggle of her words to express it: the urgent life that is not the life of forms. It is the same life that lurks in "the secret shade" of the first passage and makes a mock of her rationalizing. In the above passage it is given full play as a nightmare of loss of identity, loss of the world of forms, and it has the same sensual force for her, "like a piece of cool silk dragging across my naked legs." In a sense, when Dewey Dell says in the first passage that "it won't be me," she's right: there is something within her that connects her to a reality larger than her self or any other selves. In the second passage this reality is not the implied force that blows down the careful cardhouse of her words; it is, instead, described in words that seek to follow its force, in a flurry of negatives, in a language that tries to cast itself aside in its effort to evoke the spirit of this "something" that blows in and out, abstract and yet sensual as wind, bearing the familiar world before it. It is a lyrical evocation, an affirmation of what language can do. If it lacks irony, it is no less a function of Faulkner's comedy. Here and elsewhere, Faulkner establishes the nature of a reality that brings language to a test that it can either ironically fail or joyfully pass—or both together, in a paradox that is the source of the novel's comedy.

In the following passage, the conjunction of the world of forms and the reality of formless energy provides us with the novel's most dense and peculiar comedy. Darl is describing the search for Cash's tools, lost in the flooded river.

Jewel and Vernon are in the river again. From here they do not appear to violate the surface at all; it is as though it had severed them both at a single blow, the two torsos moving with infinitesimal and ludicrous care upon the surface. It looks peaceful, like machinery does after you have watched it and listened to it for a long time. As though the clotting which is you had dissolved into the myriad original motion, and seeing and hearing in themselves blind and deaf; fury in itself quiet with stagnation. (156)

We will come to this passage later. What I wish to stress now is that the ironical vision of human activity (the life of forms as a "ludicrous" machinery, a surreal sight gag) is a function of the vision of "myriad original motion," the Bergsonian flux of being. People are machines rehearsing the careful details of their lives in a reality of change that renders these details futile, these lives absurd. That the machines behave "with infinitesimal and ludicrous care" increases the effect of the comedy by underlining the contradiction between the two worlds. The shaping of form is celebrated in *As I Lay Dying* just as it is revealed as illusory, pointless, mechanically obsessive. It is not a question of simply making Jewel and Vernon Tull look ridiculous. Their search here is imagined as comically as are Dewey Dell's reasons for lying with Lafe, but it is also invested with the same strength as her desire. In searching for the very tools that have proved so inept and inconsequential in constructing a form (Addie's coffin) that can hold tight against floodwaters, these men affirm their place in reality even as that reality negates it. And so the world of forms, the world in which human activity, if not human nightmares, takes place, is seen in a constant struggle with the reality for which the flooded river is a central symbol. It is through a comic vision that Faulkner can best imagine the contradiction in this struggle, because comedy keeps the contradiction so constantly before us, providing the joy of shaping in the face of dissolution, and an irony that dissolves that very shaping. The strength and weakness of human life is rendered fully.

In the next section I will discuss the ways in which Faulkner's reality of flux undermines the illusory life of forms in an action of destructive irony. Faulkner's comedy varies in accordance with the range of forms. He punctures Cora Tull's reasoning and Anse's hypocrisy with the benignity of a folk raconteur. Or he exposes the Reverend Whitfield's pretensions with the relish of a satirist. Or he calls into question the very nature of how our conscious lives are structured by words, with the detached thoroughness of a metaphysician. But in all this ironic comedy there is— implied or articulated or dramatized, depending on the character who is narrating—a force imagined that is stronger and deeper than all the forms, whether they be trees, promises, human identity, or, most significantly, words themselves. This force makes its pressure felt at the edges of almost all the witnessing consciousnesses (the exceptions are the most mundane and peripheral characters), and pervades some of them, like the wind that blows through Dewey Dell's mind.

As I describe the dissolution of forms, I will seem to be approaching the conclusion that Faulkner's vision is fundamentally anarchic or nihilistic. And indeed, I'll be shaking all the dark leaves in what is often a phantasmagorical landscape. But then, in my next section, I will discuss how Faulkner gives strength to what he so strictly calls into question: the shaping of form. Ultimately, it is a creation that he performs as an artist, he who speaks through every monologue, writing them from an overall consciousness that becomes our own. My separation of these two aspects of the comedy is for purposes of clarity and convenience. It is, of course, a separation impossible to sustain, given that *As I Lay Dying,* as a comedy of language, is concerned with the relation of irony and celebration. So I'm content if the next two sections overlap. In my final section, I'll express this relation more conclusively, in a discussion of Cash as a comic character.

2. The Dissolving of Form

The world of forms is the relatively superficial one in which the Bundrens, on a promise to Addie, bear her body to Jefferson, bury it among her ancestors, and prepare to return with a new Mrs. Bundren. This is what R. P. Adams calls "the traditional epic journey . . . a parable of creation, the motion of travel implying a process in which the separately inert materials or elements of the world combine into living forms."[6] It is indeed a world of forms, of doing what you set out to do because you have given your *word,* and of doing it as best you can.

The other world is given its clearest and most cogent expression in Addie Bundren's monologue. It is a vision of reality as formless energy, "dark voicelessness" flowing through the land, the nothingness of being. This reality is not linear; it is not a progress, however difficult, from the hills to Jefferson. It is, rather, a reality in which all directions, all motion and stasis, are one. This world renders the world of forms literally ab-"surd," arising from and dissolving into the wordless irrationality of pure existence.

Images of these two worlds are presented to us at the very beginning of the novel, in the first of Darl's many monologues. Jewel and Darl are walking single file up a path "as straight as a plumb-line" and worn by feet "in fading precision." There is a cotton-house in the center of the field and the path circles it. Jewel stares straight ahead, with his wooden face and "rigid gravity," ignoring the circularity of the path. He will be the only Bundren concerned *solely* with carrying out the purpose of the journey. He steps in a single stride through the opposite window and into the path again without breaking stride. Darl, the only Bundren who will decide that the journey should not be completed, and who attempts to act on that decision, follows the circular path, and so falls behind in their progress. It is Darl who, along with Addie, recognizes the absurdity of available forms and is, finally, unable to cope with them. The comedy of Jewel's walking through the cotton-house as though it were not there exposes the house as an empty form. With fallen chinking and broken roof, it "leans in empty and shimmering dilapidation in the sunlight." As a form, it is precisely situated, yet crumbling and empty. Jewel stops to drink at a natural spring as they near the Bundren house, while Darl walks on to the house, where he drinks from a bucket and meditates on its "form." Jewel and Darl are posed, in opposition, as respectively, the character least interested and most interested in forms, and the most and least able to act. Darl's monologue, already conceived with intense visual formality, ends properly with a vision of his brother Cash's fitting two boards together and filling the air with the rhythmic

Chuck.   Chuck.   Chuck.

of his adze, Cash who is surrounded by his boards and nails and tools, obsessed with using them precisely.

We have seen that the cotton-house is empty and in the process of dis-solution. The next monologue, Cora Tull's, interrupts the spatial and chronological flow established by Darl's monologue, and provides us with another comically empty form: the discourse that issues from her mind. In her first paragraph she discusses, in tedious detail, the economic rationale behind her baking cakes to earn money to increase the net value of her chickens. She figures it all out, and then her paragraph ends, "So I baked yesterday, more careful than ever I baked in my life, and the cakes turned out right well. But when we got to town this morning Miss Law-ington told me the lady had changed her mind and was not going to have the party after all" (7). So her rationale dissolves, and in the face of the unforeseeable, Cora, never at a loss, turns to her faith ("riches is nothing in the face of the Lord"), and the precision of her form, repeating throughout her monologue that the cakes "turned out real well." We realize, halfway through her ruminations, that she is present at Addie's deathbed while worrying about her cakes. After thinking that salvation and grace are not upon Addie, she says to the other women, "They turned out real nice. . . . But not like the cakes Addie used to bake." The comical-ly incongruous juxtaposition of trivial and empty concerns with the pro-found facts of human existence is a favorite method of Faulkner's. In the face of inevitable change his characters, like Chekhov's, attend to the ir-relevant details of their lives. The trivial and the profound function as terms in a metaphor, commenting on each other, finding their common ground in the absurdity of form. Death, we will discover in *As I Lay Dying*, is as absurd as cakes that will neither be sold nor eaten.

The rhythmic sound of Cash's sawing fills the first third of the novel. Even when Cash is not center-stage, his sawing is always in the background, a great drone. Cora says that they can always hear him working (8), and Jewel in his first monologue says, "It's because he stays out there, right under the window, hammering and sawing on that goddamn box. When she's got to see him. Where every breath she draws is full of his knocking and sawing where she can see him saying See. See what a good one I am making for you" (14). This passage metaphorically connects the sawing (which Cora thinks "sounds like snoring") to Addie's breathing. It infuriates Jewel because it reminds him of his mother's dying. And when Dewey Dell comments on the sawing, she says, "And Cash like sawing the long hot sad yellow days up into planks and nailing them to something" (25). Sawing, breathing, days: these are the rhythmic motions of life in linear time, the ticked-off progression of events. Anse "spits with decorous and deliberate precision," recalling Cash's precision with the adze and saw, and the "fading precision" with which feet have worn down the path. Precision is the triumph of form, of the obsession with form, and form includes our very breathing, the measure of our lives: trivial, empty, ending in naught. Cash is "labouring on towards darkness"; when he slants two boards into "their final juxtaposition," "shaping with his empty hand in pantomime the finished box" (47), Addie dies.

Empty and *dead* are words often used by Faulkner to describe the world of forms. Dewey Dell's long monologue describing her crisis over her pregnancy, a crisis brought on by Dr. Peabody's presence, is filled with a simultaneous awareness of life and death. She says that Anse, eating, "looks like right after the maul hits the steer and it no longer alive and dont yet know that it is dead" (58), an hilarious image of stunned mechanism. As Dewey Dell experiences her own dissolution—in her hysteria—she experiences the life inside her, she feels her "bones and flesh beginning to part and open upon the alone." "I lean a little forward, one foot advanced with dead walking . . . I begin to rush upon the darkness . . ." (59). Her awareness of her sexual being is an awareness of death. At the end of her monologue she thinks, "The dead air shapes the dead earth in the dead darkness, further away than seeing shapes the dead earth. It lies dead and warm upon me, touching me naked through my clothes" (61). *Seeing,* the human observation of a life of forms, shapes only a dead reality. Life is dead, a long twilight pantomime. The air on Dewey Dell is dead *and* warm, she feels "like a wet seed wild in the hot blind earth," which is also a "dead earth." Here the intimate closeness of life to its dissolution is expressed lyrically; her life becomes more alive in its contact with reality, and more dead, too. She can feel ecstatically what her father, in his mechanism, his utter absorption in the life of forms, cannot.

In the monologue immediately following hers, her brother Vardaman, also in a crisis (over his mother's being put in a box), is intensely aware of shadows. The shadow is the empty shape of ourselves. When Darl soon picks up the description of Cash's finishing the coffin through the night, it becomes a phantasmagoric event, the solitary lantern illuminating the figures and movements of a dream. Cash places "the planks with long clattering reverberations in the dead air," which "smells like sulphur" (71–2). Upon the "impalpable plane" of this dead air, "their shadows form as upon a wall." The life of forms is, like the shadows on Plato's cave, an empty illusion. In the lantern-light, Cash bevels the edge of a board "with the tedious and minute care of a jeweller." When they hoist the coffin and carry it inside, it seems empty and lifeless to them, yet they speak of it as though it were only sleeping, waiting to awaken (75). The coffin, composed of planks that Vardaman has previously described as "bleeding," is a form as alive or more alive than the men who carry it. The monologue ends with Darl considering whether he *is*—how he, as a form, can "empty" himself for sleep. And immediately after this monologue comes Cash's reasons for bevelling the coffin. If Vardaman says, immediately, "My mother is a fish" (79), Cash is saying here that his mother is a body that exerts stress. The forms of life are interchangeable, equally "dead" in their empty living, attended to carefully by other dead forms.

Much later in the novel Darl muses, "How do our lives ravel out into the no-wind, no-sound, the weary gestures wearily recapitulant: echoes of old compulsions with no-hand on no-strings: in sunset we fall into furious attitudes, dead gestures of dolls. Cash broke his leg and now the sawdust is running out. He is bleeding to death is Cash" (196–7). The no-wind, no-sound, no-hand, no-strings suggest, once again, the illusory quality of the world of forms. We are like dolls, dead effigies made of sawdust, the sawdust recalling Cash's sawing. Dewey Dell thought earlier that Cash's "sawdusted arms looked like sand" (57), and it has already been mentioned that Vardaman sees the plank Cash is sawing as "bleeding." In Darl's words above, the blood-sawdust metaphor is completed, and the suggestion of ourselves as puppets guided by no puppet-master with no strings, just dead forms making dead gestures, is made clear.

Forms in *As I Lay Dying,* being empty and frail, are always at the point of dissolution. Vardaman describes his confrontation with Jewel's horse in these words: "It is as though the dark were resolving him out of his integrity, into an unrelated scattering of components . . . I see him dissolve —legs, a rolling eye, a gaudy splotching like cold flames—and float upon the dark in fading solution; all one yet neither; all either yet none. I can see hearing coil toward him, caressing, shaping his hard shape . . ." (55). The sense of shape, the sense of wholeness is an illusion, liable to dissolve into its component parts. The imagery of flotation, wherein the illusory quality of forms is described, appears elsewhere. Darl describes Addie's face, in death, as "fading into the dusk as though darkness were a precursor of the ultimate earth, until at last the face seems to float detached upon it, lightly as the reflection of a dead leaf" (49). The earth is a darkness that dissolves the forms of life, the things which float dreamlike upon the surface. Recall the "dark void" that Dewey Dell feels rushing under her as she lies, as if floating, in her bed. Flotation imagery is, of course, most prevalent in the river episode, the dark current analogous to the dark void, both precursing the ultimate darkness. Darl considers the undergrowth and the river seen through it, into which he will soon plunge: "Above the ceaseless surface they stand—trees, cane, vines— rootless, severed from the earth, spectral above a scene of immense yet circumscribed desolation . . ." (135). "Spectral," of course, suggests shadow, illusion, empty forms. Darl and Cash are trying to determine where the road, or ford, used to be before the current rose, in order that they may move across it. Darl sees Cash "looking back along the floorless road shaped vaguely high in air by the position of the lopped and felled trees, as if the road too had been soaked free of earth and floated upward, to leave in its spectral tracing a monument to a still more profound desolation than this above which we now sit, talking quietly of old security and old trivial things" (136). The mules, too, once the river overcomes them, lose "contact with the earth." And when, after everything— wagon, men, mules, coffin—has been floated around, Darl describes Jewel and Vernon recovering Cash's tools, in a passage I've already quoted, as torsos searching ludicrously upon a surface that has severed them. Having been baptized in the current, Darl is becoming increasingly aware of the absurdity of the world of forms: precision is ludicrous. The scene looks peaceful to him, like machinery, a description analogous to his doll image. Reality is not shape; shape is an illusion. We are merely clottings in the motion of the river, a clotting that will dissolve. Seeing and hearing are blind and deaf, and shaping is absurd. Darl's description of Dewey Dell's wet dress shaping "for the dead eyes of three blind men those mammalian ludicrosities which are the horizons and valleys of the earth," suggests that the ludicrousness of forms is connected with their regenerative capacities, their ability to continue and multiply (Darl obviously has Dewey Dell's pregnancy in mind, he being the only Bundren who knows about it).

Darl's vision of the "myriad original motion" takes us to Addie's single monologue, which comes soon after the one of Darl's quoted above. In Addie's monologue the subject of *language* as something that shapes the world of forms becomes prominent. Addie's vision of reality is that of "nothingness," that is, of no forms. Forms are to her only what perception and language shape, and perception is blind and deaf, language is composed of shapes to "fill a lack." The subject of language has occurred earlier. Jewel's desire for a time of quiet with his mother is a desire for the sound of the adze to cease (15), but also, in retrospect, for the sound of words to cease. Faulkner points this up by having Jewel remain quiet through the rest of the novel, except for some muttered curses and peremptory calls to action. In the next section after Jewel's first, Darl describes his trying to cope with this problem: " 'It's laying there, watching Cash whittle on that damn . . .' Jewel says. He says it harshly, savagely, but he does not say the word. Like a little boy in the dark to flail his courage and suddenly aghast into silence by his own noise," (18). The fact of death makes words seem like childish noises flung into the darkness, talismans which, in moments of awareness, are realized as imprecations. Almost immediately, Anse speaks of how he gave his word that he would get Addie to Jefferson "so she could rest quiet." Getting her husband to make this promise is Addie's vengeance: "But then I realized that I had been tricked by words older than Anse or love, and that the same word had tricked Anse too, and that my revenge would be that he would never know I was taking revenge" (164). In this passage *words* become *word,* the paradigm word that absorbs all meanings because all meanings are equal in their meaninglessness. Her revenge is that she causes Anse (and the others) to shape their deeds to this word, and so make them suffer for it, for being dutiful to a word that is just noise. Anse's word is absurd despite Addie's intention, because he has already promised her he'd keep the team ready, and is in the process of breaking that word. Darl's monologue near the beginning ends, appropriately, with his describing how the voices in their house, because of the wind, sound as though they come out of the air above their heads (19). They are words of the wind, disembodied, floating in nothingness, clottings of sound. Later Dewey Dell, speaking of herself and Lafe, says, "and then I saw Darl and he knew. He said he knew without the words like he told me that ma is going to die without words, and I knew he knew because if he had said he knew with the words I would not have believed that he had been there and saw us" (26). She, too, realizes the divorce of words from knowing. Later on Vardaman, seeking silence after his mother's death so that he can cry quietly, thinks he can hear and know the silence of the wood and the dark, but not "living sounds," not the sounds of others in the house, nor of Jewel's horse.

The next morning the sounds of the bereaved are heard as they sing, and when the song ends, the voices quaver and fall, as all voices must, into silence. Tull describes Whitfield's voice: "His voice is bigger than him. It's like they are not the same. It's like he is one, and his voice is one, swimming on two horses side by side across the ford and coming into the house, the mud-splashed one and the one that never even got wet, triumphant and sad" (86). Here the voice is truly disembodied. The reference Tull makes is to Whitfield's crossing the river on the way to Addie's dying. *He* is the one who emerges mud-splashed with sin, his and Addie's sin, and it is his *voice*, singing hymns, that emerges triumphant. In Whitfield's only section he says that because he was borne "safely above the flood" (and the flood was not very severe when he crossed it, as Tull says elsewhere), that he is forgiven his sin with Addie, is cleansed of it, though he arrives muddy from the waist down (170), like some sort of ecclesiastical satyr. His reasoning is as comically empty as Dewey Dell's. He says that God "knew that when I framed the words of my confession it was to Anse I spoke them, even though he is not there." His words, then, never even get wet; they are perhaps the emptiest in the novel. Whitfield triumphs, to his own mind, through his words. As Addie says at the beginning of her section, "people to whom sin is just a matter of words, to them salvation is just words too" (168).

Addie's monologue, then, is prepared for, in terms of the cold eye it casts on language. To Addie, words are the Fallen world, evidence of a separation from reality, which to her is the "dark voicelessness" flowing through the land, "the dark land talking the voiceless speech." She says, "And when I knew that I had Cash, I knew that living was terrible and that this was the answer to it. That was when I learned that words are no good; that words dont fit even what they are trying to say at. When he was born I knew that motherhood was invented by someone who had to have a word for it because the ones that had the children didn't care whether there was a word for it or not" (163). The same is true of fear, pride, love, time, Anse, "what you will," just shapes to "fill a lack," forms to fill the silence. Like other forms, these words are disembodied

and dead: "the high dead words in time seemed to lose even the significance of their dead sound" (167). When Addie learns that living is terrible, she learns at the same time that words are no good. She asks Anse to
promise to bury her in Jefferson because she knew that her father had
been right, that "the reason for living was to get ready to stay dead a long
time" (161). Addie feels that she, like Anse, had been dutiful to the dead
echo of the "word," but that after having Darl, she believed that her duty
was "to the alive, the terrible blood, the red bitter flood boiling through
the land" (166). Although this flood is associated with the earth and with
blood, the life force, the alive, its life is not the life of forms. It is, rather,
the formless energy underlying forms. This reality is dark because light is
necessary for forms to be perceived, like the lantern used to light Cash's
work on the coffin, which shapes the phantasmagoric shadows. This reality is "voiceless" because words are the names for forms. It is "nothingness" because forms are substantive. And it is "alive" because it is the
force behind all life-forms, gravid and deep. Addie is dead to the life of
forms, but that life, to her, was dead anyway, a ghostly shaping disembodied from the real. So Addie, in a sense, in reality, has not died. Death
has no dominion over her.

Recall the remarks by Peabody, someone who, as a doctor, has worked
close to the energies of life: "She has been dead these ten days. I suppose
it's having been a part of Anse for so long that she cannot even make that
change, if change it be. I can remember how when I was young I believed
death to be a phenomenon of the body; now I know it to be merely a function of the mind—and that of the minds of the ones who suffer the
bereavement. The nihilists say it is the end; the fundamentalists, the beginning; when in reality it is no more than a single tenant or family moving out of a tenement or a town" (42–3). What is suggested here is that
there is no fundamental change from what we have come to call "life" to
"death," in the sense of one ending and the other beginning. There is a
change; the body dies, dissolves, but it is like a departure, a movement
"out of a tenement or a town," which are only forms. It has often been
pointed out that Addie is still alive in the minds of the other Bundrens,
"the ones who suffer the bereavement." This is so, but she is "alive" in a
sense more profound than that.

In an essay entitled "Human Survival of Biological Death,"[7] Lawrence
LeShan discusses the differences between the "world-pictures" of classical physics and field theory physics—differences which may clarify
Addie's vision of reality. From the viewpoint of classical physics, which is
the "common-sense, Newtonian mechanics method of structuring reality," events " 'happen' as time flows inexorably and steadily from the

future, through the present and into the past." From this viewpoint, "it is an inexorable conclusion that biological death means the annihilation of the consciousness and self-awareness of the individual," that is, biological death is a fundamental end in a linear concept of time. From the "gestalt" viewpoint of field theory, however, "the primary, most 'real' aspect of an entity is its part in the larger pattern. . . . To perceive it at all, apart from the total field, is to perceive it as a subsystem, an artificially separated aspect of a field of stresses, a pattern." From this theoretical vantage, field theory physics' concept of time is Einsteinian: "events 'are,' and we—so to speak—stumble across them as we perceive narrow successive 'slices' of the space-time totality." Space and time are continuous; boundaries—ends and beginnings—are not the most "real" aspect of the world-picture. A concept of the individual consciousness, of the "I," must be consistent with the rest of the world-picture, given the initial, gestalt reasoning. "It must follow the general conceptual rules of field theory, and function in accord with the general dynamic laws which we have attributed to the model. . . . To do this, we must conceptualize the 'I' as boundaryless in the continuum; as not being 'separate from' or 'isolated from' the rest of 'what is'; as not being limited by specific events such as the perceived ceasing of biological activity." There are no such "termination events as birth and death." And so, "in the sense that all things that 'were,' 'are' or 'will be' exist forever in the continuum, the individual continues to 'be' after biological death."

Addie Bundren's vision of what is real and alive is very much like this vision of field theory (the mystical aspects of which LeShan acknowledges and explores). The world of classical physics is the world of forms, existing in linear time. To Addie, all these forms, named by words are absurd, and what is real is beyond linear time. It is the life of the land, the terrible blood, or, in Darl's words, the original motion. Speaking of her affair with Whitfield, Addie says, "Then it was over. . . . But for me it was not over. I mean, over in the sense of beginning and ending, because to me there was no beginning nor ending to anything then" (167). And Darl describes Addie's hands, moments after she dies, as seeming to be "spent yet alert . . . guarding with horned and penurious alertness the cessation which they know cannot last" (50). And indeed in the next monologue she continues to live, for Vardaman, in the fish he has killed and, later, in all fish, swimming in the current, because "it hadn't happened then. And now she is getting so far ahead I cannot catch her" (52).

The life of forms is a perpetual dying, a dissolving into reality. Addie remains present and dying throughout the novel, not merely because her family continues to be obsessed with her, but because she is still a part of the world of forms, is still present inside the precision of Cash's form, the coffin, unburied and an active force in the family's life. It is Darl who comes to realize this and who determines to destroy, as soon as possible, the form that contains her as well as the form of her physical body, which still "talks in little trickling bursts of secret and murmurous bubbling" (202). Vardaman has a conversation with Darl next to the coffin at Gillespie's and under an apple tree, symbol of the Fall into linear time, mortality:

> I put my ear close and I can hear her. Only I cant tell what she is saying.
> "What is she saying, Darl?" I say. "Who is she talking to?"
> "She's talking to God," Darl says. "She is calling on Him to help her."
> "What does she want Him to do?" I say.
> "She wants Him to hide her away from the sight of man," Darl says.
> "Why does she want to hide her away from the sight of man, Darl?"
> "So she can lay down her life," Darl says. (204–5)

Addie is still alive to the life of forms, is still "looking" at them through the wood, and Darl has determined to stop her travail, and return her to what is real to her (and to him). So he tries to burn Gillespie's barn, in which the coffin is being kept overnight. The flames of the barn "sound like an interminable train crossing an endless trestle" (209): and endless change, an endless departure. Unfortunately for Darl, Jewel rescues the coffin from the flames, and Darl ends up lying on it, crying, once again under the apple tree (214).

In my discussion of field theory I broached the subjects of space and time, as they might apply to *As I Lay Dying*. Linear time defines the world of forms. Time and form come together in Cash's "sawing the long hot sad yellow days up into planks and nailing them to something." Time and form (here the emptiness rather than the precision of form) come together when Tull, referring to Anse, says, "When the shadow touches the step he says 'It's five o'clock' " (31). Time and form come together when Addie places *time* among the empty words, and describes the "high dead words in time" (167). This is the "time" in which the journey takes place, as a completed progression, shaped by the echo of Anse's word. But along the way we experience time, especially through Darl's consciousness, not as a linear progression, but as a circular continuum. One of the main effects of Faulkner's peculiar narrative method is to allow us to experience, *at once,* the journey as a few days on the road to Jefferson, and the journey as something revolved in the minds of the travellers.

Darl describes the buzzards that hover over the commencement of the journey as "motionless in tall and soaring circles" (98). They will appear, again and again, drawn to the smell of the corpse, always hovering in circles. Darl begins to laugh. And soon, when from his position facing backward he sees Jewel approaching on his horse, Darl thinks, "We go on, with a motion so soporific, so dreamlike as to be uninferant of progress, as though time and not space were decreasing between us and it" (101). A wagon proceeds from where it has been to where it is to where it will be, yet a linear concept of time flows in the opposite direction, as LeShan notes, from future to present to past. From his position facing backward Darl experiences these two opposing progressions simultaneously, and the result is that time, like space, becomes merely *is,* "uninferant of progress." Much later, when they reach the crest of a hill and look out over Jefferson at last, Vardaman asks, "Is that Jefferson?" and Darl replies yes, and then describes what Vardaman sees: "He lifts his head and looks at the sky. High against it they hang in narrowing circles, like the smoke, with an outward semblance of form and purpose, but with no inference of motion, progress or retrograde" (216). This description of the buzzards is also one of the journey, indeed of all motion in a vision in which time and space are continuous. If we describe a linear progression in terms of a line, then a line with no "inference of motion, progress or retrograde" can be said to form a circle—a line which has completed itself by returning on itself. When Darl confronts the dark current of the river, he thinks, "It is as though the space between us were time: an irrevocable quality. It is as though time, no longer running straight before us in a diminishing line, now runs parallel between us like a looping string, the distance being the doubling accretion of the thread and not the interval between" (139). This is a good deal like LeShan's "narrow successive 'slices' of space-time totality," the slices being the spatial accretions of circling time. It is the most severe obstacle they encounter in their journey, and all the Bundrens, in one way or another, are made to struggle in its "original motion."

The imagery of circles is especially prominent in Darl's monologues. Early in the novel he speaks of getting up at night and drinking from a cedar bucket, "the still surface of the water a round orifice in nothingness" (11). Drinking from this nothingness is an intensely pleasurable experience for him. Like his mother, Darl is drawn to this dark and sensual reality, out of which emerges the life of forms: human identity, isolate and bereft. For him the world of forms is strange; it is not home. When he cries "I dont know what I am. I dont know if I am or not" (76), he articulates the paradox of feeling that he is both of and not of the world in which he finds and then loses himself. He is both attracted to and repelled by sexual regeneration, by the fact that something comes out of nothingness and must exist in some measure apart from it, empty when it is full, dying when it is endlessly alive. When Dewey Dell ministers to the stricken Cash after the river accident, Darl's description of her breasts as "mammalian ludicrosities" and her leg as "one of that caliper which measures the length and breadth of life" (97–8), he brings together images of sexuality and form (her leg being like one of Cash's tools). His obsession with his sister's pregnancy is an obsession with the "ludicrous" idea of continuing to generate a life of forms. We will discuss, later, the climax of this subject in his vision of the spy-glass.

Dewey Dell herself, in an important monologue very much like Addie's (114–6), intensely feels her pregnancy as the family passes the New Hope signboard, New Hope being the place which, if Anse decides to go and bury Addie there on account of the flood, signifies to her, her failure to obtain an abortion in Jefferson. "Now it begins to say it. New Hope three miles. New Hope three miles. *That's what they mean by the womb of time: the agony and the despair of spreading bones, the hard girdle in which lie the outraged entrails of events*" (114–5). "That" refers grammatically to New Hope, which links the idea of New Hope with the womb of time, which is agony and despair. Her loathing of having her secret discovered, because of the shame, allows Faulkner to muse on the despair of living and giving life. The "spreading bones" and "hard girdle," which refer to the womb, also suggest the grave, which is what her womb will become if she obtains an abortion. She then says that she sits naked (in Darl's sight because Darl knows) "on the seat above the un-hurrying mules, above the travail," and travail refers, of course, to the coffin and Addie, but also suggests the labor of giving birth. The travail that is dying and death is the travail that is birth and living: the travail of the journey itself. In this monologue, more intensely than in any other of hers, Dewey Dell experiences the essential unity of life and death, which the world of forms must envision as separate and opposite. Worrying about her child, about whether or not she should ask Anse to turn and go to New Hope, makes her think of the black void that she felt rushing under her at night. In the myriad original motion of reality, life and death are inextricably entwined. Later on in her monologue, this experience is expanded into the remarkably Beckett-like passage I quote on page 54. Here she experiences a small death, the dream of life becomes a nightmare. Her sense of form dissolves: her sense of her own identity, her sense of the division between sleeping and waking, her sense of time. All she experiences is *change:* "something was passing," blown by wind. This is, at the same time, an experience of her own sensuality: the wind as silk across her naked legs recalls Darl's feeling the cool silence blowing upon his parts as he masturbates (11).

Sex, the fact and idea of two-ness, is evidence of the Fall from the unity of being into the world of forms. Part of the travail of living is to extend life. It is when she knew she had Cash that Addie knew that "living was terrible." When she had Cash she felt she was "violated" by the world of forms, and that this violation took place "outside the circle" (164)—that is, the circle of unities, time and space, progress and retrograde, life and death.

The tension between the world of form and the world of flux is often expressed in vertical and horizontal imagery. Addie says, "I would think how words go straight up in a thin line, quick and harmless, and how terribly doing goes along the earth, clinging to it, so that after a while the two lines are too far apart for the same person to straddle from one to the other . . ." (165). The failure to straddle these two worlds, of words and doing, suggests the comic irony of saying one thing and doing another, the comedy of the incommensurable. It is easy to imagine the situation as a sight gag, the two worlds further and further apart until the straddling is impossible. It is clear which world Addie identifies with. She hates her father for ever having "planted" her, like another tree to be swept away by a flood.

It is also clear which world Anse identifies with. He is a man of stasis, not motion: that is part of Addie's revenge. In his first and only major monologue, Anse reveals himself to be obsessed, not with his wife's impending death, but with the road on which he will soon have to travel. He says, "When He aims for something to be always a-moving, He makes it longways, like a road or a horse or a wagon, but when He aims for something to stay put, He makes it up-and-down ways, like a tree or a man" (34–5). Man is a rooted form. Anse does not mind having been planted, and he would like to remain so. He didn't want a house near a road, because a road keeps "the folks restless and wanting to get up and go somewheres else when He aimed for them to stay put like a tree or a stand of corn." Anse imagines that Addie's sickness is caused by the road. In death she is "long ways," closer to her vision of reality, and her death initiates the journey that will bring the others closer to it, too, though each will cope with the experience very differently.

At this point we encounter a seeming contradiction: the journey as linear form and the journey as the shape of the real, horizontal and dynamic. A look at the tableau scenes should clarify this. In many of his novels, as is often noted, Faulkner's tableaux are modelled after the scene of Keats' Grecian urn: motion, usually "terrific" motion, is "frozen,"[8] as in a stop-action photograph, for our aesthetic contemplation. We experience motion and statis simultaneously. The first tableau in As I Lay Dying (Faulkner uses the very word to describe this scene) contains Jewel and his horse. Darl narrates. "Jewel is enclosed by a glittering maze of hooves as by an illusion of wings. . . . For an instant before the jerk comes onto his arms he sees his whole body earth-free, horizontal, whipping snake-limber, until he finds the horse's nostrils and touches earth again. Then they are rigid, motionless, terrific. . . . They stand in rigid terrific hiatus . . ." (12). Here two extremes are held in terrific tension, the rigidity of motionlessness conforming to the horizontal and dynamic nature of reality. What is rigid and static becomes disembodied, earth-free, and what is dynamic is arrested in form. This tension is implicit in Addie's comment (quoted above) about the impossibility of straddling words and doing. In Faulkner's tableaux this tension is resolved in a dynamic form. Peabody's horses are "like they are nailed by the hind feet to the center of a whirling-plate" (54), and a buzzard is "as still as if he were nailed" to the sky (116)—"nailed" recalling Cash at his carpentry.

The *form* that this tension suggests, the form of the tableau, is circular. The circle is the image of "dynamic immobility." The most constant tableau, once the journey has begun, is that of the buzzards hanging motionless in the sky in "little tall black circles of not-moving" (185). The circle is the perfect union of time and space, the image of change without end or beginning.

Darl describes Anse's face as "a monstrous burlesque of all bereavement" (74); so is all the Bundrens' endeavor. Addie's revenge is to make Anse and the others caricature the life of forms without even knowing it, pursue their more or less venal concerns under a cover of words. Addie says Anse would never see she was taking revenge, and he never does. His comical stoicism derives from his obsession with form. The other Bundrens, though they experience their moments of futility and despair, align themselves with Anse's doggedness for one reason or another. But not Darl. All the principal tableaux take place in Darl's monologues. In them we come to recognize the essential unity of motion and stasis, in his vision of the journey as absurd.

The conversation between Darl and Vardaman at the outset of the journey reveals Darl's recognition that to be and not to be are one and the same condition.

"Then what is your ma, Darl?" I said.

"I haven't got ere one," Darl said. "Because if I had one, it is *was*. And if it is *was*, it can't be *is*. Can it?"

"No," I said.

I am. Darl is my brother.

"But you *are*, Darl," I said.

"I know it," Darl said. "That's why I am not *is*. *Are* is too many for one woman to foal." (95)

Darl recognizes that he is the product of two-ness, mother and father, the real and the illusory, being and words. Whitfield does not recognize that his words and his reality are like two horses. Anse never recognizes that his words and his "doing" are two different things. But Darl increasingly recognizes the dualism, and in the end his consciousness splits. Cash sees that "it's like there was a fellow in every man that's done a-past the sanity or the insanity, that watches the sane and the insane doings of that man with the same horror and the same astonishment" (228). This describes Darl's last monologue, in which he speaks of himself in the third person, sees himself operating in the world of forms, and laughs. What he knows is what he used to see in his spy-glass, "a woman and a pig with two backs and no face" (244), the engendering of life as an obscenity. Here is his last vision of the rest of the family, seen as he is pulled out of the station:

> The wagon stands on the square, hitched, the mules motionless, the reins wrapped about the seat-spring, the back of the wagon toward the courthouse. It looks no different from a hundred other wagons there . . . yet there is something different, distinctive. There is about it that unmistakable air of definite and imminent departure that trains have, perhaps due to the fact that Dewey Dell and Vardaman on the seat and Cash on a pallet in the wagon bed are eating bananas from a paper bag. "Is that why you are laughing, Darl?" (244)

On the one hand the Bundrens are motionless, absorbed, like other townspeople, in the world of forms. On the other hand, they are about to depart, just as he, Darl, is departing for a cell in Jackson. The life of forms, a Fallen world in time, will continue to move from *is* to *was*, and from *is* to *are*, engendering itself, carried along in the flux of being, going nowhere. And the other Bundrens don't realize the "insanity" of this. They placidly eat bananas, and soon, Anse will come along with a new wife, "hangdog and proud." Just before Darl's final monologue, Vardaman, faced with the fact of change (the toy train he wants is no longer in the store window), is mollified by Dewey Dell:

> "Hadn't you rather have bananas? Hadn't you rather?"
> "All right." *My brother he went crazy and he went to Jackson too.*
> *Jackson is further away than crazy.* (241–2)

Jackson is further away than the insanity of eating bananas, absorbed in a life that is a trivial illusion. Darl, too, will wind up in a cage in Jackson, the life of forms reduced to an image of entrapment.

In Darl's mad laughter we hear the extreme response to the vision of life that the irony of the novel expresses. The life of forms is a ludicrous comedy: machinery carefully and purposefully bent on illusory motion in illusory time, Buster Keaton's nut-cracking machine endlessly toppling into an awful Bergsonian motion. Empty words, hollow-sounding in the wind. But like one of the hideous throng in Poe's "The Haunted Palace," Darl laughs but smiles no more. His vision is despairing, not comic. He has, finally, detached himself from the world of forms, and so from the tensions and contradictions of the comic realm. His laughter has none of the humor of someone who feels attached in some way to what he laughs at, who feels implicated in its absurdity. If the comedy of *As I Lay Dying* can be expressed in the image of people trying with patience and astonishment to hold onto the shapes of things (and the names of shapes of things) while the ground slowly moves out from under them, freezing them in postures of desperate coping, then Darl can be said to be someone who finally floats away, laughing and hating the sound of his mirthless laughter, yearning for the community of the ludicrous even as he is so aware of its ludicrousness.

But the comedy of the novel resides, not only in our awareness of the frail illusoriness of the world of forms over and against the vivid pull of reality, but of its dogged strength, its connection with this reality—a strength that is best expressed in Faulkner's very style, the power of his own "empty" words.

3. The Creation of Form

In my previous chapter I argued that *Ulysses* becomes more and more comic as Joyce increasingly asserts his narrative voice, and the novel's styles become more densely textured. This happens because, as language becomes more powerful, the comic contradiction between its distance from reality and its ability to evoke it is more forcefully dramatized. If each one of Joyce's styles fails to grasp the stream of life that flows through the novel, the narrative as a whole, in its development from a more or less conventional third person to flowing interior monologue, expresses the life of the world in language. What is ironic in each individual conception (the gap between reality and language) becomes joyful in Joyce's overall conception. What binds the various voices together is Joyce himself, the master builder, building relations, increasingly creating the book as a system at the same time that he expresses a reality beyond the ability of systems to express. Hugh Kenner, in *The Stoic Comedians*, discusses *Ulysses* as a self-contained system, as something insisting on its actuality as book, with pages that we can turn back to for reference. Kenner says that Joyce's novel "is built about the antithesis between the personal matrix of human speech and the unyielding formalism of the book as book."[9]

In *As I Lay Dying* this antithesis is even more marked because of the structure of individual and isolated consciousnesses, expressed in a series of interior monologues—which brings us closer than Joyce's method to the "personal matrix of human speech." But as many have noted in discussions of this and other Faulkner novels, Faulkner's subsuming of his characters' voices under his own is more striking than his individualizing of these voices. Like Joyce, Faulkner makes his narrative presence heavily felt, and with similar effects on his comedy. At the same time that he articulates and dramatizes the emptiness and deadness of words, he makes us constantly aware of the vivid life of his own language—a language, like Joyce's, in constant motion. In this way the action of his irony is not final, not conclusive. Faulkner's vision of the life of forms is not self-destructive, as Darl's is. Rather, he shows us the power of language, of form, and so develops an ongoing contradiction. Reality, then, becomes as creative as it is destructive, a force to express as well as a force that evades and denies expression.

Faulkner's style in *As I Lay Dying* attempts to overcome in metaphor the mere *naming* of things, the dead uses of dead words, in order to describe a world in flux—in short, to convey in words what cannot be conveyed in them and so take on the beauty and absurdity of an impossible task. Through his use of metaphor he dissolves things into dynamic relations, and these relations, rather than the things themselves, form the strange landscape of the novel.

The sun, an hour above the horizon, is poised like a bloody egg

its eyes roll in the dusk like marbles on a gaudy velvet cloth

his face on which the freckles look like English peas on a plate

Some of these are striking in themselves; some are striking in their detail: *English* peas, for example. As individual images, they make us attentive to Faulkner rather than to the consciousnesses of his characters. Darl refers to Addie's coffin spanning two sawhorses as a "cubistic bug" (209), and the failure of voice, here as elsewhere, is intentional: we are in the presence of Faulkner the artist, shaping his material as his characters shape their experience. Most of the metaphors are repeated, connecting throughout the novel, such as the image, already discussed, of sawdust.

What Faulkner's metaphors do is delineate and clarify the life of forms while dissolving it into relation. A good example is the spy-glass Darl got in France during the war, in which are "a woman and a pig with two backs and no face" (244). The spy-glass recalls a paragraph of Tull's after he crosses the flooding river with Vardaman and looks back. This wonderful and overlooked passage is worth quoting in full.

> When I looked back at my mule it was like he was one of these here spy-glasses and I could look at him standing there and see all the broad land and my house sweated outen it like it was the more the sweat, the broader the land; the more the sweat, the tighter the house because it would take a tight house for Cora, to hold Cora like a jar of milk in the spring: you've got to have a tight jar or you'll need a powerful spring, so if you have a big spring, why then you have the incentive to have tight, wellmade jars, because it is your milk, sour or not, because you would rather have milk that will sour than to have milk that wont, because you are a man. (132)

What Tull sees through the spy-glass of his mule, which acts here as a kind of synecdoche of Tull's life on his farm, is a vision of form. If the form is tight and wellmade, it can withstand the pressure of the current of being that is liable to sour it. If the form (the jar, the farm, one's life) is wellmade, the milk it contains, an image of fecundity, will not sour, and the life of forms will continue. This is in direct contrast to Darl's vision of the obscenity of the act that engenders. What Tull does is celebrate, lyrically, the creation of forms that are a function of the strength of reality to dissolve them, pry them open, ruin them. Tull's jars are tight and wellmade because they are so threatened. He accepts the challenge of the spring. The joy of keeping one's life together is derived from the danger that life encounters: it is better to have milk that will sour. Tull can feel this because he has just halfway submerged himself in the river in trying to get across the sunken bridge, and so he has become attentive to the frailty of forms. His vision is not without an accompanying irony: Cora is a comically blind character and, though here associated with fecundity, hasn't provided Vernon with a male child. Still, his vision is a powerful and poignant one. Through the metaphor of the spy-glass, a lyrical and obscene vision of the life of forms are united in a form that is Faulkner's own, the action of his metaphor.

Tull's passage is also significant in regard to the relation between Life and living. Life is destructive of form, like a current it sweeps forms away. It is the void into which we all dissolve. Living is the aspect of Life that is formed, and because it is formed, it is separated from Life. Living is what Beckett called *habit,* the "boredom of living,"[10] profoundly without life. When Addie nursed Jewel, "the wild blood boiled away and the sound of it ceased. Then there was only the milk, warm and calm, and I lying calm in the slow silence, getting ready to clean my house" (168). The wildness of Life gives way to the calm of living, and Addie too prepares to make her form well, clean her house before she leaves it. Earlier in her section, Addie expresses a much darker vision:

> He did not know that he was dead, then. Sometimes I would lie by him in the dark, hearing the land that was now of my blood and flesh, and I would think: Anse. Why Anse. Why are you Anse. I would think about his name until after a while I could see the word as a shape, a vessel, and I would watch him liquefy and flow into it like cold molasses flowing out of the darkness into the vessel, until the jar stood full and motionless: a significant shape profoundly without life like an empty door frame. . . . (165)

Here the Life that is a part of us, the land that is a part of our flesh and blood, is shaped, poured into a form, and so becomes dead and motionless. The Life that shapes us dies in the shaping. The jar here recalls the jar in Tull's passage that was full of the milk of Life, only here that Life is dead—indeed, it is as though it were not there at all. For Addie, a well-made door frame is just as profoundly dead as any other.

This, then, is the paradox of form: it both contains and kills the real. Faulkner, through his metaphors, is able to express what *things* contain in common: Life, or being. And yet at the same time a metaphor is composed of words, is a form—only an active form, in flux. Wallace Stevens' notion that "a poet's words are of things that do not exist without the words" is relevant here. Most of the metaphors in *As I Lay Dying* give rise to others, connect and develop in a system that attempts, impossibly, to dissolve language into reality.

While riding with Jewel to accomplish their three-dollar job, Darl recalls his quizzing of Dewey Dell ("You want her to die so you can get to town: is that it?"), and immediately describes the surroundings as follows:

> The sun, an hour above the horizon, is poised like a bloody egg upon a crest of thunderheads; the light has turned copper: in the eye portentous, in the nose sulphurous, smelling of lightning. When Peabody comes, they will have to use the rope. He has pussel-gutted himself eating cold greens. With the rope they will haul him up the path, balloon-like up the sulphurous air.
>
> "Jewel," I say, "do you know that Addie Bundren is going to die? Addie Bundren is going to die?" (39)

In this passage we move from shape to light to smell to light to related shape (egg, balloon) to what is finally both light and smell: "sulphurous." In this synaesthesia, a welter of sensations are brought together. There is also a train of associations from Dewey Dell's abortion plans to "bloody egg" to Peabody's being "pussel-gutted" to Addie's death, associations that bind life and death together. Darl's consciousness is united with the landscape. Peabody underscores this in the next monologue when he describes Vardaman sitting in the "sulphur-coloured light" and thinks, "That's the one trouble with this country: everything, weather, all, hangs on too long. Like our rivers, our land: opaque, slow, violent; shaping and creating the life of man in its implacable and brooding image" (43–4). Man *is* the land, the river, the weather. Peabody has on his mind Addie's impending death, and in the next monologue Darl, after imagining Addie's death *in absentia*, continues to torment Jewel about it as Jewel attempts unsuccessfully (as we later learn) to extricate the wagon full of lumber from a ditch. In the passage in which the wagon is described (48), water, earth and sky are dissolved into a unity, the color of which is the color of the lumber, both in the wagon and, earlier, in Cash's hands. (Peabody, in the previous monologue, thinks that Cash's coffin boards "look like strips of sulphur.") And Dewey Dell has previously described Cash's "sawing the long hot sad yellow days up into planks." One could go on. The imagery is incremental, creating a world of intense *relationship:* of form (the lumber) and formlessness (the streaming elemental mass).

Metaphor, and particularly metaphor that shifts and grows, engendering out of itself new relations, allows us to glimpse the real. We need not be blinded by it because we truly *see*, blinded, that is, to the world of forms. Like Tull, we can walk into the water, but still be on a bridge that, despite its instability, emerges on the other side, "on something tame like the hard earth again that we had tromped on before this and knowed well" (131). We are brought to face "the Great Unknown" (Cora's term, which points up how useless words are to describe it or conceive it), but we may still have our faith in God, triumph, New Hope, redemption—the words go on. Like Whitfield we are borne safely above the flood, and can emerge with our voice "triumphant and sad." But we can listen to our own voice, and hear its echo in darkness, and laugh at it, as we do Whitfield's.

An analysis of Faulkner's concept of family in *As I Lay Dying* will clarify metaphor as a revelatory rather than an opaque or dead form of language. Since Addie's simultaneous presence and absence dominates the novel, her monologue will be a good place to begin.

Near the beginning she speaks of her feeling of estrangement from her students in the days before she met Anse. Her students were "each with his and her secret and selfish thought, and blood strange to each other blood and strange to mine." They left her class to go home to their various homes. This sense of each person as a separate entity, strange to other entities, was most painful to Addie in the early spring, with the smell of rot in the air, a time when everything seemed one with renewed life. It was then that she remembers her father saying that "the reason for living was to get ready to stay dead a long time," very possibly because to die would be to return like a rotting leaf to the earth again and become one with Life. Only by enduring the life of forms, and being strange to others, could she prepare to stay dead. She looked forward to when her students failed so she could whip them and make herself part of their "secret and selfish life." This kind of communion, in the face of her solitude, is unsatisfactory, and she takes Anse for a husband. Still, her aloneness is not violated, not even by Anse in the nights, until Cash comes, and then she knows that Cash's life inside her was the answer to the terror of living. The life inside her is both a revelation that living is terrible, because it had been caused by a word (*love*) and "words are no good," *and* an answer to the aloneness caused by words because it *is* another life, inside her. She has become two. That words cause isolation is clear when she says, "we had to use one another by words like spiders dangling by their mouths from a beam, swinging and twisting and never touching. . . ." With Cash, her aloneness "had been violated and then made whole again by the violation: time, Anse, love, what you will, outside the circle." She is two with Cash, but when Cash is born, she is alone again, and has created a new form, with a name attached to it: "Cash." When she finds she has Darl inside her, she realizes the "trick" involved: a word, such as *love*, which creates a communion, a two-ness, only results in an increased isolation. It is after having Darl that Addie makes Anse promise to bury her with her kin in Jefferson; she will make him suffer, too, force him to shape a family journey on the basis of a word.

Then Addie talks about the emptiness of forms (165) and how the shape of her body where she was a virgin was "the shape of   ," that is, nothingness until she gave birth to Cash and Darl, new forms into which her life had poured and then died, become strange to her: "And then I would think *Cash* and *Darl* that way until their names would die and solidify into a shape and then fade away." Our previous discussion of sexuality is relevant here. Addie, who identifies her blood and flesh with the wild blood of the land, must, in order to feel at one with that Life, to feel that Life inside her, be violated by a word (*Anse*) which continues the whole pain and isolation of the world of forms, in which words and doing can't get together.

The human condition is a condition of two-ness: words and deeds, isolation and communion. This two-ness is experienced simultaneously and in relation, at the same time that the relation is one of opposition, like the faces of a coin, the image that Darl is obsessed with in his final schizoid state. We fumble at deeds like "orphans to whom are pointed out in a crowd two faces and told, That is your father, your mother" (166). Two-ness results in one-ness, we are all orphans searching for two-ness again, and so it goes on. It is Darl who comes to realize this, who is most an orphan and most alone, who says, "I cannot love my mother because I have no mother" (89), because his mother has not loved him. While tormenting Jewel as they haul lumber, Darl thinks, "It takes two people to make you, and one people to die. That's how the world is going to end" (38). But it will only end for him, because the world of forms goes on because people will continue to search for communion because they are alone because, because. . . .

With her realization that her living with Anse has created more words and shapes (Cash, Darl, not hers) Addie desires *not-Anse*. She believes she has a "duty to the alive, to the terrible blood," so she takes Whitfield as a lover. She believes that sin is like "the clothes we both wore in the world's face, of the circumspection necessary because he was he and I was I" (166)—sin is that which separates people. To be naked with Whitfield will be to sanctify the sin of isolation, "since he was the instrument ordered by God who created the sin, to sanctify that sin He had created." Here Addie's own words suggest an unintended (on her part, not Faulkner's) comedy. Her reasoning is not unlike her daughter's reasoning about succumbing to Lafe: the contradiction between her abstract rationalizing and her actual deed is comic, especially when we discover, in

Whitfield's own monologue following hers, that her lover is a man made out of words, an hilarious hypocrite. Whitfield rationalizes his actions with a transparent religious rhetoric, to the point where his "wrestling thigh to thigh with Satan" is all too uncomfortably related to his affair with Addie. "I framed the words which I should use," he says in reference to confessing his sin to Anse, "framed" suggesting how formed his language is, and how dead. He ends his monologue calling God's grace upon the Bundren's house because Addie died not telling, and so spared him his confession. Addie seems to realize Whitfield's character when she says, "I would think of the sin as garments which we would remove in order to shape and coerce the terrible blood to the forlorn echo of the dead word high in the air." Although they remove their garments, although they bring their blood together, they are shaping it to the dead word: Whitfield, sin, sanctification, what you will. And the result is Jewel. Addie's narrative has taken on, darkly, the character of a comedy of frustration. Life, for Addie, is a tricky joke.

With Jewel the inextricability of isolation and communion becomes clear. Addie says, "My children were of me alone, of the wild blood boiling along the earth, of me and of all that lived; of none and of all. Then I found that I had Jewel." Anse to her was "dead" and so Cash and Darl were hers alone. But they were also words and shapes, the children of Anse, despite his dead-ness. With Jewel, "the wild blood boiled away and the sound of it ceased," and he, the closest of all the children to her, is the most shaped to a dead word. Darl, from whom she feels most isolated, is the most like her, with the land running out of his eyes. Jewel is a "wooden" and "rigid" figure. The closer one comes to communion, the more isolated one becomes, and vice versa. The more one is isolated from the real (as Darl is), the more conscious one is of it, the more one knows it, feels its presence. The more one lives close to reality (Jewel), the more one is blind to it.

If reality is the formless union of all living forms into Life, then a family is an image of the real, because its members have a bond, share a blood. A family is a communion. But a family is also shaped by dead words, is a product of two-ness, and its members experience the isolation of the orphaned. The Bundrens act as a family, and accomplish their family goal, at the same time that they remain comically isolated in their own consciousnesses, with their jealousies, hatreds, fears and venal concerns. Anse, whose concerns are the most selfish (getting new teeth), is the most interested in their acting as a family unit, with their own wagons and mules, "beholden" to no-one. And it is he who shapes the family together again at the end. Jewel, the bastard, the member most isolated from the others, is the most intense and successful about getting his mother buried.

Dewey Dell, because she is wrapped up in her own family problems and hence least concerned with carrying out the express purpose of the trip (were it not for her baby, she would ask Anse to bury Addie at New Hope), is most interested in carrying the journey out. It is she who is instrumental in casting Darl out of the family for threatening the completion of the journey. The ironies go on and on, bringing the negative and positive elements of the novel into a relation so close that the words "negative" and "positive" are not descriptive.

Sitting in the wagon looking at the river before they decide to enter its currents, Cash and Darl "look at one another with long probing looks, looks that plunge unimpeded through one another's eyes and into the ultimate secret place where for an instant Cash and Darl crouch flagrant and unabashed in all the old terror and the old foreboding, alert and secret and without shame" (135). To relinquish one's secrecy and expose one's nakedness is an act of terrific ambivalence. It involves a retreat into further secrecy, and this leads to a renewed desire for communion, and so on, no end or beginning. The ultimate tendency of this is a death-wish, a desire for the final isolation (from form) and communion (with Life), which turns out not to be "final" at all, but just another "departure." What results is a darkly comic ongoingness that Beckett would appreciate.

The Bundren family continually asserts itself as a community of individuals. Darl is impressed by Jewel's risking his horse in the river and offering to pay for Vernon's mule, since Vernon won't risk his own. It is immediately after the conversation over risking mules that Darl's long and touching account of how Jewel got his horse begins. This account (121–9) is the high point of our sense of the Bundrens as a family. Everybody but the unwitting Anse supports Jewel in his secret efforts to raise cash. Darl thinks, "It was as though, so long as the deceit ran along quiet and monotonous, all of us let ourselves be deceived. . . . But now it was like we had all . . . flung the whole thing back like covers on the bed and we all sitting bolt upright in our nakedness, staring at one another and saying 'Now is the truth. He hasn't come home. Something has happened to him' " (127). Here acting as a family has *covered* their nakedness, and then the communal and familial sense of fear has *exposed* it. This is the paradox of family. In the entire monologue, Darl is recounting the family experience with an affectionate nostalgia at the same time that he is painfully aware of what it reveals about the closeness of Addie and Jewel. This last awareness reveals to him that Jewel doesn't have a father. At the end of the monologue Darl finds Addie crying by Jewel's side as he sleeps, and says, "then I knew that I knew" (129). Darl knows the secrets of others, and his eyes expose their nakedness. Through his knowledge he is most acutely aware of the family as family, and through it he is most detached from the family. In his final detachment, on the train to Jackson, cast out of the family *because* of his knowledge (Dewey Dell tells on him and so covers her own nakedness), Darl thinks for the first time that "Darl is our brother, our brother Darl. Our brother Darl in a cage in Jackson . . ." (244). In the splitting of his consciousness, he is both member and commentator, inside and outside.

The scene where everybody (except Anse) helps Cash recover his tools from the river reveals a broader sense of community. Holding onto a rope they submerge themselves in the current to recover the symbols of form, sharing the same sense of community that Tull felt with Vardaman as they crossed the sunken bridge holding hands. The sense of community is felt in the immersion in the destructive element. It is an act of faith, and we also see it, in the ironic context of the novel, as a ludicrous fiction. The "clotting" which is them dissolves into flux and emerges clutching planes, saws, hammers, squares, chalk-lines, the tools with which they will construct their coffins and cells.

So Faulkner is ambivalent about form, whether it be Cash's carpentry, the endurance of family, or the way that language frames reality. This ambivalence does not, as the preceding analysis reveals, result in a constant comedy. The somber energy of Addie's monologue is a case in point. We discover what comedy is there by juxtaposing it (as Faulkner does) with Whitfield's monologue. Like Wallace Stevens, Faulkner often separates the elements of the contradiction, the emotions that make up the ambivalence, and so can express, eloquently and non-comically, either the power of reality to undermine, or the power of language to construct. It is a way of making these subjects vivid and potent, so that the comedy that can result from their simultaneity is far more vivid and potent than it would otherwise be—and more essential, because more inclusive.

It is important that Faulkner ends his novel with a comic family scene. With Addie buried and Darl sent away, the remaining Bundrens prepare to leave. Anse tells the others to meet him at a corner, and he shows up with a new Mrs. Bundren, the woman he had borrowed shovels from, and a gramophone. The last scene of the novel is so carefully balanced between irony and lyricism that it leaves the reader in a perfect comic suspension, in which contradictions are both defined and absorbed. Here is an assertion of form (of the family) and ongoingness that the reader takes, by this time, as both utterly futile and absurd, and yet necessary.

Anse's bringing a new wife while Addie's grave is still fresh is, in the first place, his response to his wife's "revenge" on him. At the time Addie made him promise to bury her in Jefferson Anse said, "Nonsense . . . you and me aint done chapping yet, with just two" (165). If Addie feels, like her father, that "the reason for living was to get ready to stay dead a long time," then Anse has his small triumph over her. Anse's belief in "chapping" is, however, and not surprisingly, practical. Very early in the novel Cora Tull, in what may be her only true prophecy, says that Addie had been behind Anse's working and would be for thirty years more, "Or if it ain't her, he'd get another one before cotton-picking" (32). And so he does, obtaining a new farm-hand along with his new teeth and gramophone. Cash, who is above all his father's son, mentions the teeth before the woman.

There are more ironies. Cash mentions the gramophone "all shut up pretty as a picture," an image of closed form that we have already discussed as, in Addie's words, "profoundly without life like an empty door frame," "just a shape to fill a lack." What further proof of Addie's contention that the shapes of abstract words like *love* are dead, than the fact that Anse can replace her so quickly and—it would seem—so easily? Cash's mention of Darl is significant, too. The family Bundren has betrayed and cast out its own, only to take in a stranger for continuance. Cash's claim that this world and life are not Darl's is both a truth and a rationalization, both an expression of empathy and a convenience.

What do we make of "this world," the world of forms and of the attachment to forms? It is, in one sense, an absurd and empty pantomime of Life, or an adjustment to the trivial. As Darl says in his last monologue, "there is about" the Bundrens waiting to leave "that unmistakable air of definite and imminent departure that trains have" (244), all of them calmly eating bananas, waiting for Anse to take them back to the comforts of "this world." We behold in the waiting Bundrens the simian display of habit.

Cash describes his father as "hangdog and proud," and the other time when Anse behaves this way is when he has bought a team from Snopes with a mortgage on his farm equipment, Cash's money that he'd been saving for a gramophone, and Jewel's beloved horse for swap. Armstid describes Anse as "kind of more hang-dog than common, and kind of proud too. Like he had done something he thought was cute but wasn't so sho now how other folks would take it" (179–80). "I do the best I can," says Anse, and the best he can do is swap goods that mean a great deal to the rest of the family in order to get to Jefferson, not even to bury his wife as he promised, but because, as he tells Jewel, "For fifteen years I aint had a tooth in my head" (181). So doing, as we have noted, is the accomplishment of selfish ends. The futility and/or triviality of the goals are underscored by the fact that it matters not how incompetent, venal or stupid the means. Anse *does* get his teeth, buries his wife and gets a new one, and gets Cash his gramophone. As in a comic folk tale, people survive and cope *despite all,* and our chuckle is at the strength of their indefatigability, a quality beyond justice and circumstance. When Armstid tells his wife Lula, who is outraged by the smell of the corpse, that Anse is doing the best he can, she replies, "Do? . . . Do? He's done too much, already" (179). Lula places in perspective the idea of doing. It may or may not be meaningful to do anything; most often, for the Bundrens, it is not. Doing just shut things up, and not always pretty as a picture.

So the comedy of the final scene rests in part on our ironic awareness of the absurdity of Anse's action. He has deprived Jewel of his horse, caused Cash to limp on a short leg for the rest of his life if he's lucky, and sent Darl off to an asylum. One is ready to agree with Peabody that the cure for the whole family would be to stick Anse's head in a saw. All this irony suggests that Anse's being "proud" of providing his family with a new mother and a gramophone, after fulfilling his promise to Addie, is only the appearance covering a reality of empty gesturing, the creation of "a significant shape [in this case, the enduring family] profoundly without life."

And yet the full comedy of the scene would not be accounted for, were we not to accept Cash's view that this world—in which the Bundrens, or most of them, endure—this world, that is, not Darl's nor Addie's—has its tenacious strength and meaning, too. The family does continue, however much each member continues to stew in his own solipsism. It knits itself together in whatever way it can, and keeps on going. The creation of forms is as necessary as their destruction, and we end the book as ruefully impressed by Anse's accomplishments as we are appalled at his hypocrisy and selfishness.

4. Cash on a Balance

The sense of a comedy that survives the strictures of irony is conveyed strongly by the fact that it is *Cash* whose monologue contains the final scene, it is from his angle of vision that we see it. It is Cash who can enjoy "this world," as Darl cannot. It would have been easy for Faulkner to end his novel with Darl's final, mad monologue; that he didn't is important. Cash's role helps us to understand Faulkner's comic double vision of form.

Cash's absorption in his work makes him a classic example of a character of humor. He is, particularly in his abrupt early monologues, a

burlesque of a man absorbed in the life of forms. It is not surprising that
he is the last Bundren to offer a monologue. Cash speaks through his carpentry. When his dying mother cries out to him, he answers her by fitting
two boards together, himself framed by her bedroom window. He wants
to show her what a good job he's doing, that he's joining her coffin on the
bevel. This may be an expression of his love for Addie; he may be sublim-
ating his grief in his work, and in this sense the form he constructs is expressive. But Faulkner stresses the bizarre quality of his *idée fixe*. It is
comically ironic that Addie, who meditates on the emptiness and dead-
ness of frames, should be offered, in her very last moments, a "final juxtaposition" of planks, and a charade of what the finished box will look
like (47). Both Darl and Vernon Tull testify to Cash's tedious but impres-
sive skill and care, his obsession with making things right. But Cash's first
monologue is an hilarious list of reasons for making the coffin on the
bevel. For example,

5. In a bed where people lie down all the time, the joints and seams
   are made sideways, because the stress is sideways.
6. Except.
7. A body is not square like a crosstie.
8. Animal magnetism.
9. The animal magnetism of a dead body makes the stress come
   slanting, so the seams and joints of a coffin are made on the
   bevel. (77–8)

What is comic here is not simply the mechanism of the list, though it is
odd enough that he offers no hint of *what the coffin will contain*. It is also
comic that his reasoning is so absurd. Cash wants to be thorough and rational, to pursue and organize the reasons for his decision, but one beholds here his rationality as something imposed on muddle. Clearly
Cash's obsession is not based on reason, any more than his father's is.
Both get their tasks done, but not necessarily neatly. Together, Anse and
Cash lay Addie in her coffin "reversed," so as not to crush her dress (82).
Neatness is seen as a comic mechanism, rather than as an aesthetic or
moral value.

Cash's next two monologues are brief exclamations about the coffin's
not being "on a balance" in the wagon. His fears are borne out when it
slips from the wagon into the river. Later, after Cash has calmly accepted
Anse's decision to pour concrete over his leg, Peabody tells Cash that he
will have "to limp around on one short leg for the balance of his life"
(230). In deference to Anse, Cash has made a bad job of his own leg, he
has acquiesced in his own unbalancing. Cash's concern with neatness

and skill is matched by his ineffectuality. Like Hugh Kenner's Man of Sense as Buster Keaton, he refuses to be surprised.[11] He holds to his obsession tenaciously and to no avail, as things slip away from him.

Cash's last two monologues are relatively voluble. He has become, rather startlingly, articulate. Many critics have seen this change as growth, maturation, character development. But Cash does not essentially change. His injury has afforded him the opportunity to meditate at leisure on his obsessions. He does not put them aside. He is constantly ruminating on the subject of form, trying to see the chaotic events around him in terms of form. He is building an outlook, just as he built a coffin. By bringing Cash to the fore, Faulkner is able to develop the comedy in his character and make it resonate through the novel.

It is interesting that most of the critics of *As I Lay Dying* regard Cash as the hero, based on his last two monologues (the crazier early ones are pretty much ignored). Olga Vickery's 1950 essay established the idea of his heroism, and most critics have been making variations on her judgment ever since. She says, "Combined with his own firm foundation in action and the concrete details of his trade, this increase of sensitivity and imaginative perception makes Cash the one character in the novel who achieves his full humanity in which reason and intuition, words and action merge into a single though complex response."[12] A more recent critic echoes Vickery in these words: "The abstraction which is language is in fact a fulfillment, not an evasion of existence. Properly used language affirms being. Thus it is only when Addie's eldest son Cash begins to use words to express doubt, concern, pleasure that we are assured of his full humanity."[13] Cash achieves this "full humanity" by his use of words; if Addie casts doubt on words and their relation to reality, she is merely *wrong*. Even Calvin Bedient, whose essay on *As I Lay Dying* is still the best, says that "Cash exemplifies the pride that saves us and is itself the substance of identity."[14] Cash is "the worker as hero," shaping and asserting "the human in the teeth of its negation—the nothingness awaiting life, the shapelessness surrounding it," for in the world of the novel, "the hero's role must be to shape and define." That is, the world of the novel is Cash's "this world."

Clearly, for these and so many other critics, the world of forms has a *given* value, and since Cash is the principal spokesman for the virtues of form, the man with the tools of the trade, he must be the voice of humanism crying out in the wilderness, bearing the burdens of identity, maturity, the ethic of work, the proper use of language, reason, duty, property and pride. This is not to mention music appreciation. To regard Cash so is, of course, to disregard him as ever being a comic character, to dis-

regard the comedy of the novel in general, and to disregard Addie's and
Darl's visions as anything but interesting and feeble opposition, at best
something to be considered and overcome, at worst insane. But if we are
attentive to Faulkner's comedy, we can see his interplay of points of view,
and his complex vision of form.

What is it that Cash thinks that has touched off all this humanist rhetoric? Cash's main subject in his last two monologues is Darl, and his own
complicity in turning Darl over to the authorities for burning Gillespie's
barn. He says, "Sometimes I aint so sho who's got ere a right to say when
a man is crazy and when he aint. Sometimes I think it aint none of us pure
crazy and aint none of us pure sane until the balance of us talks him that-
a-way. It's like it aint so much what a fellow does, but it's the way the
majority of folks is looking at him when he does it" (223). Cash is sympathetic to Darl; he admits elsewhere that he, too, wished Addie had been
borne off by the river. He admits craziness is an aspect of humanity. But
his obsession with balance, the very thing that makes his judgment so im-
pressive, has a questionable relevance to Darl's situation. How has Darl
been tipped to insanity by "the majority of folks"? If, as this suggests,
Darl has been *made* crazy by being grabbed and carted off by a collusion
of Bundrens and townspeople, then how can he, Cash, justify his part in
it? What he says has an abstract reasonableness, but nothing to do with
why he didn't tell Darl that others knew he had burned the barn, when
Darl, obviously feeling he and Cash had a close bond, thought sure he
would have (227). As Cash says elsewhere, it was either send him to Jackson or have Gillespie sue them (222). So he helps betray his brother for
pecuniary reasons, again behaving as his father's son. "I can almost believe he done right in a way. But I dont reckon nothing excuses setting fire
to a man's barn and endangering his stock and destroying his property.
That's how I reckon a man is crazy. That's how he cant see eye to eye with
other folks. And I reckon they aint nothing else to do with him but what
the most folks say is right."

Cash's morality, then, is part and parcel of a very social world of
forms: money, property, and the opinion of most folks. Vickery says that
Cash "is forced to conclude that society's judgment is the only possible
one," and doesn't question the wisdom of this conclusion. It's at least a
question. Peabody takes a dim view of it, and he's a member of the community. He says to Cash that it never bothered Anse "to throw that poor
devil down in the public street and handcuff him like a damn murderer"
(230). This is surely a condemnation of what Cash himself, in the monologue before Peabody's, calls "a shoddy job." As Jewel screams for Darl's
death, Cash says, "A fellow cant get away from a shoddy job" (227), and

this is Cash's job, too. "It was bad. It was bad so. I be durn if I could see anything to laugh at. Because there just aint nothing justifies the deliberate destruction of what a man has built with his own sweat and stored the fruit of his sweat into" (228). Cash is certainly right here; it is a terrible thing to burn a man's barn. But Cash's concern here is, again, with the value of form over and above understanding his brother. What matters is "what a man has built . . . ," and the use and comfort it gives.

Cash says, "It's like some folks has the smooth, pretty boards to build a courthouse with and others dont have no more than rough lumber fitten to build a chicken coop. But it's better to build a tight chicken coop than a shoddy courthouse . . . " (224). A form, especially a wellmade form, is a comfortable thing. If we do not question Cash's aesthetic judgments, we must question Cash as the bearer of them. If it was shoddy to have Darl borne off the way they did, how could it have been done *well*? No, there's an emptiness in Cash's language. If he has bevelled the edges of his ruminations, the result is still a wellmade frame around a central nothingness. Like his father he is sunk, passively, in the life of forms, tipped into *that* particularly comic insanity by most folks. That Cash is Anse's boy is clinched in one of the comic high points of the novel, the end of his and Peabody's conversation as Peabody is fixing his leg.

". . . . Does that hurt?"

"Not to speak of," he said, and the sweat big as marbles running down his face and his face about the color of blotting paper.

"Course not," I said. "About next summer you can hobble around fine on this leg. Then it wont bother you, not to speak of. . . . If you had anything you could call luck, you might say it was lucky this is the same leg you broke before," I said.

"Hit's what paw says," he said. (230)

The critics admire Cash for his stoical endurance, but here that endurance is comical, a dogged clinging to a fragile world designed to deny the Addies and Darls of the world.

And so in the final scene of the novel, Cash can offer us, without intentional irony, but instead with barely grudging appreciation, the restoration of the world that is not Darl's. He has neatly and comfortably separated the two worlds, but Faulkner has not. Faulkner has them contradicting each other, and in the comedy of this contradiction, is able to write a tight, wellmade novel that conveys a reality beyond itself in the very process of denying it. It is both the vividness and deadness of art, of the wellmade form, that it tries to express what it cannot express.

It is a sense of the comic that will prevent us from asserting *As I Lay Dying* as a work of self-destructive nihilism based on the irony engendered by the unbridgeable gap between language and reality. For in comedy ironies are never final, there is a bedrock of being that language puts us in touch with in the process of calling itself into question. It is not forms themselves that are affirmed as expressions of humanity, the moral categories that language creates: pride, maturity, responsibility, what you will. What is affirmed, if affirmed is the proper word, is the reality that gives to forms the strength they have. Cash ends the novel describing the regrouping and endurance of the Bundren family, because it is he who can express what value such a life would hold, a life that must needs exclude so much—as Tull says, comically, long before the end, "they would risk the fire and the earth and the water and all just to eat a sack of bananas" (133). This world survives, like the other world of formless reality that the other Bundrens perceive in their most hectic and abandoned moments—it is ugly and strong.

As I Lay Dying does not end with Joyce's lyrical Yes, but in its final freeze-frame of Anse and the new Mrs. Bundren, full of pride, we behold an image of ongoingness that is as strong as it is absurd. Cash can "frame" it because he is the framer, and it hangs there both dead and alive, like language itself, ready to survive the very ironies it creates. The formless is formed once again, necessarily, nothingness made something and that something revealed as celebrated as nothingness. Faulkner neither merely affirms nor merely denies the human. He does both at once, and that comic paradox expresses the range, the depth, the complexity of his vision.

Wallace Stevens: The Poet as Comedian

The comedy of hollow sounds derives
From truth and not from satire on our lives.[1]

1. Introduction

Although Wallace Stevens is the most comic of all great modern poets, and although he had, in the course of his long career, a good deal to say about the nature of poetry, he did not address the subject of comedy in more than passing remarks. I have not made a count, but I would guess that the words *comedy* and *comic* appear more often in his poetry than in his lectures, essays and letters. Surely his poems, particularly his early poems, are more comic than his prose, and this is a fact of some significance, because for Stevens comedy was a poetic mask, or voice. The comic was for him a marvelous way of expressing the speculative philosophy that informs his poetry. I wish to demonstrate the relationship between his philosophy and his comic voice. The peculiarly asocial nature of Stevens' poetry—a nature he poignantly realized when he wrote, in his "Adagia," that "Life is an affair of people not of places. But for me life is an affair of places and that is the trouble"[2]—allows me to demonstrate, more conclusively than I can when discussing fiction, that a vivid comedy can be achieved beyond the realm of the social.

In the light of my introductory chapter, it is important that Stevens was influenced by Bergson's metaphysics and not by *Laughter*. It is Bergson's metaphysics to which he turned in his first major elucidation of his ideas on reality and the imagination, "The Noble Rider and the Sound of Words" (1942). In this lecture, having established that there is a "universal interdependence" of reality and the imagination, Stevens discusses the meaning of reality. Stating that "its connotations are without limit," he goes on to quote from *Creative Evolution:* "Bergson describes the visual perception of a motionless object as the most stable of internal states. He says: The object may remain the same, I may look at it from the same side, at the same angle, in the same light; nevertheless, the vision I now have of it differs from that which I have just had, even if only because the one is an instant later than the other. My memory is there, which conveys something of the past into the present." Stevens goes on to quote from Dr. Joad's commentary on this passage: " 'Similarly with external things. Every body, every quality of a body resolves itself into an enormous number of vibrations, movements, changes.' " Joad then asks, since philosophy and modern physics have dismissed the idea of *substance* as being that which is changed, " 'How, then, does the world come to appear to us as a collection of solid static objects extended in space? Because of the intellect, which presents us with a false view of it.' "[3] Reality, Stevens then says, which is the "subject matter of poetry," is not this collection of objects but "the life that is lived in the scene that it composes" (NA, 25). It is "things as they are," and things as they are in a state of constant flux. Reality for Stevens is change, the restlessness of the mind (a restlessness *sui generis*) in a landscape of diurnal and seasonal flux, light and shadow, summer and winter. Reality and the imagination are "interdependent" in the sense that each one is dependent on the *motion* of the other. The imagination is not the intellect, which perceives " 'solid, static objects extended in space' "; it is the motion of consciousness adapting itself to the motion of the object, which at the same time is seen as the imagination sees it—that is, in motion. Later in his essay Stevens, referring back to Joad's commentary, says that, "as in the case of an external thing, nobility [which is the quality of the imagination] resolves itself into an enormous number of vibrations" (NA, 34). So reality and the imagination "adhere" to each other in a state of change. This has little to do with reason or intellect; indeed, as Stevens makes clear in an earlier essay, it is an "irrational" transaction (OP, 217).

It is Bergson's vision of reality as a mobile, evolutionary, ever-becoming continuum of change that had the greatest influence on Stevens' thought. Stevens' poetry is a meditation on the mind's ability and inability to imagine such a reality. When the mind is able, we experience "The joy of meaning in design / Wrenched out of chaos," we experience the poet as "the true creator" (OP, 100). But even as we experience this joy, we recognize that it involves a wrenching, a necessary distortion of the real, the poet's words become something else than the reality they were meant to express, something else than true. In this way the mind is seen as unable to express reality—that

> We are ignorant men incapable
> Of the least, minor, vital metaphor, content,
> At last, there, when it turns out to be here. (CP, 305)

The "it" in the last line is reality, which evades our expressions of it. If, in the experience of joy, we regard reality as chaos, in the experience of defeat we regard it as truth, the only real power. These are two aspects of the same indivisible flux.

In the passage quoted above, the last lines of "Crude Foyer," we have a fine, if dead-pan, expression of Stevens' comic vision. We can imagine the poet as a comedian, content that he has fixed something that has, however, utterly eluded him, that turns out to be even closer than he thought: *here*, not there! He is the ignorant man pretending knowledge. He is like the Buster Keatonish "Doctor of Geneva" (CP, 24), a burgherly and lacustrine man confronting the cold and swelling cataracts of the Pacific. The Doctor pretends to feel no awe as he pats his hat and tugs his shawl, and even when he gets sprayed, he can only use his handkerchief and sigh. The comedy derives from the contradiction between his tepid and orderly habits of thought and behavior, and the churning reality that deluges him. In "Crude Foyer," Stevens' voice calls "false happiness" the idea that one can attain, "at the end of thought," an absolute place of contentment from which one can

> read the critique of paradise
> And say it is the work
> Of a comedian, this critique;

Stevens' ironic point is that the true vision, as opposed to this "false" one, *is* one of a comedian, and *is* a critique of paradise, of anything absolute. The poet as comedian, Stevens implies, knows that he is "ignorant," that reality cannot be penetrated "merely by thinking" of a "foyer of the spirit" in which we are content. There is no such *focus* (the Latin word from which "foyer" is derived); there is only "the eye as faculty" and the eye is deceptive, and reality is relative and the poetry that must express that reality is a struggle, a process involving failure, frustration, contradictions that yield the comic. In "Of Heaven Considered as a Tomb" (CP, 56), Stevens refers to life on earth as "our old comedy," and it is a comedy— and we comedians—because, unlike heaven, it is a world of change.

Stevens' comedian-poets are not comic because they fail to adhere their imaginations to reality (such failure can be bitter or anguishing, as it sometimes is in his poetry), or because they succeed (success would obviate the comic), but because they both fail and succeed at the same time.

The poet wishes to imagine, to shape reality with words, and so to place it "beyond the compass of change, / Perceived in a final atmosphere; / For a moment final" (CP, 168). But reality has moved from there to here, and so made him fail. But he does not accept failure, he tries again and again, and in the comedy of his attempts to shape the shapeless, his gestures are both ironic and joyful. For in his continual failure he makes us recognize the reality that made him fail, and in this way he succeeds. The poet as imaginer is a constant, even "the absence of the imagination had / itself to be imagined" (CP, 503), and so in the constancy of its failed assertions the imagination expresses what eludes it.

In "Poems from 'Primordia,' " published in 1917, we come across this very early example of Stevens' comic spirit.

The horses gnaw the bark from the trees.
The horses are hollow,
The trunks of the trees are hollow.
Why do the horses have eyes and ears?
The trees do not.
Why can the horses move about on the ground?
The trees cannot.
The horses weary themselves hunting for green grass.
The trees stand still,
The trees drink.
The water runs away from the horses.
La, la, la, la, la, la, la, la,
Dee, dum, diddle, dee, dee, diddle, dee, da. (OP, 8)

The poem begins by declaring the relation between the horses of consciousness ("eyes and ears") and the trees of reality. Then it poses their differences in a series of questions (a proper function of consciousness) followed by abrupt, simple declarations of how the trees *are*. The contrast is comical. Finally the horses are seen as weary because the world does not seem made for them; they must struggle for their nourishment while the trees simply drink. The high-spirited singing in the last lines makes the poem comic in two ways. The song is a song of the water running, expressing the sheer gaiety of being in a music beyond language, "away from the horses." Noise and motion are intimately related in Stevens' poetry, as his persona declares in "The Place of the Solitaires":

There must be no cessation
Of motion, or of the noise of motion,
The renewal of noise
And manifold continuation . . . (CP, 60)

It is also a song of the poet, contained in the poet's lines, nonsense syllables but language nonetheless, attuned to the gaiety of being. It is thus a comic song that expresses both difference and reconciliation. It appears again and again in Stevens' poetry, running through it like a thread of scat and instrument-thumping. It says "*Voilà la vie!*" (OP, 14), and this is *la vie* of both reality and consciousness. As the poet ploughs North America, digging into its enormous soil, he sings "Tum-ti-tum, / Ti-tum-tum-tum!" (CP, 20). The "disaffected flagellants" of "A High-Toned Old Christian Woman" (CP, 59), fat and gay and secular poets all, are "Proud of such novelties of the sublime, / Such tink and tank and tunk-a-tunk-tunk," proud of their own fresh and ornamental fictions, expressed as a "jovial hullabaloo" that comes from a sublimity within themselves, not from gazing at heaven. Theirs is the gay nonsense that contains the uproarious, irrational life of the real. It often echoes the sounds of birds, an answering call from the poet: rou-cou, rou-cou, a song of accord (CP, 63, 519). It seems to be for Stevens what the music of language can become, a forsaking of sense for sound, a song beyond words, yet with its own expressive sense. Above all it is *playful*, expressing as it does a play between consciousness and the abandonment of consciousness, the beginning and end of language.

Stevens' early poetry (up to and including *Harmonium*) is particularly full of this odd music—not only of nonsense syllables, but of words used so much for their sounds that they seem to verge on nonsense: "Chieftain Iffucan of Azcan in caftan / Of tan with henna hackles, halt!" (CP, 75). Or "piebald fiscs unkeyed," a phrase from "The Comedian as the Letter C" that Stevens himself pointed out as an example of his "play" on the sounds of the letter C,[4] the sound of the comedian-poet reduced to sound but tuned to reality. The gaudy (that is, joyful, rejoicing) play of Stevens' language is, of course, the most notable feature of his early poetry. It makes the poetry both ornamental and veracious, both a sign of its fictive qualities (its removal from reality, its consciousness of its own peculiar powers as language) and of its musical connection to the life of things, to the "gaudium of being" (OP, 71).

For Stevens the experience of simultaneous success and failure in poetry is the experience of belief in a fiction. As he says in one of his most famous adages, "The final belief is to believe in a fiction, which you know to be a fiction, there being nothing else. The exquisite truth is to know that it is a friction [sic] and that you believe in it willingly" (OP, 163). He means "fiction" both in its sense as making and counterfeiting, the fictive act as a necessary but absurd fabrication. There is nothing else but fiction because we cannot escape our imaginations. So we must both recognize, ironically, that the imagination *is* a counterfeiter of reality, and believe in it—that is, take its fictions *as real,* and so celebrate it. This truth is "exquisite" because it is both precious and keen, delicately poised between irony and joy.

It can be said that Stevens' early poetry stresses the *fiction* and his later poetry the *belief,* although the poise between the two is already there, potentially available for comedy. The early poetry is more comically aware of itself as playfully fictive. It seems that Stevens, in his poetic career, had to realize himself as a poet through realizing himself as a comedian. It was through his comic personae that he was able to understand the paradoxes in his ideas. We can see this most clearly through a close examination of his two longest, most important, and—not incidentally—his funniest early poems, "Le Monocle de Mon Oncle" (1918) and "The Comedian as the Letter C" (1922).

2. "Le Monocle de Mon Oncle"

The occasion of "Le Monocle de Mon Oncle" is a traditionally comic one. The uncle who relates the poem is a middle-aged man who doubts that he will be adequate to the task of having an affair with a young woman. He knows that, as a studious man of forty called upon to play once more the role of amorist, he can strike a comic figure. His love can no longer be as abstract as a youth's; he feels the changes in his physical life too strongly. Given the reality of his situation, how can he express his romantic longings without sounding ludicrous? Stevens elevates this occasion into a rumination on the nature of poetry without ever losing the comic potential in its contradictions. He does this by making the young woman the uncle's poetic Muse, come to haunt him once again, eternally youthful and desirable. She is what Frank Doggett calls "the archetypal image of women projected as a personification upon the world of one's impressions"[5]—the One of Fictive Music, the Interior Paramour. She is the love of the world within him, as well as the world appearing to him as a lover, requiring poems from him to express his love. So the poem is not simply an account or expression of his affair with her, it *is* that affair— and given the situation, a properly comic one, with a comic language.

The first four lines contain in miniature the comic drama of the poem. They are a botched apostrophe to his Muse. The uncle wishes to write a magnificent, abstract apostrophe in traditional style and can't do it:

"Mother of heaven, regina of the clouds,
O sceptre of the sun, crown of the moon,

There is not nothing, no, no, never nothing,
Like the clashed edges of two words that kill." (CP, 13)

The first two lines represent his trite and rhetorical attempt to celebrate her, and the second two lines burst this bubble with a clumsy explosion of negatives. The uncle can no longer trust the noble, abstract language he feels is appropriate to the occasion; it is too unreal, like "Plato's dear, gorgeous nonsense" (NA, 3) in Stevens' essay, "The Noble Rider and the Sound of Words." It won't do. He realizes too well the negative ability of such language to "kill" what is real, and as an aging man he is too grounded in reality to allow such language to express his desire. His own language must be as earthy—even as a-metrical and ungrammatical as his third line—as it is romantic. But it must be romantic, because he feels the impulse; hence he includes the two lines that he undermines, and initiates a comic tension. This mock-apostrophe is a fine example of the comedy of language because in it, the uncle is able both to proclaim his love "in magnificent measure" (l. 5) and to mock his words, thereby creating an unresolvable contradiction that is both expressive and ironic.

In the last lines of the first verse—

The sea of fuming thought foists up again
The radiant bubble that she was. And then
A deep up-pouring from some saltier well
Within me, bursts its watery syllable.

—the uncle explains the forces that yielded his mock-apostrophe. One aspect of his mind "foists up" (a comic verb suggesting the inauthenticity of this voice) radiant, if insubstantial, imagery. But another aspect, deeper in his consciousness, "bursts" this imagery with its insistent reality ("salt" is a favorite word of Stevens for the piquant taste and quality of the real). These two voices clash throughout the poem, in an expression and then an ironic undercutting of his romantic situation. But the voices merge, too, in a joyful strength as the uncle makes real his romantic impulse, and writes his poem.

One form that the ironic clash of voices takes is anticlimax. A good example occurs in the first lines of verse II:

A red bird flies across the golden floor.
It is a red bird that seeks out his choir
Among the choirs of wind and wet and wing.
A torrent will fall from him when he finds.
Shall I uncrumple this much-crumpled thing?

Here the uncle's ruddy and graceful imagination, symbolized by the red bird, is reduced to a "much-crumpled thing." In the first four lines it seems a thing apart from him, an inherited abstraction, seeking its place in the weather of reality. But the allusion of "choirs" to Shakespeare's Sonnet 73 suggests that, when the bird is connected to its source, the aging uncle, it will have alighted on "Bare ruined choirs, where late the sweet birds sang." This, and the comic exaggeration in the fourth line, prepare us for the deflation of the fifth line, in which the bird, acknowledged now as the uncle's own, becomes as much-used as he is. A description of beauty becomes a question. Can the power of his imagination be renewed? The image is devastating, since a much-crumpled thing can be uncrumpled but not fully restored. This near-despair is echoed a few lines later in "No spring can follow past meridian." But at this point, when his age seems an impossible barrier to renewal, he conjures his Muse: "Yet you persist with anecdotal bliss / To make believe a starry *connaissance*." The verb in the last line is perfectly poised between irony and joy: the awakened desire for transcendence in an aging man is both make-believe and belief-making. And so the comic rhythm continues, in a deflation and reflation of his desire.

The uncle's awareness of his mortality is constantly played off against the requirements of a "starry *connaissance*." Stevens has his irony cut both ways in order to establish the uncle's physical life as a source of both limitation *and* value. In verse IV he says that when his paramour-Muse was Eve, the apple that she offered him—presumably in the innocence of his youth—was "Untasted" (as yet) and so imagined as "sweet." But now he is no longer in that "heavenly, orchard air," he has tasted the "acrid juice" of the apple and Fallen into time, just as "This luscious and impeccable fruit of life / Falls . . . of its own weight to earth." The implied question is, should he bite now? She is offering it again, and to accept it is to realize, more sharply than ever, his bondage to time. And yet it is, after all, the "fruit of life," and the pleasures of mortal life are more vivid than those of divine life.

> An apple serves as well as any skull
> To be the book in which to read a round,
> And is as excellent, in that it is composed
> Of what, like skulls, comes rotting back to ground.

That which rots includes, as verse IV develops, life, love, skull, apple, book—to create fictions and to meditate on them is to have bitten the apple of life and love. The book of life is a series of fictions which harmonize (as in a musical "round") because they bring us close to the rhythm of life, the changing nature of reality. If it is acrid it is also excellent.

The leap from verse VII to verse VIII also involves a comic Fall. At the end of VII the uncle imagines his paramour as "A damsel heightened by eternal bloom," an embodiment both of the ever-renewing world and his own imagination. Yet in verse VIII he declares that for him the "ancient aspect" of his imagination "blooms . . . bears its fruit and dies," and this leads him into a description of his life in time as a "grotesque" comedy of things as they are, not as they might be:

Our bloom is gone. We are the fruit thereof.
Two golden gourds distended on our vines,
Into the autumn weather, splashed with frost,
Distorted by hale fatness, turned grotesque.

This has an almost Falstaffian exuberance about it. The experience of aging is described as both painful and vivid. The Muse is realized here as something that both lives and dies in him, as well as something eternal. But if life in its mortal changes is a descent from the eternal longings of the poetic imagination, it has its own ugly strength.

Although he is but a squash ripening to rot (the fool's knowledge; life as folly), the uncle, in verse IX, calls upon his "venerable heart" to celebrate, in fictive imaginings, his faith in himself. The fifth line is a comic anticlimax to the vigor of the first four:

In verses wild with motion, full of din,
Loudened by cries, by clashes, quick and sure,
As the deadly thought of men accomplishing
Their curious fates in war, come, celebrate
The faith of forty, ward of Cupido.

What words can do! Clashing like soldiers with all the dynamism of youth, words can celebrate . . . a middle-aged man stung by Cupid's arrow! The rest of the verse sharpens this irony by contrasting his "venerable heart" with his lustiness, and then his lustiness with the studious insularity of his middle age ("I quiz all sounds . . ."). The uncle is being called upon to revive the potency of his imagination, and he's not sure he can do it. Verse IX ends almost querulously: "Where shall I find / Bravura adequate to this great hymn?" It may be that his celebration will be only vain boasting, that "the lustiest conceit" he creates will be as vain as it is poetic.

The studiousness of the uncle is often contrasted to the sensuality of the paramour's temptation, of the requirements of love. He is "a dull scholar" (VIII) reading books "to pass the time" (IV). In verse III he wonders, with a kind of nervous and bookish fussiness, why the arts of love of the past did not achieve the "end of love."

> Alas! Have all the barbers lived in vain
> That not one curl in nature has survived?
> Why, without pity on these studious ghosts,
> Do you come dripping in you hair from sleep?

Hair that is curled or clipped is a traditional image of reality transformed by art (cf. *Twelfth Night*, I.iii.83–91). All the "curling" of the past has been in vain because the paramour still comes to him, her hair hanging straight down,[6] asking, once again, to have it dressed. The uncle is clearly unnerved by her unspoken request. As a studious man, he is alarmed to find that the "studious ghosts" of the past, and their arts, offer him no guidance. One can imagine the uncle thumbing through books on the art of love while his potential lover waits, perhaps patiently, for him to discover his own.

The uncle discovers it, but only through a comedy that acknowledges the terms of his situation. In verse VI he declares flatly that "There is a substance" in men of forty "that prevails." Unlike youthful poets, burning for "a furious star" (V) or leaving "Memorabilia of the mystic spouts" (X), men of forty are not searching the heavens for transcendent knowledge. They are, rather, looking for "The basic slate, the universal hue" in nature that will merge "ephemeral blues": the immanent constancy of reality. But to discover this they must acknowledge and submit to change (in nature, in themselves), and this subjects their yearning to comical frustration.

> But in our amours amorists discern
> Such fluctuations that their scrivening
> Is breathless to attend each quirky turn.
> When amorists grow bald, then amours shrink
> Into the compass and curriculum
> Of introspective exiles, lecturing.

Here the activity of the imagination is reduced to the comic image of "scrivening" men "breathless" from their attempts to copy the difficult handwriting of reality. The fortyish imagination wheezes from keeping up with reality's changes, and shrinks finally into the studiousness of the ancient ghosts of verse III. The words above have clashed edges: *amours* suggests something illicit and romantically exciting, while *curriculum*, *introspective* and *lecturing* suggest that these amours are academic affairs.

And yet however much these balding amorists are diminished by reality, they are, in a much-qualified way, heroic in their search. They are not "fops of fancy" seeking "magic trees" and "balmy boughs" (X). They are in touch with the very reality that eludes them, and in this sense their Fall is a fortunate one. In verse V the uncle declares that "The measure of the intensity of love / Is measure, also, of the verve of earth." *Verve* derives from *verba,* words; the words of the earth express the *élan* of the earth just as intensely as "fiery boys" yearn for stars and virgins and mystic spouts. If the declarative strength of these lines is qualified, in the lines that follow, by the tedious ticking of the ephemeral firefly—a reductive image—nevertheless this firefly, like Keats's grasshopper and cricket, speaks the "poetry of earth," and that poetry never ceases. In the last lines of verse V the uncle returns to his paramour:

And you? Remember how the crickets came
Out of their mother grass, like little kin,
In the pale nights, when your first imagery
Found inklings of your bond to all that dust.

Now she is mother earth, not "Mother of heaven!" If she is bound to dust, she remains eternal. If the first four lines of "Le Monocle" are a failed apostrophe, they are set off, by quotation marks, from the rest of the poem, which is an extended, non-traditional, successful apostrophe. As he has changed, so must his vision of her, so that they may come together and celebrate the real.

Throughout the poem the uncle makes positive, lyrical declarations about his situation as a man that must face his aging. The lines about "the verve of earth" and the "universal hue" and the excellent apple are examples. Another is, "The honey of heaven may or may not come, / But that of earth both comes and goes at once" (VII). In all of these declarations process is celebrated for what it is, and the limitations of the mortal become a source of strength. If Stevens subjects his lyricism to a constant irony, it is only to expose its essential strength to tests, as Rosalind tests Orlando's love through mocking in *As You Like It.* The lyricism survives and gathers under scrutiny. By the end of verse XI, the uncle can give us these lines:

Last night, we sat beside a pool of pink,
Clippered with lilies scudding the bright chromes,

> Keen to the point of starlight, while a frog
> Boomed from his very belly odious chords.

Here we return to the two visions, radiant and salty, of verse I, only now one does not burst the other. The romantic atmosphere is in a kind of tense harmony with the frog's "chords." Stevens does not say "*but* a frog," he says "while," which softens the discord. The comedy is there—the contradiction has not been resolved—but the irony is not as deflating as it is in verse I. It is worth noting that this romantic vision is not a youthful one, but occurred "Last night." The uncle is closer to achieving his vision.

The twelfth and final verse begins with a vision of very specific pigeons rather than the abstract "red bird" of verse II. One pigeon circles endlessly, the other "flutters to the ground, / Grown tired of flight." Just so, a man of forty continues his constant search for what prevails while fluttering to the ground of the real, the ground of poetry. Both flights are necessary if he is to discover the constancy in the inconstancy of nature. If he must return to a sense of his own mortality, he need not regard himself as merely a grotesque piece of rotting flesh. That view, the uncle makes clear in this verse, is one of a youth, imagining himself removed "in lordly study," regarding man as a mere "gobbet." No, the comedy of "Le Monocle" does not, as the epigraph to this chapter says, derive from satire on our lives, but from truth—in this case, the aging man as he is, amidst things as they are, all changing. When no longer a youth, and in love with the world rather than detached from it, he pursued "the origin and course" of that love, which brought him down to earth. The course of love, as Frank Doggett remarks, "is only the course of nature."[7]

> but until now I never knew
> That fluttering things have so distinct a shade.

I think these last lines mean that although he flutters in his descent in excitement and perhaps confusion, the image he projects, however much a shadow, is both individual and clear. Things that change, including the uncle, have within them a substance that prevails. The Muse as paramour has helped the uncle to discover and realize this substance, in both his life and his language, and to this extent "Le Monocle" is a joyful poem. But its joy is at one with its irony, its necessary disruption of what is fixed. The uncle's sardonic comedy is a means to discovery, not destruction. It is interesting that the paramour does not appear in the last verse—though she remains, of course, the person to whom the lines are addressed. Perhaps she is the poem itself now, and the last verse a consummation of their affair.

As Joseph Riddle says, "Le Monocle" affirms an "earthy poetry,"[8] vital and virile, in which reality is revealed rather than transcended. And yet the experience of this reality makes one seem mortal, vulnerable, pathetic, even ridiculous. Stevens alternates moods, so that the ironic and the celebratory aspects of the poem are continually clashing for comic effects, commenting on and qualifying each other. In this way he is able to express, simultaneously, youth and age, imagination containing and being contained by reality, the universal and the ephemeral, "the origin and course / Of love."

This complex comedy is realized in Stevens' mixed language of radiance and salt, starlight and frogs, dainty muleteers, mysticism and grit. Language, the medium through which the poet's love of the world is realized, is both powerful and precious, intense and ephemeral. There is a substance that prevails, and it is also the substance that rots us away: reality is both creative and destructive as it is embodied in the poet and his words. Language, and the romance of the uncle with the world, is both undermined and asserted as something ongoing, in a rhythm of success and failure. The uncle's monocle is a lens by which he can perceive reality more clearly, see the distinctness of shade, and yet a lens, an obstruction, a preciosity, designed for a single and incomplete vision. The monocle is the poem itself.

3. "The Comedian as the Letter C"

I have spoken of Stevens' figure of the poet as a diminished person, someone dwarfed by the spectacle of a reality too large or elusive, too demanding for him to express. Like Chaplin and Keaton, Stevens' uncle and Doctor of Geneva are figures of diminution with reserves of strength. If, like buffoons, they fall down, they get up again and continue, and in this dogged continuing they are creatures of romantic aspiration as well as butts of the jokes the world plays on them.

One of Stevens' gayest and most diminished poets is the inchling of "Bantams in Pine-Woods":

Chieftain Iffucan of Azcan in caftan
Of tan with henna hackles, halt!

Damned universal cock, as if the sun
Was blackamoor to bear your blazing tail.

Fat! Fat! Fat! Fat! I am the personal.
Your world is you. I am my world.

You ten-foot poet among inchlings. Fat!
Begone! An inchling bristles in these pines,

Bristles, and points their Appalachian tangs,
And fears not portly Azcan nor his hoos. (CP, 75–6)

Here the inchling is shouting up at the Chieftain, a "universal" poet who
would order the world, himself as Creator, even the sun his servant. The
inchling, with whom we are made to sympathize, feels the Chieftain has
grown fat and tall with his own importance, a comical version of Hoon, a
character of Stevens who, seven poems earlier in *Harmonium,* states
grandly, "I was myself the compass of that sea: / I was the world in
which I walked, and what I saw / Or heard or felt came not but from myself" (CP, 65). The inchling mocks this cocksureness. He himself is a
"personal" poet who realizes that the world the Chieftain feels he has en-
compassed is only the Chieftain's world, a pompously self-created world,
and not reality. The inchling is dwarfed by reality. Although he is a
comically inappropriate bantam lost in the woods, he nevertheless
"points" reality, sharpens our sense of *its* grandeur without altering or
reducing it. By his very failure to encompass reality the inchling is able to
express it, and that makes him a comic figure of a very different sort from
the Chieftain. The Chieftain is either, in his avatar as Hoon, an impres-
sive figure in his own right, or, in this poem, a ridiculous personage
undermined by irony. But the inchling realizes his strength in his very
failure, his limitations, by making acute the reality that diminishes him.
He is the comedian of language because, in the efflorescent gaiety of his
language is the seed of nonsense, the acknowledgement of language as
only a sequence of human sounds, and the recognition that, while language creates meaning (the lines make perfect sense, after the reader's
initial double take), meaning is a matter of language.

Crispin, the comedian-poet-protagonist of "The Comedian as the Letter C," is Stevens' fullest realization of the poet as a successful comic failure. In Crispin's quest—and the poem, despite its many diversions and
jeux d'esprit, is a remarkably lucid narrative—he is reduced from Chieftain to inchling again and again as reality continually and rudely intrudes
on his poetic formulations.

In R. W. B. Lewis' remarks in his essay, "The Aspiring Clown," the
title of which is taken from "The Comedian" (see p. 14), the tension between defeat and joy is noted in the modern comic tradition. But if one
considers that there can be a simultaneous expression of defeat and joy,
then there is no reason to associate defeat with "living with despair," as
Lewis does. He does not say what he means by defeat, and I want to sug-

gest, in the context of "The Comedian" in particular and Stevens' poetry in general, that defeat is the condition of the artist who imagines that he can order reality in ways that it has been ordered in the past. And further, that defeat is the condition of all modern artists, who must try to make order out of a world increasingly imagined as disorderly.

The artist as clown is defeated by the pressure of modern reality, a pressure that is metaphysical as well as social and political.[9] But unlike the tragic figure, who stands and falls in his defeat, the clown stands and falls and gets up again for another fall, each defeat the occasion for a possible triumph, each triumph the occasion for another defeat. Crispin, in the tradition of the robber robbed, is the barber "clipped," and what are clipped are his relations, his imaginative means of coming to terms with a reality that always eludes his mental grasp. To be so clipped is a defeat only in terms of a particular view of relation, a particular idea of what constitutes the vocation of the poet. In another sense, the clipping is a pruning, necessary for further growth, a process toward a knowledge that accepts the failure of each particular relation. In this way the poet discovers a gaiety, Lewis' "positive joy," which brings him into relation with change. The "C" to which the comedian is clipped is both a reduction and "the sign of poetic beginning . . . the first tone of the scale."[10] This is the poem's fundamental paradox.

Part I of "The Comedian," "The World Without Imagination," is the most clearly and heavily ironic in its diminution of Crispin from "sovereign ghost" in Bordeaux to "skinny sailor" at sea. This reduction is immediate and sustained:

Nota: man is the intelligence of his soil,
The sovereign ghost. As such, the Socrates
Of snails, musician of pears, principium
And lex. Sed quaeritur: is this same wig
Of things, this nincompated pedagogue,
Preceptor to the sea? Crispin at sea
Created, in his day, a touch of doubt. (CP, 27)

In its fussy and finicky assertiveness, this academic voice immediately calls attention to itself, and puts itself in question. The diction and rhetoric have just had the dust of the library blown off of them. But the voice is capable of undercutting itself, as it does with the inclusion of "ghost," the pairing of Socrates and snails, the comic surprise of "wig," which suggests judge and censurer, and the deflation of "nincompated pedagogue." In undermining itself, the voice deflates Crispin even before he appears. The question asked is purely rhetorical: a crazy pedagogue is not going to be preceptor to anything, and the idea of being a preceptor to the *sea* is absurd in its own right. In the face of the question, Crispin's creating a "touch of doubt" is a comic understatement; we know that Crispin is at sea in more ways than one. What we encounter in these first lines is a collusion between persona and Crispin, both nincompated pedagogues, both poets.

The poet as pedagogue, like Chieftain Iffucan, can't bring the world to order, can't establish *leges* and *principia* whereby relations are classified and shelved. Such a poet can only create a "mythology of self," swell himself up as Creator. As a poet in Bordeaux, Crispin no doubt found the occupation of barber to the world's hair to be a facile one, for the world there consisted of "simple salad-beds," "honest quilts" and apricots: a lacustrine world, easily bounded. But, leaving Bordeaux and setting off for a New World, Crispin is truly at sea: the waves are "Inscrutable hair in an inscrutable world," the "snug hibernal" of his "terrestrial" existence is lost, and his mythology of self is "Blotched out beyond unblotching." He enters a winter of the spirit, now a "barer self / In a starker, barer world. . . ."

In this poverty of spirit his words are "washed away" by the magnitude of the ocean's sound, "Ubiquitous concussion, slap and sigh, / Polyphony beyond his baton's thrust." This sound, however much it is beyond Crispin's making sense of it, is not merely chaotic noise but a polyphony. However turbulent and gusty and overwhelming, it seems to be speech, inscrutable but teasingly there, "a vocable thing, / But with a speech belched out of hoary darks / Noway resembling his. . . ." This is a reality with all its old myths (Triton, for example) cast off.

> What was this gaudy, gusty panoply?
> Out of what swift destruction did it spring?
> It was caparison of wind and cloud
> And something given to make whole among
> The ruses that were shattered by the large.

If the myths are gone, there remains a "panoply," a "caparison"—both suggesting ornamental coverings. There is still something for the imagination to adhere to, to articulate: not mere sound but a *tone*, not formlessness but an inscrutable form, or potential for form. Something is "given" for Crispin to "make whole" among the shattered images of the past. Despite his diminution, his poverty, Crispin "was made new." If his imagination could no longer "evade / In poems of plums, the strict austerity / Of one vast, subjugating, final tone," it still could not be denied, it still must find "what will suffice" (CP, 240). There is still a lion locked in the stone of the real. Crispin is severed from his Bordeaux past, from "the last distortion of romance," and if the storm he encounters on his way to a brave new world can be compared to Shakespeare's tempest, he proceeds to a realization.

I have discussed, in this book, the reality of change and the artist's necessary adaptation of his form to that reality in order to apprehend it intuitively. Some of the central lines of "The Comedian" are in Part III: Crispin "conceived his voyaging to be / An up and down between two elements, / A fluctuation between sun and moon." Sun and moon are well-known Stevensian symbols of, respectively, reality and the imagination. Before the powerful source of life the poet is, or should be, an inchling, but in the moonlight of his imagination he is "King of the Ghosts" (CP, 209). Crispin, the servant of two masters,[11] is throughout the poem inflating himself and then being deflated. He continually aspires to grasp reality, and reality, in its many guises, continually defeats him, overwhelms or eludes him, and with its power to change, leaves him diminished . . . until his aspiration swells again. His voyaging, "the hubbub of his pilgrimage," never ceases. Once in America his "Western voyage ended and began"—that is, his outward, physical voyage becomes an inward one as he tries to take root in a local reality. It is in Part IV, in America, that Stevens says, "he humbly served / Grotesque apprenticeship to chance event, / A clown, perhaps, but an aspiring clown." It is a paradigmatically comic person who tries to be an apprentice to chance, someone who must go through a series of "sweating changes" (III) in his attempt to keep up with the unpredictable. An apprentice to chance is, indeed, a good working definition of a clown, a figure at once inept and capable of unpredictable violence, sudden change.

The reduction of poet to clown is qualified by "aspiring." As Father Lynch says, "Our way of ferreting out the true comic image will be to identify all the false images of comedy: the clown, the fastidious man, the too-much-humor that makes a fool of man, the laughter of hatred. What, then, is really funny? Things are really funny because wonderful realities can come of their lowermost depths."[12] "Aspiring" takes us beyond the false image of the clown as a merely reductive figure. For Stevens "aspiring" suggested more than a quality of pride or purpose that would only make the clown seem more ridiculous, although this connotation is certainly there.

In "The Figure of the Youth as Virile Poet" Stevens quotes Bergson on "the morality of aspiration," which implicitly contains "the feeling of progress. The emotion . . . is the enthusiasm of a forward movement. . . . But antecedent to this metaphysical theory . . . are the simpler representations . . . of the founders of religion, the mystics and the saints . . . they begin by saying that what they experience is the feeling of liberation . . ." (NA, 49). Stevens' comment that "just as Bergson refers to the simpler representations of aspiration occurring in the lives of the saints, so we may refer to the simpler representations of an aspiration (not the same, yet not wholly unlike) occurring in the lives of those who have just written their first essential poems" (NA, 49–50). Aspiration, then, is a feeling of liberation extending to the spiritual and poetic experience that includes "not only desire but the fulfillment of desire, not only the petition but the harmonious decree" (NA, 50), that involves the feeling of "a man who needed what he had created, uttering the hymns of joy that followed his creation" (NA, 51).

So Crispin's celebrations of "rankest trivia" are "his first central hymns" (IV). The last stanza of another poem, "Anecdote of the Abnormal," offers a further comment on Crispin:

> Crispin-valet, Crispin-saint!
> The exhausted realist beholds
> His tattered manikin arise,
> Tuck in the straw
> And stalk the skies. (OP, 24)

Crispin-valet contains the irony, Crispin-saint the joy necessary for poetic expression. Though exhausted and tattered, Crispin aspires, is constantly made new and vivid, is constantly evolving his aesthetic. This aspiration increases his Chaplinesque clownishness even as it deepens it. Without the irony, the aspiration would seem merely pompous, in the manner of Chieftain Iffucan. Without the joy, the clown would be a trite and superficial image of buffoonery, an easy mark.

For Stevens poetry as comedy yields the truth of poetry. I have used the word *deflation* often. A comic deflation is distinct from a comic destruction. A *deflatus* is the letting-out of air, as from a sail or balloon. The form remains; reconstitution is possible. Indeed, the deflation is necessary for the preservation of the form. A *deflatus* is a decreation, and this is what Crispin constantly undergoes. To demonstrate the special comedy of Crispin's aspiration and deflation, I will concentrate on the major events of Parts II to VI, then closely analyze the concluding lines.

In Part II, "Concerning the Thunderstorms of Yucatan," Crispin seems to have emerged from his ordeal at sea a better man and poet, "made desperately clear, / Fresh from discoveries of tidal skies." He arrives "much trumpeted," which suggests that the sea's "hallucinating horn" not only diminished but proclaimed him. The humbled Bordeaux poet has become, rather too rapidly, a poet swelling himself to the heroic dimensions of a barbaric and grandiose reality. We expect this braced and confident Crispin to be deflated and he is, in a series of ironies that make us aware of how much his newfound self is an acquired thing, a new poetic pose. His restless venturing "Into a savage color" is immediately followed by "How greatly had he grown in his demesne, / This auditor of insects!" Stevens revels in evoking the rich, exotic, "elemental" reality of Yucatan, and then suddenly reminding us that this reality is only something "For Crispin and his quill to catechize," a "new reality" of "parrot-squawks" for the "affectionate emigrant." This contrast between the elemental and the studious is most comical when the thunderstorm drives Crispin from his inspecting and note-taking to seek refuge.

> Crispin, here, took flight.
> An annotator has his scruples, too.
> He knelt in the cathedral with the rest,
> This connoisseur of elemental fate,
> Aware of exquisite thought. . . .

The tragedian would rage, like Lear, against the storm; the comedian ducks in out of the rain. So much for "elemental potencies." Crispin is a "connoisseur" in the sense that his knowing of "elemental fate" is an intellectual knowing; in his "exquisite thought" such fate is apprehended, not in the turbulence of reality.

And yet despite his fear of the storm, its "proclamation," its "span / Of force, the quintessential fact," is a force that renews him. His mind is

> free
> And more than free, elate, intent, profound
> And studious of a self possessing him,
> That was not in him in the crusty town
> From which he sailed. . . .

The self that is taking possession of him is the very self of reality,[13] a self that exists in change. He remains, of course, "studious." He must. "Studious" here is comic in a deeper sense than simple diminishing, and yet that irony is a part of its meaning. Crispin will become aware, as we will, that a poet must be a "connoisseur," seeking his images, his ideal, even when forced back to Square One. Reality, in all its changes, *is* a matter for study. The thunder, "lapsing in its clap, / Let down gigantic quavers of its voice, / For Crispin to vociferate again." That vociferation will be a comically small assertion indeed, merely the cry of a valet who seeks to own the quintessential fact, "The thing that makes him envious in phrase," and yet we recognize it as the necessary cry of an inchling in the wilderness, aspiring to ring his voice from the tops of the pines.

Crispin's heroism is that he does not remain satisfied. If he scampers into the cathedral he does not remain there. His flight to America in Part III, "Approaching Carolina," is also a seeking of "relentless contact," of a possible "blissful liaison, / Between himself and his environment." So he travels to another New World, from the dense profusion of Yucatan to the "polar-purple" of a northern clime. The clipped comedian-poet seeks a clipped world, "gauntly drawn," to which he can become attuned. But in the approach to Carolina his fiction of his New World disappears, because Carolina is enjoying its springtime, "A time abhorrent to the nihilist / Or searcher for the fecund minimum." If Yucatan was a "jostling festival," America, first glimpsed, is a "gemmy marionette"; instead of the "sinewy nakedness" that he sought, *voila!* another teeming atmosphere, only this time raw and burly.

> He savored rankness like a sensualist.
> He marked the marshy ground around the dock,
> The crawling railroad spur, the rotten fence,
> Curriculum for the marvelous sophomore.

This last line is deliciously ironic. Once imagined as something to be grasped, reality becomes "curriculum," something reduced to the dimensions of form. Seeking to avoid the studious, Crispin only enters his second term. Yet his education *is* continuing, and Stevens, rather than ending Part III with this deflation, concludes on the upbeat. If Crispin is only a sophomore he is still marvelous. He rises to the occasion. The dock scene

>   made him see how much
> Of what he saw he never saw at all.
> He gripped more closely the essential prose
> As being, in a world so falsified,
> The one integrity for him, the one
> Discovery still possible to make . . .

This is both comic and true. We understand the seriousness and worth of his intent, at the same time that we understand that he may not be up to it. Part III ends in a spirit of quest that carries us and Crispin onward.

> To which all poems were incident, unless
> That prose should wear the poem's guise at last.

In the mutual interdependence of the prose of reality and the poetry of the imagination, a "guise" is both false and necessary, revealing.

In Part IV "The Idea of a Colony" is projected, a new aesthetic signalled by the opening line, "Nota: his soil is man's intelligence." This truly is something "worth crossing seas to find," a clear improvement on his European idea of the poem's first line, "Nota: man is the intelligence of his soil." The imaginative man is, rather, the weatherman of the local weather, the atmosphere which he breathes and in which he resides. The last three parts of "The Comedian" concern the consequences of this discovery, as Riddel has noted.[14]

The idea of Crispin's colonization is made precise in Part IV. He wishes to come into contact with an essential prose "more exquisite than any tumbling verse." He wants

> to drive away
> The shadows of his fellows from the skies,
> And, from their stale intelligence released,
> To make a new intelligence prevail. . . .

—that is, to dissolve all old orders and confront the *present* time and place. (It is, of course, from the release of old intelligences that new ones are created; decreation is a necessary aspect of creation.) Living in the present, and considering immediate things, be they "rankest trivia," Crispin relentlessly seeks to contact reality as common things rather than exotica. In this he is

> The florist asking aid from cabbages,
> The rich man going bare, the paladin
> Afraid, the blind man as astronomer,
> The appointed power unwielded from disdain.

The appointed power is that of the poet, the power of words to order reality as the poet desires, the power of Hoon. But for Crispin, such power is "unwielded from disdain," as he humbles himself before the reality of the American soil, an inchling in pine woods. This disdain is, as we shall see in the next chapter, close to Beckett's argument in his "Three Dialogues" that the artist should realize himself as a failure, turning away from the power of his relations. For Crispin and for Stevens, the poet exists in his soil and allows the relations immanent in reality to appear, and disappear, and appear again, in a round of rediscovery. On these "premises" Crispin "Projected a colony," a soil to shape him. He will be "pine-spokesman" for the pines around him. No longer content "with hapless words / That must belie the racking masquerade, / With fictive flourishes . . . ," Crispin will accept reality's gaudy changes, whether as "masquerade" or "jostling festival" or "gemmy marionette."

We recognize Crispin's colony as a heady aspiration, noble and naive. It is, after all, vast America, extending south to where

> Sepulchral señors, bibbling pale mescal,
> Oblivious to the Aztec almanacs,
> Should make the intricate sierra scan.

If the aesthetic here is a good one—they drink a native liquor and are not bound by the past—it is also comic in a crucially debilitating way. The imbalance between bibbling señors and "intricate sierra" is telling. How can they make it "scan"? Can such a vast reality be available for poetic grasp? The old problem of trying to convey reality in form and measure reappears, and one senses that Crispin is, after all, a stranger in America (like the Spaniards), founding not a New World but a colony, under the jurisdiction of laws he wanted to leave behind. It is clear that, in order to be truly native—the notion that"The natives of the rain are rainy men" is part of his "prolegomena"—Crispin will have to give over his intelligence to the soil.

This is exactly what happens in Parts V and VI, "A Nice Shady Home" "And Daughters with Curls." As the titles indicate, Crispin's noble aspiration diminishes into an ignoble and quotidian actuality. We see Crispin reduced by the pressure of a reality he sought to contact, and the Idea of a Colony shrinks to the Idea of a Back Yard: "Crispin dwelt in the land and dwelling there / Slid from his continent by slow recess / To things within his actual eye. . . ." If the soil should be his intelligence, Crispin becomes all too governed by its suzerainty. The quotidian life "saps" him "like the sun"; the inchling disappears into the tall pines. Crispin may be "pure and capable," but his will is "infected" by the sheer pleasantness of his surroundings:

> a fig in sight,
> And cream for the fig and silver for the cream,
> A blond to tip the silver and to taste
> The rapey gouts. . . . (V)

As "gouts" suggest, this life is not healthy.

The ironies of this domestic life are many. Crispin becomes "magister of a single room." His costume discarded, he fades into the good, confining life. If "The words of things entangle and confuse," what lies beyond those words, surviving "in its own form" beyond change, is only, like a plum, something to be swallowed, guzzled in contentment (V). Crispin's quotidian situation clarifies the metaphysical problem. How can one relentlessly contact reality except in its changes? Since the poet must fix a pattern in the flux, he must thereby inevitably closet himself. Crispin has latched himself in, closed the door, and been lulled to a "congenial sleep." A "long soothsaying silence" descends, as he is no longer entangled and confused by words. But how, except in words, can we express reality? Are Parts V and VI parodies of Bergson's concept of intuition? Has Crispin truly come to adapt himself to the being of reality, to truly know beyond the knowledge of the intellect? Or has he been decreated to the point where no further creation is desired, no further aspiration felt?

Part VI begins with what Helen Vendler rightly calls a parodic invocation.[15] The Muse is called upon to celebrate comically rather than lament tragically, the changes that Crispin is enduring:

Portentous enunciation, syllable
To blessed syllable affined, and sound
Bubbling felicity in cantilene,
Prolific and tormenting tenderness
Of music, as it comes to unison,
Forgather and bell boldly Crispin's last
Deduction. Thrum with a proud douceur
His grand pronunciamento and devise.

Like the opening lines of "Le Monocle," these celebrate something that is being taken away, and so the source of the gaiety of the language is the source of its irony. What is it that is so grandly devised by Crispin? Why, "The chits came for his jogging . . . ," four daughters are born. Most of Part VI is devoted to a celebration which maintains its buoyancy as it is being deflated. The daughters are Crispin's "poems," "Leaving no room upon his cloudy knee, / Prophetic joint, for its diviner young"—and we may regard this "return to social nature" as "Anabasis or slump, ascent or chute." The daughters are the capacious blooms sprung from his new soil, the four "personae" of a new masquerade or festival, "intimate / As buffo . . . in hilarious dark." Crispin, seeking nakedness, has comically sprouted all over, has bloomed like the Yucatan landscape.

Vendler, who has commented most fully on this difficult section, regards it as strongly ironic: "The revulsion from the proliferation of life . . . is nowhere clearer than in this account of Crispin's daughters."[16] She speaks of Stevens' "active repugnance" in their presence. This is partially true, but in lines like "All din and gobble, blasphemously pink," I discern, along with the spectacle of the everyday, the "active force" as opposed to the "inactive dirge": a certain joy (if that is not too strong a word) in the expression of Life. The four "chits" sound an harmonious chord; they are "four blithe instruments," "four voices several / In couch" which "spread chromatics." If theirs is not the music of poetry, but of life, are the two related? Can they be reconciled?

The last verse paragraph of "The Comedian" offers us the clearest expression of the poem's essential dualism: "Crispin concocted doctrine from the rout." If we take "rout" to mean rabble or disorder, then Crispin can be seen as the poet creating order from disorder. Even if the order derives from the harmony of bearing daughters instead of creating poems, or of presiding over a cabin instead of a colony, it is nevertheless an order, and close to the fecund life of the real. If Crispin-Candide is still tending his salad-beds, they are at least his own and not someone else's, nor the wilted salad-beds of the past. But if we take "rout" to mean a substantial, even a disastrous defeat, Crispin's *own* defeat, then we are presented with the ironic notations of a fatalist:

> The world, a turnip once so readily plucked,
> Sacked up and carried overseas, daubed out
> Of its ancient purple, pruned to the fertile main,
> And sown again by the stiffest realist,
> Came reproduced in purple, family font,
> The same insoluble lump. The fatalist
> Stepped in and dropped the chuckling down his craw,
> Without grace or grumble.

While Crispin has discovered a new and rougher soil, he has in a significant sense come full circle, reality remaining "insoluble." If reality changes—from an "ancient purple" in Bordeaux to a naked fact to a domestic purple—it remains the same lump. Crispin, in swallowing it whole, is swallowed by it.

How are we to regard Crispin's adventures? Stevens offers us two possibilities:

> Score this anecdote
> Invented for its pith, not doctrinal
> In form though in design, as Crispin willed,
> Disguised pronunciamento, summary,
> Autumn's compendium, strident in itself
> But muted, mused, and perfectly revolved
> In those portentous accents, syllables,
> And sounds of music coming to accord
> Upon his lap, like their inherent sphere,
> Seraphic proclamations of the pure
> Delivered with a deluging onwardness.

This is one sense of the anecdote, a joyful one: Crispin *has* contacted reality, the harmony of family life is a harmony of the real, of the "inherent sphere" in which the family dwells. The anecdote of Crispin is "Autumn's compendium"; he has come to live as the seasons do, breeding new life. The anecdote is "muted, mused, and perfectly revolved," a Stevensian description of the essential poem.

> Or if the music sticks, if the anecdote
> Is false, if Crispin is a profitless
> Philosopher, beginning with green brag,
> Concluding fadedly, if as a man
> Prone to distemper he abates in taste,
> Fickle and fumbling, variable, obscure,
> Glozing his life with after-shining flicks,
> Illuminating, from a fancy gorged
> By apparition, plain and common things,
> Sequestering the fluster from the year,
> Making gulped potions from obstreperous drops,
> And so distorting, proving what he proves
> Is nothing, what can all this matter since
> The relation comes, benignly, to its end?

This is the ironic sense of the anecdote: Crispin, faded and profitless, is still only a "sovereign ghost," distorting reality, falsely illuminating it. His "relations" are not perfectly revolved, but "obscure." It doesn't matter anyway, the anecdote is a bubble, Pop! A benign bubble, harmless and entertaining, blown up by a clown.

The final line of the poem sums up the ambiguity produced by these two *sentencia:* "So may the relation of each man be clipped." In one sense the barber is barbered: his relations, doctrines, prolegomena, have come to naught. And yet the tone of the line points to another sense: so *may* it be, which suggests that the relation will be and should be clipped, if Crispin is himself to be clipped (in the sense of "embraced") by reality. To return to the imagery of hair in "Le Monocle," although it is true, in "The Comedian," that "not one curl in nature has survived," still the poetic profession of trimming and pruning nature, and being trimmed and pruned by nature, endures. The poets die, the poets' beauty lives. If the comedian is pruned to C, that is the first note of the scale. To "clip" is to fasten or clasp as well as to cut. The poem helps us to understand that the two processes are one.

At this point I would like to remark on the relation between the narrator and Crispin. Crispin's adventures are related in the past tense, and to that extent narrator and protagonist are distinct: Crispin is a fictional character, the narrative voice provides an outside commentary. But the narrator's language, as I mentioned when discussing Part I, is most of the time imitative of what we suppose Crispin's to be: finicky, gorged, almost obscure. Though it has a narrative suppleness, and can be direct and concise, still we are constantly aware of it as language. The anecdote of Crispin is the poem; what we think of Crispin we think of the poem. The final verse paragraph is as much a description of a poem as of a man: they come together in "anecdote." When we ask what the poem means, or if it means, we are asking about Crispin and his adventures. The poem as autobiography[17] supports this. The relation between narrator and Crispin, between the poem itself and what the poem discusses, exemplifies the poem's ambiguity. Crispin is Stevens' marionette, whom Stevens can operate at will, commenting on him ironically, making him appear foolish. Crispin is the poet reduced to vain gestures, a parodic figure. And yet Crispin *is* a poet, and so serves as a comment on Stevens.

The poet as comedian is both Stevens and Crispin, both an essential figure creating and celebrating relations, and an absurd figure whose relations are false. The poem contains "pages of illustrations" that "These / Two things are one" (CP, 215). As Daniel Fuchs says, "To the extent that Crispin is Stevens, he is a poet in spite of himself writing a poem about the inadequacy of words in an outpouring of verbal opulence."[18] I would add that the irony of proving words inadequate is also a function of the *distance* between Stevens and Crispin.

Stevens, commenting on "The Comedian" to Hi Simons, made the following observation:

> It is true that the letter C is a cypher for Crispin, but using the cypher was meant to suggest something that nobody seems to have grasped. I can state it, perhaps, by changing the title to this: THE COMEDIAN AS THE SOUNDS OF THE LETTER C . . . as Crispin moves through the poem, the sounds of the letter C accompany him. . . . You have to read the poem and hear all this whistling and mocking and stressing and, in a minor way, orchestrating, going on in the background. . . .[19]

The comedian as the sounds of the letter C is the comedian as a man "Made Out of Words," to once again use the title of a later poem (CP, 355). C as a pun on "sea" is apposite here. The imaginative man, the poet, the comedian, sounds the sound of reality as a note of the scale. The sea, in him, becomes music (cf. "The Idea of Order at Key West," CP, 128–30). But the words also "entangle and confuse," and Crispin's anecdote is a "distortion." The narrator, too, who exists as the poem, is a man made out of words, and encounters the same dilemma.

Many critics have remarked that Crispin is an artist *but* a failed one, overcome by the pressures of the quotidian. I am arguing that Stevens felt that the modern poet is by nature a failure. In a postscript to the same letter quoted above, Stevens says,

> About the time when I, personally, began to feel around for a new romanticism, I might naturally have been expected to start on a new cycle. Instead of doing so, I began to feel that I was on the edge: that I wanted to get to the center: that I was isolated, and that I wanted to share the common life. . . . People say that I live in a world of my own: that sort of thing. Instead of seeking therefore for a "relentless contact," I have been interested in what might be described as an attempt to achieve the normal, the central.[20]

Crispin, sharing the common life with his wife and daughters, approached the "central," a favorite word of Stevens for the meeting place of reality and the imagination. To approach is to fail in the sense of having one's poetic relations "clipped." Crispin has proved "nothing," he has proved that "what he proves / Is nothing": the poem embodies and transcends its own destruction because it *lives* that destruction. Bergson describes the direction of consciousness "to the precise point where there is a certain intuition to be seized":

> We shall gradually accustom consciousness to a particular and clearly-defined disposition—that precisely which it must adopt in order to appear to itself as it really is, without any veil. But, then, consciousness must at least consent to make the effort. For it will have been shown nothing: It will simply have been placed in the attitude it must take up in order to make the desired effort, and so come by itself to the intuition.[21]

Crispin has been shown "nothing" only in the sense that the poem shows us "nothing." Stevens denies us the final spectacle of Crispin's experiencing an intuition, because that intuition is, for Stevens, "the ideal," and a poem, like a metaphor, has only "its aspect of the ideal" (NA, 81–2), can only be notes *toward* a supreme fiction.

Stevens' technique, in this poem more than in any other, is to make us aware of words as sounds, sounds that often entangle and confuse us. In this way we come to know the Comedian *as* these sounds. We become aware of both the gaiety and the falsity of language, and realize that these two things are one—just as Crispin is both failure and poet. One can say of Stevens' comedy what Hugh Kenner says of Beckett's: "If it can deal with everything it touches because it operates solely with the laws of thought, by the same token it can really deal with nothing, because thought is not prior to things, and things escape."[22] That is a description of Crispin's ultimate *deflatus* and *afflatus*.

4. Masks and Change

French Morse has pointed out how the mask of Crispin, like other masks Stevens assumed in his early work, was a means for him to come to terms with his own poetic role and its relation to his life.[23] And Fuchs remarks wisely that Stevens' masks, "however playfully they are sometimes assumed, are not poses but the self-dramatization of urges deeply felt and insights intricately perceived."[24] Fuch's main problem in his useful book, *The Comic Spirit of Wallace Stevens*, is his failure to relate adequately the masks and the urges. He analyzes well the comedy deriving from the masks, particularly in his first chapter, and he has many interesting things to say about Stevens' central concerns. But he doesn't substantially relate the two, and so his discussion of the latter is not a discussion of comedy. Vendler's comment on summarizing Stevens' poems could be used to describe Fuch's problem: "Such summaries do not match the tone of the poem as we have it, and conclude in paying homage to the 'seriousness' of its intent while honoring the surface of the poem, if at all, as the sparkling but almost irrelevant iridescence over the serious 'topic.' "[25] However misleading or "false" Stevens' masks might be, they are signs of the urges behind them. There is always something of the essential Stevens behind his comic masks, because his essential ideas are comic. As the lines from "Like Decorations in a Nigger Cemetery" that serve as an epigraph to this chapter imply, language, however hollow, derives from truth, the truth of necessity and desire and aspiration. Hence the "comedy" of language is not merely satirical, an ironic judgment on our habits of ordering. Rather, the irony that operates in the comedy is a necessary, descending curve in an ongoing cycle.

Stevens' early poems are often comic because he conceived the role of the poet as that of a comedian of masks in "a theatre of the mind."[26] The drama enacted thereon is a series of scenes describing the present and fleeting moment, in images created and decreated. In "As at a Theatre" (OP, 91) the acts or scenes are seen as new shapes, poetic images. Each new image is "like / A new knowledge of reality" (CP, 534), the fitting last words of *The Collected Poems*. There is no final, no fixed knowledge, only a prologue to another new knowledge. In this way, "knowing / And being are one. . . . We come / To knowledge when we come to life" (OP, 101).

These last lines are from "The Sail of Ulysses," a late and awkward poem written, no doubt in some haste, for the Phi Beta Kappa Exercises at Columbia.[27] If it is more dissertation than realized poem it is interesting as a skeletal disclosure of ideas. Speaking of the poet, Stevens writes,

> His mind presents the world
> And in his mind the world revolves.
> The revolutions through day and night,
> . . .
> Are matched by other revolutions
> In which the world goes round and round
> In the crystal atmospheres of the mind,
> Light's comedies, dark's tragedies,
> Like things produced by a climate, the world
> Goes round in the climates of the mind
> And bears its floraisons of imagery. (OP, 102)

This is something of a rough gloss on "Notes Toward a Supreme Fiction": the poem must be abstract, revolved in the crystal of the mind; it must change, as reality changes in its diurnal and seasonal revolutions; it must give pleasure, express in its abstraction and its changes the "gaudium of being," the eternal joy of life in its continual creativity. The movement toward the dark, toward winter, is for Stevens a tragic movement, but the tragedy is not final, it gives way to "Light's comedies," and the series continues. This vision of series I have called comic rather than tragicomic because the final expression is one of joy: "After the final no there comes a yes" (CP, 247), and this "ember yes" does not triumph over the "cindery noes" (CP, 529), it contains them and pushes on. As Baird says, "We must assert that the comedian from the moment of his first appearance was the reveler who felt the shadow,"[28] who felt the encroachment of night and winter, the decreation of the imagination by reality. Yet the reveler continues to revel,

> The cancellings,
> The negations are never final. The father sits
> In space, wherever he sits, of bleak regard,
> As one that is strong in the bushes of his eyes.
> He says no to no and yes to yes. He says yes
> To no; and in saying yes he says farewell.
> He measures the velocities of change. (CP, 414)

The father is, of course, a mask of the poet, of him who "fetches pageants out of air, / Scenes of the theatre" (CP, 415).

From the metaphor of "theatre" in Stevens' poetry (particularly from "The Auroras of Autumn," quoted above, and from "Of Modern Poetry" and "Repetitions of a Young Captain"), we can construct the following scene. The poet is an actor on the stage of his mind. There are no props, no lines, nothing is readymade, the past is a souvenir. The theatre is a ruin, the wind howls outside. There is, in fact, "no play. / Or, the persons act one merely by being here" (CP, 416). By merely "being here" the actor must discover what will suffice, what the speech of the place is, what stage to construct. He must create "the spectacle of a new reality" (CP, 306) from the cinders of old ones. He exists, to cite the title of an oddly neglected poem, "In a Bad Time":

> He has his poverty and nothing more.
> His poverty becomes his heart's strong core—
> A forgetfulness of summer at the pole.
>
> Sordid Melpomene, why strut bare boards,
> Without scenery or lights, in the theatre's bricks,
> Dressed high in heliotrope's inconstant hue,
>
> The muse of misery? Speak loftier lines.
> Cry out, "I am the purple muse." Make sure
> The audience beholds you, not your gown. (CP, 427)

If in his poverty he is Melpomene, the muse of tragedy, that should be, as Stevens' voice says, only a mask, the mask perhaps of a tragic clown. For he is commanded to declare the power of his imagination, even in a time of calamity. His essential self, beneath his gown and mask, is creative, even if it must, given the time, create a sense of misery. The strength in his heart's core is that he has imagined well his bad time, and this is an overcoming of misery, a lofty aspiration. There is a gaiety underlying the most abject poverty. In the face of our poverty, of our being "O most miserable," we have the "gaiety of language" (CP, 322), there being nothing else.

Stevens' masks, then, may be comic or tragic, gay or sad, as the conditions require, but beneath the masks is a fundamental poetic self, strong in its search to express reality even if each of its particular expressions, its particular poses, is inadequate, strong in its ability to change and so to convey the reality of change. Stevens' poems are dramatic even when they do not include theatrical metaphors. To respond to Stevens' comedy is to respond to the modulation of voices (personae, masks) in his poems. His

comic irony deflates voices and orders and words so that the comic joy of
the impulse that creates voices and orders and words can be expressed—
an impulse that, more than any single voice, puts us in touch with "the
gaudium of being." Many of Stevens' comic poems after *Harmonium*
achieve their comedy, not so much in the sheer exquisiteness of their language, nor in the adventures of clownish protagonists, but in the comic
drama of their argument, their play of voices. Two fine examples of this
later comedy are "Connoisseur of Chaos" and "So-and-So Reclining on
her Couch."

The connoisseur of "Connoisseur of Chaos" (CP, 215–16) undergoes
a gradual change that is essential to the poem's argument, which also
changes. The poem begins as a logical argumentation expounded by a
very confident preceptor-figure pointing, as it were, to the blackboard:

I
A. A violent order is disorder: and
B. A great disorder is an order. These
Two things are one. (Pages of illustrations.)

The parenthetic addition is a comic intrusion that carries the confidence
of the persona to a pompous extreme. But even before this notation, the
comedy of blatant paradoxes being presented in outline form is evident.
We proceed to specifics:

II
If all the green of the spring was blue, and it is;
If the flowers of South Africa were bright
On the tables of Connecticut, and they are;
If Englishmen lived without tea in Ceylon, and they do;
And if it all went on in an orderly way,
And it does; a law of inherent opposites,
Of essential unity, is as pleasant as port,
As pleasant as the brush-strokes of a bough,
An upper, particular bough in, say, Marchand.

It becomes immediately clear that the argument is proceeding along
aesthetic rather than logical grounds. The persona turns out to be discussing metaphor, relation, and his *exempla* seem almost effete. The confident "and it is . . . and they are . . . and they do . . . And it does" are more
assertive than convincing. We are being presented with a vision that
seems intuitive and private, yet the syntax is logical: *given* the following
relations, *then* it is clear that "essential" relation or order exists. Yet that
conclusion, too, "is as pleasant as port," a conclusion that could apply to

good wine, or to a painting. The voice of the pedant is shading into the voice of a rather fussy connoisseur.

III

After all the pretty contrast of life and death
Proves that these opposite things partake of one.
At least that was the theory, when bishops' books
Resolved the world. We cannot go back to that.
The squirming facts exceed the squamous mind,
If one may say so.

It becomes clear that this proof is only "pretty," that the order asserted is tenuous indeed, a creation of the classroom lecture. A stronger, firmer voice asserts that it is an old theory, no longer useful, that we cannot return to resolving the world so tidily. Yet even as this saltier voice is asserting itself it says, fussily, "If one may say so." Then it modulates again:

And yet relation appears,
A small relation expanding like the shade
Of a cloud on sand, a shape on the side of a hill.

We recognize this voice as more nearly Stevens' own. The fastidiousness of the preceding argument has been undermined by a vision of chaos ("squirming facts"), and then out of this chaos emerges a vision of relation that is neither pretty nor stale nor logical. It is an immanent rather than an imposed order, expressed clearly and directly.

IV

A. Well, an old order is a violent one.
This proves nothing. Just one more truth, one more
Element in the immense disorder of truths.
B. It is April as I write. The wind
Is blowing after days of constant rain.
All this, of course, will come to summer soon.
But suppose the disorder of truths should ever come
To an order most Plantagenet, most fixed . . .
A great disorder is an order.

The new, strong, simple yet lyrical voice continues at the same time that it returns to the logical apparatus. An old order is violent because it is imposed, creating disorder because it falsifies natural order. This much is clear, yet it "proves nothing": the rational voice is undermined even as it is affirmed. So it is not surprising when, after "B." the voice becomes personal and reflective rather than strictly logical. A great disorder is an order: though the seasons change, the wind blows, we know that summer will come, and the year will make its inevitable way. The cyclical nature of this vision, or order, leads the voice to suppose a possible, but only possible, fixed ideal, the knowledge at the imagined end of aspiration.

> Now, A
> and B are not like statuary, posed
> For a vista in the Louvre. They are things chalked
> On the sidewalk so that the pensive man may see.

Clearly, an argument *has* been developed, only its premises are not rationally fixed—nor are objects of the past fixed for the dilletante's contemplation. They are "chalked" on a modest and quotidian part of the scene in which one lives, transient rather than fixed, available for everyone rather than mounted in a museum. Just so, the fastidious logic of the poem has dissolved into a vision of aesthetic order, culminating in the final lines:

> V
> The pensive man . . . He sees that eagle float
> For which the intricate alps are a single nest.

This vision is not restricted to art and has nothing to do with logic, though the "V" remains to sustain the comedy. The pensive, the imaginative man, can attain a vision so inclusive as to resolve the most vast and "intricate" apparent chaos into order, into a "nest" for the eagle, the principle of relation, not to be denied. Here is a joy beyond poor Crispin's inability to "make the intricate Sierra scan," a momentary realization of aspiration.

Emerging from the comic *deflatus* of the persona, then, is a joyful *afflatus*, an inspired affirmation of the power of poetry to express relation. But we must remember that "These / Two things are one," that the vision of the eagle depends on the vision of chaos ("intricate Alps"), that the dialectic goes on in change. The voice of the logician-dilletante is ironically undercut so that what is true in it, the search for relation, can be released: there *is* a dialectic, and it *is* aesthetic. What is affirmed rises from the diminution, rises during the process of diminution, in a modulation of voice. The comedy that underlies the comic persona is a joy in the expression of relation. The various voices modulate, finally, into the voice of the true connoisseur, the "poet-knower" (to use Baird's phrase) who contains and transcends the instructing dilletante. The irony of the poem is never destructive, it is a process of discovery of what is true.

"So-and-So Reclining on her Couch" (CP, 295–6) is similar to, if not as complex as, "Connoisseur of Chaos." We encounter again the pedant, about to instruct us concerning some aesthetic principles. He points to his subject, a desirable young woman reclined in odalisquean splendor on a couch, as "This mechanism," initiating a comedy that derives from the contradiction between the mechanistic and the real. In this way an instruction in aesthetics is hilariously undermined by the immediately aesthetic sensuality of the woman, all too perceived by the lecturer. He points out "The curving of her hip, as motionless gesture, / Eyes dripping blue, so much to learn," intending to regard her as an *objet d'art,* but her actual beauty makes his desire seem comically dry. The lesson involves some of Stevens' ideas, but here they are mocked by the reality they try to describe. She is a real object, Projection A; Projection B is "the slightest crown / Of Gothic prong" suspended above her, the sense of her as idea, imaginatively tipped, as it were. The conclusion is as follows:

> She floats in the contention, the flux

> Between the thing as idea and
> The idea as thing. She is half who made her.
> This is the final Projection, C.

> The arrangement contains the desire of
> The artist.

This final Projection is the poem itself, in which she exists in an interdependence of reality and the imagination. But the comedy of the poem is that things (the woman as woman) and ideas (the woman as mechanism) are made to clash in contradiction. The arrangement does *not* contain the true desire of the persona, and he becomes addled, affected by her actual presence, and proceeds to undermine his own argument:

> But one confides in what has no
> Concealed creator. One walks easily

> The unpainted shore, accepts the world
> As anything but sculpture.

An aesthetic of poetry having been established, the real conclusion is offered that the aesthetic is not to be trusted, that one "confides" in the natural order of things rather than in the artist's order, however cleverly concealed. Reality intrudes, as it did in "Connoisseur of Chaos," and the voice modulates to present it, ironically undercutting its own pretensions. The world (that is, the woman) is "anything but sculpture," anything but a thing—which is what we suspected all along. The poem ends,

                                        Good-bye,
    Mrs. Pappadopoulos, and thanks.

This is at once the voice of the pedant dismissing his subject, addressing her formally, thanking her for being his "thing," *and* the voice of the realist granting her her reality (her name, her marital status), so that she is no longer So-and-So born at twenty-one, not merely an object for aesthetic contemplation. Both voices have made their point, and both thank her for it. The good-bye is both a polite acknowledgement that the point has been made, and a farewell to an idea, an indication that no final Projections can ever be established. You are real, Mrs. Pappadopoulos, and you will change, and we will change with you. The poet is a man of forty chasing you, desiring you. He has an idea of you as an ideal woman constantly young, yet he knows you are as mortal as he is. For him, you will change but you will not change. He is a clown, a real and commonplace man pursuing that which squirms away, evading his grasp, a self lost in a world he cannot fully understand—as such, a paradigmatic comic figure. But he is also an aspiring clown, he has a vision that transforms him and his surroundings. He will make, like Hart Crane's Chaplin, "A grail of laughter of an empty ash-can,"[29] and know it to be a fiction.

    For although he knows he must and should say farewell to ideas, he also realizes that "The cancellings, / The negations are never final" (CP, 414). If the cancellings make us aware of our poverty, reduce and diminish us, we cannot be content with that. "A season changes color to no end, / Except the lavishing of itself in change" (CP, 416), and we must change with it, live in change.

5. Metaphor and Change

To understand Stevens as a comic poet is to understand his poetry in general, including the many poems that are not comic, because his comedy derives so directly from the fundamental paradoxes in his thought and language. For Stevens, as for Bergson, language is both false because all that it is capable of expressing is form, and true, because words can be extensible and mobile. Bergson said that language has contributed to the liberation of the intellect because "the word, made to pass from one thing to another, is, in fact, by nature transferable and free." Thus the intelligence "profits by the fact that the word is an external thing, which the intelligence can catch hold of and cling to, and at the same time an immaterial thing, by means of which the intelligence can penetrate even to the inwardness of its own work."[30] In his many remarks on the nature of metaphor, Stevens shows how close his thought is to Bergson's. Metaphor is the most mobile use of language, "the creation of resemblance by the imagination" (NA, 72).

Through the creation of resemblances poetry becomes "a part of the structure of reality" (NA, 81), because the resemblance between things is "one of the significant components of the structure of reality" (NA, 72). This component is "significant because it creates . . . relation. . . . It binds together. It is the base of appearance" (NA, 72), and this binding creates in us a sense of a possible "*noeud vital*" (NA, 44, 49), the essence of reality and the center of poetry, a "mystical *vis*" (NA, 49) very like Bergson's *élan vital*. Metaphor suggests, by theoretical extension, what binds all things together. And what all things have in common is change, the movement of a possible *vis*, imagined as a flow of being in later poems such as "Metaphor as Degeneration" and "The River of Rivers in Connecticut." "A poet's words," said Stevens, "are of things that do not exist without the words" (NA, 32). This is close to Bergson's notion that language is both "immaterial" and external. A metaphor contains external objects, yet creates something in their resemblance that reveals the inner workings of the mind intuitively responding to the fluidity of reality.

And yet, language, including metaphorical language, falsifies reality in its necessary adherence to forms. Distrust of the evasions of metaphor is a subject of much of Stevens' poetry and prose. As he says in "Bouquet of Roses in Sunlight,"

> Our sense of these things changes and they change,
> Not as in metaphor, but in our sense
> Of them. So sense exceeds all metaphor.
>
> It exceeds the heavy changes of the light.
> It is like a flow of meanings with no speech
> And of as many meanings as of men. (CP, 431)

The "sense" of things is a sense beyond "speech," a naked sense of the actual unmediated by words. And yet, "above everything else, poetry is words" (NA, 32), and words create an unreality. So the problem is, paradoxically, impossibly, how to get beyond words with words.

A major response to this problem, for Stevens, was through the "repetitions of resemblances," or a "gradus ad Metaphoram" (NA, 81). If metaphors, like voices, can be continually created and decreated, then "the ideal" of apprehending being can be approached in an "ascent through illusion" (NA, 81). Bergson said as much in these words: "No image can replace the intuition of duration, but many diverse images, borrowed from very different orders of things, may, by the convergence of their action, direct consciousness to the precise point where there is an intuition to be seized."[31] So Stevens' poetry is often, as many have pointed out, a *series* of images, or metaphors, or propositions, each one an "illusion" in and of itself, each one provisional, but in the movement of their creation and decreation, the "inward life of things," to use Bergson's phrase, is expressed. This is the source of Stevens' heavily apposite style, evident in most of the poems quoted in this chapter.

I have tried to point out how Stevens was able to realize this continual creation and decreation, whether of images or poet-figures or voices, in a comedy of language. Each attempt to express reality is ironically revealed as a frail illusion, and each attempt has its joyful truth that can only be released in the repetition of attempts—just as the strength and beauty of the comic protagonist or clown is realized in the intimate relation between his awkward stumbling and his recovery from it, his clumsy grace, his continually failing aspiration.

Even in one of Stevens' very late poems, "Long and Sluggish Lines" (CP, 522), when he imagined himself, at "so much more / Than seventy," wandering among the too-familiar trees that "look as if they bore sad names / And kept saying over and over one same, same thing" —even in this poverty he feels "an opposite, a contradiction" to the sameness, and imagines "A comic infanta among the tragic drapings, / Babyishness of forsythia, a snatch of belief. . . ." The mind is beginning again, in its comic and continual rebirth, to stir: "The life of the poem in the mind has not yet begun."

Samuel Beckett: *Watt*

To contrive a little kingdom, in the midst of the universal muck,
then shit on it, ah that was me all over.[1]

1. Introduction

As the above passage indicates, we are in the presence here of a much harsher voice. Samuel Beckett's comedy is far more ironic and less joyful than Stevens' or Faulkner's or his mentor Joyce's. In fact, joy does not have the relevance to Beckett's work that it has in Joyce's and Stevens'. And yet there is a dark lyricism, what Beckett would call a "nightsong," running through his work that give his comedy its depth, its necessary ongoing human pulse. Unlike Faulkner, Beckett does not give his sense of absurd endurance the levity and charm of a folk tale. His vision is more abstract, his characters more often thinking heads than figures in a landscape. Yet despite all his protagonists' desires to *stop* thinking, to cease using words, they "go on." Although Beckett's "I'll go on" is a cry of despair over the doggedness of human consciousness, it is a signal, too, that no despair is final, that there is something like the "contradiction" in Stevens' "Long and Sluggish Lines," the comic stirring among the trappings of misery. Something is kept alive, however much that something and that life are resented. So Beckett's often bitter, often hilarious, always potent irony is never destructive, though his characters wish it were. The little kingdoms of words get contrived—and contrived beautifully—no matter how often they are shat upon. Contrivance, the fabrication of worlds through words, is—as in our other comic authors —a continual and indestructible force that carries with it a dark song of an essential reality beyond words. This ongoingness makes the irony comic: no matter how intentionally destructive or persistent it is, no matter how terrific in scope, it cannot have the last say.

It may seem strange to study Beckett after Wallace Stevens, writers who are seldom if ever paired. Yet however different the surface characteristics of their work, there is in both a profound sense of the paradox of human consciousness: that it grows in power in its attempts to transcend or eliminate itself in an effort to express what it cannot express. In Stevens' late poem, "The Rock," he wrote these eerily Beckett-like lines, creating a scene like the one between Watt and Sam that I will discuss later.

> The lives these lived in the mind are at an end.
> They never were.... The sounds of the guitar
>
> Were not and are not. Absurd. The words spoken
> Were not and are not. It is not to be believed.
> The meeting at noon at the edge of the field seems like
>
> An invention, an embrace between one desperate clod
> And another in a fantastic consciousness,
> In a queer assertion of humanity:[2]

Here it is stated that words are absurd, that the mind's life is "at an end" because nothing that has been spoken has mattered. And yet it has *not* ended, human consciousness asserts itself again, and the poem gains in strength as it recognizes this vitality. Nothing is final, permanent, concluded—deep in the cold comes this "queer assertion." The paradox of the situation is rendered in the lines that follow soon after the above passage:

> As if nothingness contained a métier,
> A vital assumption, an impermanence
> In its permanent cold, an illusion so desired
>
> That the green leaves came....

Out of nothingness comes a calling, a trade, a career of words. In the absence of form is contained the seed of form, illusory but necessary. But how can nothingness contain a métier? To paraphrase one of Beckett's Addenda to *Watt*, how can words enclose nothingness? The dilemma here is too somberly declared to be comic, but the unsolvable paradox that yields both Stevens' and Beckett's comedy of language is there, available.

Here is a typical example of Beckett's comic style, from the "Texts for Nothing":

That's right, wordshit, bury me, avalanche, and let there be no more talk of any creature, nor of a world to leave, nor of a world to reach, in order to have done, with worlds, with creatures, with words, with misery, misery. Which no sooner said, Ah, says I, punctually, if only I could say, There's a way out there, there's a way out somewhere, then all would be said, it would be the first step on the long travelable road, destination tomb, to be trod without a word, tramp, tramp, little heavy irrevocable steps, down the long tunnels at first, then under the mortal skies, through the days and nights, faster and faster, no, slower and slower, for obvious reasons, and at the same time faster and faster, for other obvious reasons, or the same, obvious in a different way, or in the same way, but at a different moment of time, a moment earlier, a moment later, or at the same moment, there is no such thing, there would be no such thing, I recapitulate, impossible. (*Stories*, 118)

A voice calls for the end of talk while talking. It calls for an end to creatures while going about its creaturely métier, inventing a persona, an "I." It trashes its words while inventing more, faster and faster. The passage is a verbal equivalent of a clown's continually stumbling without being able to fall. The voice, in fact, imagines a way out of language only as a way out of life: just as steps tramped through mortal time are seeking a conclusion, so words are steps toward the wordless. Only "destination tomb" can end this voice, and Beckett's voices never die because they keep on talking. Their language, like the language above, becomes more comical as it tries to realize itself as language—that is, as something syntactically and substantially logical, a *form* of expression, a figuring out of things maniacally and fastidiously—because the contradiction between the logic and the absurdity and arbitrariness of language becomes more pronounced. Beckett's comedy is, in many respects, our purest example of the comedy of language because his obsessive preoccupation is with the very fact of address. Often, as in the "Texts for Nothing," there is nothing else but a voice ruminating on what issues from it: words, words.

2. The Aporetical Style

"What am I to do, what shall I do, what should I do, in my situation, how proceed?" Beckett's Unnamable asks himself, and immediately follows this question with another: "By aporia, pure and simple?"[3] Aporia is the awareness of opposing and incompatible views of the same subject; it also means the doubt or skepticism implicit in such an awareness. Aporia thus connotes irresolution or impasse (the Greek *aporos* means "impassable"). One poises, in suspension, two mutually exclusive ideas, points of view, etc. This may suggest a kind of stasis, but if one is true to one's aporetics, no stasis is possible. If the Unnamable had *stated*, "By aporia pure and simple," he would have decided on an answer of how to proceed, and the issue would be, in a way, resolved. No, in aporia all answers are further questions. Indeed, the Unnamable soon says, "I say aporia without knowing what it means. Can one be ephectic otherwise than unawares?" About this, J. D. O'Hara has judiciously written, "Obviously if one is deliberately skeptical, if one deliberately suspends judgment as a matter of policy, then one's action is in itself a judgment; pretending to be skeptical, one has actually committed oneself to a belief."[4] This is so, but O'Hara, for his own relatively unplayful purposes (his subject is not Beckett's comedy), does not quite follow through with the joke: the Unnamable obviously *does* know what aporia means, he uses it quite precisely, is obviously aware of suspending judgment (being "ephectic"). And so the problem continues in a vicious circle, the questions go on, like the voice of the Unnamable, whose refrain is "I can't go on, I'll go on."

Beckett's Malone, near the beginning of *his* novel, reveals his familiarity with aporia: "Perhaps I shall not have time to finish. On the other hand perhaps I shall finish too soon. There I am back at my old aporetics. Is that the word? I don't know" (Trilogy, 181). He, too, claims not to understand what he really does understand about not understanding what he really understands, and so on. The more one unravels such paradoxes, the more comic one's own prose becomes, because language, with its syntax and sentences, is designed to elucidate the elusive, not to confront the fact of elusiveness itself. Language isolates what it can out of flux and ignores flux itself. The more language attempts to fix what it cannot fix, what cannot *be* fixed, the more it parodies its own mechanism. This is how much of the comedy of *Watt* works, particularly in the extended passages in which Watt (a unit of energy asking questions) tries to fix in words a reality (the reality of Knott) that eludes him. The result is a vaudeville of language, an explosion of hectic and futile reasoning.

A visual equivalent of Watt's mental processes at work is Buster Keaton's "great infernal nutcracking machine," which Henriette Nizan has described:

> The machine which stands on a table must be at least three feet high. It looks extremely complicated. This is how it works: a crane, put in motion, picks a choice nut from a gunny sack. The crane raises the nut to the top of a slide and drops it; the nut begins its slide, and after meandering from small a to big A, then from small b to big B, it

drops into a basket. The basket conveys it from C in C′ to a trans-
porter bridge. From there, after a lot of comings and goings intended
to soften it, the nut crosses several canals and inclined planes, and
then, suddenly set on its vertical, comes to a raised platform on
which it descends, progressively, until it arrives at last beneath a
kind of steam-hammer in the form of a mallet which, at the proper
moment, rises, comes down, and ... misses.[5]

The machine, if it did crack the nut, would still be comic in a Rube Goldbergian way. It is profoundly comic because it does not crack the nut, and
so realizes itself as a kind of pure machine: functionless, solipsistic, engaged solely in its own processes. Watt confronts incidents "of great
formal brilliance and indeterminable purport,"[6] a phrase that also describes, necessarily, the language that issues from his thought processes
—and also Keaton's machine. The "formal brilliance" of the machine is a
function of its not cracking the nut. The pleasure we feel in seeing the
machine operate is a function of our ironic awareness that it will not fulfill its express purpose. And vice versa: the irony of our awareness is a
function of our pleasure in seeing it operate. The comic experience is two-
fold and simultaneous: (1) we see, ironically, that the machine does not
"work," and (2) we see, in a sudden expansive vision that is the soul of
play, that it *does* work insofar as it fulfills itself on its own terms.

So too with language, which comes to comical fruition in its failed efforts to get its job of ordering done. We have left Malone at his old aporetics; if we return to them we can connect them to the idea of play.
Malone, waiting to die in his room, knows that, however much his un-
quiet thought will be "wide of the mark," it will struggle on nevertheless.
And so he conceives of his stories, his incessant language production, as
"play" or "a game" (Trilogy, 180). So conceived, his language need no
longer be burdened with "the earnestness" of seeking for some formu-
lated truth: "What half truths, my God. No matter. It is playtime now"
(Trilogy, 182).

Aporia is "play" because, in the suspension of its opposing terms and
consequent circularity of its reasoning, it puts us in touch with a form
that is closer to the life of things, a reality that simply goes on in purposeless splendor. Eugene Fink says that "play is characterized by calm, timeless 'presence' and autonomous, self-sufficient meaning," that it "has
only internal purpose, unrelated to anything external to itself."[7] He continues, "In the autonomy of play action there appears a possibility of
human timelessness in time. Time is then experienced, not as a precip-
itate rush of successive moments, but rather as the one full moment that
is, so to speak, a glimpse of eternity."[8] This is precisely what Didi's and

Gogo's vaudeville-style "play" does for them in *Waiting for Godot:* allow them to forget the tedious round of their waiting, and prepare for whatever will come at the end of that round: God, Godot, Nothing, Knott. And yet play reflects, just as it absorbs, the presentational forms of the world outside its boundaries, just as children often enact war in their play. Malone's consciousness and the language that expresses it go on, in relentless purpose, seeking to describe what it cannot describe, seeking to cancel itself out and so avoiding the cancellation. "And I even feel a strange desire come over me, the desire to know what I am doing, and why. So I near the goal I set myself in my young days and which prevented me from living. And so on the threshold of being no more I succeed in being another. Very pretty" (Trilogy, 194). We can understand Malone's (and Beckett's) voice if we realize that the tone behind "very pretty" is as appreciative as it is sardonic and bitter. Indeed, it is both. The aporetical style expresses a constant contradiction between a desire to cease speaking because language is absurd, and a desire to speak because language is necessary. The contradiction is never resolved, no point of view is ever final. Henriette Nizan's response to Keaton's nutcracking machine is appropriate: "There's nothing for it but to begin all over again."[9]

3. The Forms of Fiasco

Before analyzing in some detail Beckett's second novel, *Watt*, I think it would be useful to sketch some of Beckett's characteristic paradoxes, as a background to the central images and ideas in the novel, and in all his work, and as a preparation for describing the comedy of these images and ideas.

Beckett's most obsessive imagery is that of light and darkness. Darkness expresses security, enclosure, refuge, silence: the state of the womb, or conditions for which the womb is paradigm. Darkness is the Paradise that has been lost,[10] for we are expelled from it into light, into the world, the "outside" data demanding to be named. This expulsion is a Fall which Beckett's protagonists lament. They regard living in this world, the outer world, as atonement for an unknown sin, or "itself a sin, calling for more atonement" (Trilogy, 239), or as a series of "stations." The cross that they bear is consciousness, for as soon as they are expelled from the womb they begin to hear voices naming things. Molloy expresses this most lucidly in the passage I quoted in section 3 of the first chapter, in which his consciousness is described as a disturbance of silence, a "lie" (Trilogy, 88). The voice inside us, with which we speak, is not truly of ourselves, but is a voice inherited, as it were, from "outside." This results in a fragmentation of our identity: "I express by saying, I said," or Molloy says, or any number of given and invented names says. Richard Coe articulates this well when he says, "we do not make our words—we learn them. From others. Others speak and we hear. Not a thought in our heads, not a memory, not a fragment of our personality, which was not created and put there by other people."[11]

Birth entails, then, a loss of identity, of the self we feel is ours alone, the unnamable self. We emerge from our self-enclosed being into an illusory and patterned world, a Babel of voices outside that initiates a Babel of voices within, murmuring constantly. We enter what in *Murphy* is called the "physical fiasco,"[12] the rot of living, the valley of the shadow of death. Moran gives us a feeling for it in this passage: "I get up, go out, and everything is changed. The blood drains from my head, the noise of things bursting, merging, avoiding one another, assails me on all sides, my eyes search in vain for two things alike, each pinpoint of skin screams a different message, I drown in the spray of phenomena" (Trilogy, 111). Change is the ruling principle of the fiasco. Change brought us outside and rots us. Moment to moment, infinite fractions of moments to infinite fractions of moments, things change, perceived or unperceived.

There is no actual light without darkness, and no actual darkness without light in Beckett's landscape, only a continual movement from one to the other, a shadowing and dawning in eternal change. For we are not only expelled onto our personal *via dolorosa*, but we long to return to the security of darkness, to the sense of our being without consciousness, to mother, to "home." "Murphy, all life is figure and ground," said Neary; "But a wandering to find home," said Murphy (*Murphy,* 4). At home we can experience once again "the silence of which the universe is made" (Trilogy, 121), and be at rest at last. In Beckett's world, one is prodded out of one's rest, and one seeks rest. The protagonist of "The Expelled," on being expelled from his home, sets out on his own, failing to stay on the sidewalk (all Beckett's protagonists find motion to be an intricate and difficult business, the life of forms a precarious affair). Soon he enters a cab like a "black box" and curls up foetally in a corner of it (*Stories,* 17). In the course of most of the story he attempts to remain in the womb-like cab, and finally must leave it, making "towards the rising sun. . . . When I am abroad in the morning, I go to meet the sun, and in the evening, when I am abroad, I follow it, till I am down among the dead" (*Stories,* 25).
Most of the scenes in Beckett's landscapes take place in the dawning or dying day. Even at midday there are shadows, and at night there is usually the moon, pouring its rays upon Watt, for example, who dislikes it (33). As Sam says much later, referring to the effects of the years on the

colors of Watt's hat and coat, "So it is with time, that lightens what is dark, and darkens what is light" (218). Or again, of Malone's fictional creation, Sapo, it is said, "of a sudden he is off again, on his wanderings, passing from light to shadow, from shadow to light, unheedingly" (Trilogy, 206). Beckett's descriptions of scenic landscapes are seldom of solid objects clearly seen, but of things seen dimly and lyrically in the constant movement of light and shadow.

For Beckett's protagonists, existing in change, the movement toward light is a movement forced on them. The contingencies of the world require them to move, prodded from the foetal rest that was contentment. Analogously, the murmur of voices, the continuous babble of "intelligible sounds," makes them seek *meaning* in these sounds. Referring to the "spray of phenomena" that he encounters outside, Moran continues, "It is at the mercy of these sensations, which happily I know to be illusory, that I have to live and work. It is thanks to them that I find myself a meaning. So he whom a sudden pain awakens" (Trilogy, 111). Consciousness is a "pensum" assigned to us by the Generalized Other; we are obligated, for reasons unknown, or because we are human, to wrench meaning out of chaos. This painful undertaking is the "ancient labour" at which Watt labors.

The search for darkness, for refuge from phenomena, is initiated by a desire to be free of meanings, and of the voices that suggest them—to touch what lies beyond words, that which Beckett calls in his monograph on Proust "the mystery, the essence, the Idea" (*Proust,* 57). In *Proust* Beckett makes a distinction between "Habit" and "the suffering of being." Habit is all that we mean when we say "Life" or "living"; it is the "compromise effected between the individual and his environment," whether inner or outer, the "consecutive adaptations" to the world that we make in order to be comfortably sealed off from the "suffering of being." This suffering occurs when the individual, in rare and painful and delicious moments, comes in contact with "the real"—that is, reality stripped of the protective conceptions with which we, in self-defense, clothe it. The world then appears truly strange, and ourselves truly strangers in it.

> . . . when the object is perceived as particular and unique and not merely the member of a family, when it appears independent of any general notion and detached from the sanity of a cause, isolated and inexplicable in the light of ignorance, then and then only may it be a source of enchantment. Unfortunately Habit has laid its veto on this form of perception, its action being precisely to hide the essence—

the Idea—of the object in the haze of conception—pre-conception. (*Proust,* 11).

Habit, then, allows us to cope with the outside world; our voice, at the beck of the voices we inherit, formulates meanings, conceptions, categories, so that objects are classified—chair, book, pot, Molloy—by inherited words, the "icy words" that "hail down upon" us, "the icy meanings, and the world dies too, foully named" (Trilogy, 31). This is by now a familiar idea to us: language, which in its naming and classifying is inexorably logical, separates us both from reality and our own identity, an identity which for Beckett's protagonists is "wrapped in a namelessness often hard to penetrate" (Trilogy, 31). The attempt to penetrate it, which forms the main action of *Watt,* is what I am calling the movement toward darkness.

It is important to understand that the two movements, toward light and toward darkness, are simultaneous, in constant and comic contradiction. Perhaps the most abstract expression of this condition is in Beckett's first published work, his essay on Joyce's "Work in Progress" (*Finnegans Wake*), entitled "Dante . . . Bruno. Vico . . . Joyce":

> Thus we have the spectacle of a human progression that depends for its movement on individuals, and which at the same time is independent of individuals in virtue of what appears to be a preordained cyclicism. . . . the work of some superior force, variously known as Fate, Chance, Fortune, God . . . Individuality is the concretion of universality, and every individual action is at the same time superindividual. The individual and the universal cannot be considered as distinct from each other.[13]

For Beckett, as for Vico, we live paradoxically in and out of History. As part of a "universal" structure, we are in a sense victims of its preordination, and as individual agents we are aware of our unique identities, our unique relations with a unique world. We inherit "voices" yet we realize, if we are not completely stunned by Habit, that these voices are not our own. Richard Coe, who provides us with a sort of Ariadne's thread through Beckett's abstract thought, comments on one of Watt's ruminations in this way: "For either Tom is temporal, in which case his whole existence is determined by his place in the series; or else he is a-temporal, a-spatial, and independent of the series—he cannot very well be both. *And yet,* says Beckett, *this is precisely what he is.* Human existence *is* a logical impossibility. It belongs to the series and yet evades the series; it is at once in time and out of time."[14]

As Sartre said in his essay on Faulkner's *The Sound and the Fury*, every metaphysic implies an aesthetic, and Coe's remark bears on his thesis that Beckett's view of the human condition, and hence of art, is that they are "literally and logically *impossible*."[15] The idea of a paradoxical aesthetic brings us to Beckett's only extended commentary on his own aesthetic, his "Three Dialogues" with the French art critic, Georges Duthuit,[16] to which I have referred in previous chapters. The central paradox is this: that the artist is obliged to express at the same time that he cannot express. Part of the third dialogue, on the painter Bram Van Velde, goes like this:

> B.—The situation is that of him who is helpless, cannot act, in the event cannot paint, since he is obliged to paint. The act is of him who, helpless, unable to act, acts, in the event paints, since he is obliged to paint.
> D.—Why is he obliged to paint?
> B.—I don't know.
> D.—Why is he helpless to paint?
> B.—Because there is nothing to paint and nothing to paint with.[17]

The artist is obliged to paint (to express, create, relate things) simply because he exists in the world. Born into the light, he is compelled by the light, voices compel him, inexorably, inexplicably. To ask why he is obliged to express is like asking why certain muscles contract to effect parturition. They contract involuntarily. And involuntarily we toe the line of History, and proceed along it, receiving a language, asking questions with it, seeking answers. This is our cross to bear. The artist is "helpless" to express because he is aware of "the incoercible absence of relation," the Nothing that underlies our orders, relations, conceptions, words—and so is aware that his relations are false. "The history of painting . . . is the history of its attempts to escape from this sense of failure, by means of more authentic, more ample, less exclusive relations between representer and representee, in a kind of tropism toward the light . . . and with a kind of Pythagorean terror, as though the irrationality of pi were an offense against the deity, not to mention his creature."[18] The references to dark and light are consistent with my earlier comments. The shadowing toward darkness involves a sense of the falseness of language (whether of paint or words) and the knowledge that art, and the artist, must fail. The "tropism toward the light" involves involuntary Habit, the desire to create and possess one's conceptions, stake out one's artistic property on the vast and meaningless landscape of reality. This is the "estheticized automatism" of the individual who seeks to express and to

be part of the universal. Art, to Beckett, is or should be impossible because the artist seeks or should seek to express "nothing," attempt to enclose silence in words. As Northrop Frye says at the end of his review of
the Trilogy, Beckett's "final paradox is the conception of the imaginative
process which underlies and informs his remarkable achievement . . . to
restore silence in the role of serious writing."[19]

The mention of the irrationality of pi in the passage from the "Three
Dialogues" quoted above suggests another paradox—or, more precisely,
another expression, in different terms, of an essential paradox—the fact
that man exists, simultaneously, in rational and irrational worlds. The
domain of rational numbers is the domain of History, of forms. But as
Hugh Kenner points out, there is another domain, "which we can think
about but not enter with our minds," the domain of irrational numbers,
"more numerous even than the infinitely numerous rationals. And it is
the analogy between these interpenetrating but incommensurable domains that Beckett discerns his central analogy for the artist's work and
the human condition."[20] The closeness of this to Bergson's opposed
worlds of the intellect and intuition should be noted. The work of the intellect is with stable states, forms—by analogy, rational numbers. Intuition brings us into contact with the creative evolution of constant change
—by analogy, the irrational realm which the intellect cannot define, or
what Beckett calls, when describing Murphy's mind, the "matrix
of surds."

Beckett's description of Murphy's mind (*Murphy*, ch. 6) helps us to relate the imagery of light and darkness to the domains described above.
Murphy's "mental experience was cut off from the physical experience.
. . . It was made up of light fading into dark. . . . It felt no issue between its
light and its dark, no need for its light to devour its dark. The need was
now to be in the light, now in the half light, now in the dark. That was
all." His mind is not ethically oriented, and so its only operative principle
is constant changing from its states of light and half light and dark. In the
zone of light, mental experience is "parallel" with physical experience
(cause and effect being an obvious lie to all of Beckett's protagonists).
This climate of light is the one in which most of us spend most of our
lives. Murphy regards it as merely "a radiant abstract of the dog's life. . . .
Here the whole physical fiasco became a howling success." In the zone of
half light mental experience is not parallel with physical experience. This
is the climate in which most of Beckett's protagonists intermittently exist,
in which one contemplates one's physical experience objectively, if one
contemplates it at all. Physical life is there, nevertheless, a source of
Chaplinesque surprise. In the third zone mental experience is completely

self-enclosed, "a closed system subject to no principle of change but its own, self-sufficient and impermeable to the vicissitudes of the body." Beckett describes it in significant detail:

> The third, the dark, was a flux of forms, a perpetual coming together and falling asunder of forms . . . nothing but forms becoming and crumbling into the fragments of a new becoming, without love or hate or any intelligible principle of change. Here there was nothing but commotion and the pure forms of commotion. Here he was not free, but a mote in the dark of absolute freedom. He did not move, he was a point in the ceaseless unconditioned generation and passing away of line.
>   Matrix of surds.

This is the irrational zone. At the end of the novel, Murphy glimpses it in the eye of Mr. Endon, who is insane, and presumably achieves it in his (Murphy's) death, when the "superfine chaos" of gas soothes him to a final sleep, his body quiet at last. The third zone is not a state that can be entered except in madness or death. *Murphy* is not a comedy because, in effect, Murphy resolves his dilemma, or has it resolved for him. It is the half light in which the minds of Beckett's other protagonists play, and they play continually, their minds in a comic flux between the light of rationality and the darkness of surds.

I have been sketching some related paradoxes. Perhaps an accumulation of them is called for:

light	dark
universal	individual
words	silence
rational numbers	surds

The world of Beckett's comic fiction and drama takes place in an aporia between these poles, in which the oppositions are not resolved but are suspended in paradox. If we think of this fictional ground as, say, a magnetic field, we can imagine particles constantly ordering and reordering themselves on it. Beckett's protagonists seek rest and are compelled to move, seek silence and are compelled to speak and write their reports, are overwhelmed by a sense of the irrational yet are compelled to rationalize. Their problems are central to Beckett's problem as an artist: given that he is obliged to write, how does he write when there is nothing to write about and nothing to write with? Or, as the question is put in the Addenda to *Watt,* who may "nothingness / in words enclose?"

This is a brief sketch of Beckett's vision. How is it made the subject of comedy? Discussing *Watt,* Hugh Kenner remarks with characteristic cogency: "That things and events are extracted in self-defense from an unintelligible continuum of changes is one of philosophy's self-cancelling propositions, assailing the very fact of its own affirmation. It is thus ideally suited to Beckett's characteristic comedy of the impasse. It is first cousin to the statement, ' Every statement that I make is meaningless.' "[21] How are such reflexively self-cancelling statements related to comedy? In *Sweet Madness: A Study of Humor,* the psychologist William Fry proposes, in discussing the "vicious-circle principle" and the role of paradox in human communication, that paradox is an inescapable and pleasurable issue of human thought processes and is the essence, the very nature of "play" or humor.[22] The vicious-circle paradox of the lying Cretan is found by Fry to be operative, in less obvious ways, in simple statements like "This is unreal" or "This is a dream"—reflexive statements that, by cancelling themselves out, initiate a "shimmering, endless oscillation of the paradoxes or 'real-unreal.' Humor becomes a vast structure of intermeshed, revolving rings of reality-fantasy, finite-infinite, presence-void."[23]

This speaks directly to Beckett's comic world. Take the celebrated end of *Molloy:* "Then I went back into the house and wrote, It is midnight. The rain is beating on the windows. It was not midnight. It was not raining" (Trilogy, 176). This calls Moran's report into question, making us realize that all his statements have been fictional creations and hence lies. And, at the same time, the seeming voice of "truth" ("It was not...," etc.) is only, after all, another fictional voice, as suspect as any other. If we read the passage closely enough, we are made acutely aware of the fictional nature of any voice. It might have been raining, who can know? The conventional distinction between fictional present ("It is. . . .") and fictional past ("It was not. . . .") is broken down. The voice of Moran in his report and the voice of Moran speaking to us as he writes his report, the voice of Beckett in his fiction and the voice of Beckett commenting on his fiction—all are equally real or unreal, we cannot be certain, we are suspended in uncertainty. The discovery of this is a playful discovery, the sudden understanding of a profound joke, what Freud called "the liberation of nonsense" in the discovery that "what at one moment has seemed to us to have a meaning, we now see is completely meaningless. . . ."[24] By disembodying language from any notion of "truth," Beckett makes a game of it, or exposes it as a game—a serious and important game (for it is about a universal fiasco), but a game nevertheless.

I have discussed two basic movements in Beckett and of paradoxes generated by the simultaneity of these movements. The movement from light to dark is the expression of the meaninglessness of the world of forms, a world which exists in light. And the movement from dark to light is the expression of form through language. Near the end of *Molloy*, Moran ruminates about his bees:

> For the bees did not dance at any level, haphazard, but there were three or four levels, always the same, at which they danced. . . . I was more than ever stupefied by the complexity of this innumerable dance. . . . And all during the long journey home, when I racked my mind for a little joy in store, the thought of my bees and their dance was the nearest thing to comfort. For I was eager for my little joy, from time to time! And I admitted with good grace the possibility that the dance was after all no better than the dances of the people of the West, frivolous and meaningless . . . it would always be a noble thing to contemplate. (Trilogy, 169)

Here a comic balance is struck between the nobility and the meaninglessness of the dance, between its ability to give comfort and joy and its essential obscurity and frivolity. It is "of great formal brilliance and indeterminable purport." Beckett's protagonists seek this sense of form, of being able, nonsensically, to measure the measurelessly "innumerable," at the same time that they recognize the futility of the endeavor. "For I was eager for my little joy" is at once sardonic and lyrical, a typically Beckettian comic utterance. Beckett's world is comic in its relentless reduction of the modes of thought, the "dances" of the Western world (particularly its tropism toward logical meaning), and it is also comic in the strange gaiety with which it creates and orders a reality of its own, impossible and necessary, literally ab-surd.

4. Watt

Watt is Beckett's most wildly comic novel, perhaps because Watt himself is Beckett's most obsessed logician, his most persistent searcher for meaning—and so, inevitably, his most clownish character, with the exceptions of Didi and Gogo. His very name suggests both a unit of energy and a question: What? It is his questing spirit that runs the little mechanisms that keep him moving onward through a landscape, both physical and mental, that bewilders him. He is as much a principle as he is a character, as we see in the very first scene of the novel.

In this hilarious and much-ignored scene, many of Beckett's central concerns are introduced before Watt appears. A humpback Mr. Hackett, approaching his "seat" (a tram bench), finds it occupied and "did not know whether he should go on, or whether he should turn back" (7). This is a small introduction to a major subject, the perpetual repetition and uselessness and inevitability of motion. The text continues, "Space was open on his right hand, and on his left hand, but he knew that he would never take advantage of this. He knew also that he would not long remain motionless. . . . The dilemma was thus of extreme simplicity: to go on, or to turn, and return, round the corner, the way he had come. Was he, in other words, to go home at once, or was he to remain out a little longer?" (7–8). One conjures Chaplin or Keaton or Stan Laurel, scratching his head over the most minimal task. To "go on," for Mr. Hackett, is to advance to the "seat," "the property very likely of the municipality, or of the public," which was not his but which he thought of as his. To turn back is to go "home," back to one's room, one's solipsism. The dilemma, generally stated, is to proceed along the line of History, calling yours things that are not yours, seeking to join your voice with the choir of voices, *or* to turn back "home," toward the dark identity that pre-exists entrance into the outside world.

> Night is now falling fast, said Goff, soon it will be quite dark.
> Then we shall all go home, said Mr Hackett. (16)

After some conversation about how Tetty's experience of giving birth is "one of riddance," Hackett says, "Tell me no more . . . it is useless" (15). Clearly Hackett's experience of the world has made him identify with the child gotten rid of. He says he has always wondered "what it feels like to have the string cut" (14). Later, he speaks of how he fell off a ladder at the age of one, with nobody around, and acquired, presumably, his present deformity. His father, it turns out, was "breaking stones on Prince William's Seat," and as he remembers the fall he hears the "distant clink of the hammers" (15–6). Jacqueline Hoefer has offered a helpful elucidation of the meaning of Beckett's ladder. She proposes that Arsene's comment, much later in the novel, "What was changed was existence off the ladder. Do not come down the ladder, Ifor, I haf taken it away" (44), is an allusion to the end of Wittgenstein's *Tractatus*, where he uses the ladder as an image of the process of logical reasoning. One climbs the ladder to a point where it is no longer needed; one uses words to approach silence.[25] The ladder, then, is a symbol of the process of "going on," of taking rational steps toward the light. We are born at the bottom of the ladder, and it is our ancient, Sisyphean labor to climb it, rung by rung, word by word. Hackett has fallen off the ladder, and it is for this reason that motion is a dilemma to him. His rather pathetic situation off the ladder is contrasted, in the first of the many lyrical passages in the novel, with his father's toil, breaking stones on property not his own ("Seat" recalls Hackett's municipal "seat"). Hackett tells Nixon, "I am scarcely the outer world" (10), a description applicable to Watt, for whom motion is always a problem, and who is always, like Hackett, "a solitary figure" (16), regarded as strange by others. Nixon, referring to Watt, tells Hackett, "The curious thing is, my dear fellow, I tell you quite frankly, that when I see him, or think of him, I think of you, and that when I see you, or think of you, I think of him" (19). And later, the porter whom Watt knocks down cries, "The devil raise a hump on you" (24).

Hackett and Watt, then, are set apart from the others. Nixon avers that Watt, who has just appeared on the far side of the street, is setting out on a journey, and how he is going about it is the subject of an hilariously mismanaged conversation among Hackett and the Goffs. Nixon says that Watt was on his way to the station, and wonders why he got off the tram across the street from them. The others offer reasons, the reasons are logically rejected. The conversation becomes tedious as they attempt to determine, logically, why Watt got off, if he wished to go to the station, and why, having gotten off, he continued by foot *toward* the station, an action which rules out a possible desire to turn back.

> Perhaps, said Mr Hackett, he suddenly made up his mind not to leave town at all. Between the terminus and here he had time to reconsider the matter. Then, having made up his mind that it is better after all not to leave town just now, he stops the tram and gets down, for it is useless to go on.
>
> But he went on, said Mr Nixon, he did not go back the way he came, but went on, towards the station.
>
> Perhaps he is going home by a roundabout way, said Mrs Nixon.
>
> Where does he live? said Mr Hackett.
>
> He has no fixed address that I know of, said Mr Nixon.
>
> Then his going on towards the station proves nothing, said Mrs Nixon. (20)

Mrs. Nixon is right, of course, their analysis is proving nothing, it is comically trying to understand the irrational by rational means. It is useless to go on, yet Watt is going on anyway, impossibly trying to go "home" by a "roundabout way." Perhaps, as Hackett suggests, he has removed his individual will from the act of going on, referring it to "the frigid machinery of a time-space relation" (21). In a sense, Watt is not going on, because he has gotten off the tram, and yet he is not going back, because he continues to walk toward the station. Perhaps, as Hackett suggests, he has removed his individual will from the act of going on. Yet was it not a "decision" to take matters into his own hands in order to leave things up to chance? Watt's motives and direction are not resolved easily, indeed cannot be resolved at all. The triviality of the problem is precisely to the point: Watt is a figure who causes them (and us) to ask What? about the simplest things, to perceive dilemmas in the most ordinary affairs.

The conversation between Hackett and the Nixons derives its comedy from a clash between the realm of Habit, represented by the Nixons, and the "suffering" of life off the ladder, represented by Watt and Hackett. The relationship of these last two characters is clinched in the passage in which Hackett says he has been "intrigued" by Watt and burns with curiosity and "wonder," a sensation he doesn't think he could bear for more than a half hour (17). It is hard to bear the idea of Watt because it involves the breaking of Habit. The above passage occurs just after Watt appears, "motionless, a solitary figure" (16), like a thought, a vaguely outlined and vaguely outlandish man, or more a principle than a man. Watt is someone or something ("Hackett was not sure that it was not a parcel . . . wrapped up in dark paper and tied about the middle with a cord") that causes us to inquire into, say, the direction we travel in, the cause and effect of events like getting off a tram, that opens for us a whole world of comically futile speculation and endeavor.

> What does it matter who he is? said Mrs Nixon. She rose.
> Take my arm, my dear, said Mr Nixon.
> Or what he does, said Mrs Nixon. Or how he lives. Or where he comes from. Or where he is going to. Or what he looks like. What can it possibly matter, to us?
> I ask myself the same question, said Mr Hackett.
> How I met him, said Mr Nixon. I really do not remember, any more than I remember meeting my father. (23)

Charter members of "the outer world," the Nixons regard such questions as so many houseflies. Watt is merely a topic of passing conversation for them, someone whom Goff knows, beyond his voluntary memory, and yet does not know at all. Watt appears and disappears, here and elsewhere in the novel, like a memory or thought. He is last seen, in this episode, standing on a bridge, "faintly outlined against the last wisps of day" (18), and then, as an afterthought during their conversation,

Mrs. Nixon says simply "he is gone" (19), to which Mr. Nixon replies "is that so" and the conversation goes on. Watt is more alive in their discussion of his journey than he is an actual person. He fades away like the light of the dying day that is emphasized so often in this scene. It is appropriate that the light is "failing" (7), the day "dying" (10), "the last flowers" about to be "engulfed" (22), because the passage of light to darkness is a motif of Watt's journey, or of all his journeys, for Watt is an "experienced traveller" (20).

There is much in this first scene to prepare us for Watt's adventures. Beckett places us with spectators, considering Watt; we become, like Hackett, intrigued and wondering. Hackett serves as a kind of transition from the "outer world" of the Nixons to Watt's world, into which we abruptly plunge. Hackett is much affected by the enigma of Watt. At the end of the scene the Nixons stroll off, having settled things comfortably in their minds ("He is a university man, of course, said Mrs Nixon. I should think it highly probable, said Mr Nixon"), but Hackett remains, "crying, in the night" (24). The scene concludes, "Mr Hackett . . . looked towards the horizon that he had come out to see, of which he had seen so little. Now it was quite dark. Yes, now the western sky was as the eastern, which was as the southern, which was as the northern" (24). All directions have become one in the dark. Beckett's world is one of the "failing light" of directions, questions, reasons, speculations, all fading hopefully but futilely into a dark that cannot last. We experience, in the opening pages of *Watt*, a comic irony directed at the tedium of the patterns of rational thinking and the discourse created by the normal functioning of words, to the point where it seems a conversation out of Carroll's Wonderland. At the same time we experience a sense of the reality that lies beyond these words, something which the presence of Watt suggests to us, an involuntary memory of something real, from which we have become estranged. Mr. Nixon "did not like the sun to go down on the least hint of estrangement" (23), but we are left with Hackett crying in the night, and are about to enter Watt's world. "Estranged" is a good word for this tenebrous world; in it, we will become estranged both from the outer world, the habit of mind and behavior and language, *and* from the pure darkness to which we can no longer turn back.

It is never made clear why Watt gets off the tram across the street from Hackett. The point is made that the tram line, with its series of "stations," is a Beckettian image of the *via dolorosa* of human existence, the going on from birth to death, bearing the burden of consciousness. And the point is made that Watt gets off. When we come upon him directly, after the initial scene, he is at a station, about to get on a train. We assume, relying on the chronological conventions of the novel, and not given any signals to the contrary, that what takes place with Watt at the station is occurring some time after he got off the tram and spoke with Nixon. Only when the novel is over will this assumption be called into question, and the dilemma of direction raised again.

For those who get off trams and trains, and who fall off ladders, motion is a problem. We encounter Watt bumping into a porter and regarding as an "extravagant suggestion" the remark that he look where he's going. The porter's job is described in its tedium: "On the platform the porter continued to wheel cans, up and down. At one end of the platform there was one group of cans, and at the other end there was another. The porter chose with care a can in one group and wheeled it to the other. Then he chose with care a can from the other and wheeled it to the one. He is sorting the cans, said Watt. Or perhaps it is a punishment for disobedience, or some neglect of duty" (26). It is, of course, both. Most human tasks could be described in the same manner, and would require the same linguistic tedium to be so described, a tedium that makes the use of language seem as Sisyphean a task as futilely sorting cans. It is useless to go on, as Hackett says, because to go on and to turn back are one and the same, neither final.

Once on the train Watt meets a Mr. Spiro, editor of *Crux*, a popular Catholic monthly. (It is weirdly prophetic that two characters named Nixon and Spiro appear in rapid succession.) Spiro "must speak to a fellow wanderer" (28), and so describes to Watt some of the absurdly scholastic questions that *Crux* deals with, quoting obscure theologians, yammering along as the silent fields fly by and the voices, "singing, crying, stating, murmuring, things unintelligible" (29), prevent Watt from hearing anything Spiro says. One gets on the track and hears language, the language of reason ludicrously applied to the theological study of trivia.

Watt gets off (though typically we don't see him get off) just as Mr. Spiro is pursuing the question of whether or not a rat which has eaten a consecrated wafer has ingested the Real Body, and if he has, what is to be done about it. As a result of this congruence, we aren't sure whether, in the following passage, Watt or the rat is referred to: "Personally I would pursue him, said Mr Spiro, if I were sure it was he, with all the rigor of the canon laws. He took his legs off the seat. And pontifical decrees, he cried. A great rush of air drove him back" (30). The momentary confusion here suggests Watt as a rat who has swallowed a consecrated wafer. Like Christ, he embodies the paradox of the spiritual inhabiting the physical, here become a comical paradox. What is to become of Watt? Will that part of him that is drawing him to Knott's house be fulfilled? Spiro's rational language removes him from what is, after all, a crux of human life. He flies on through the night, along the tracks, as Watt proceeds to Knott's in a "funambulistic stagger" (31), his walk a fantastically unstable means of moving "in a straight line" (30). Beckett's protagonists, like the Expelled in the story of that name, are compelled to journey in straight lines and have a good deal of trouble doing so, to their credit. Watt soon grows weak and falls in a ditch. The notion of proceeding in a straight line is, in a post-Euclidian world, an absurd notion in any case, yet our conceptions of progress, direction, process, are hopelessly and rigorously Euclidian, worthy of the Flat Earth Society.

Lying in the ditch, Watt knew it would be difficult to get up and move on, yet there is in him an imperative to go on, as well as an inner imperative to rest and listen "to the little nightsounds in the hedge behind him . . . the breath that is never quiet" (33). What he hears is the sound of pure process, the million little changes that add up to no change, the leaves rotting and the flowers blooming, the wind blowing nowhere. Then the voices come to him again, "with great distinctness, from afar, from without, yes, really it seemed from without . . . indifferent in quality, of a mixed choir" (33), singing to him a song about surds ("Fifty two point two eight five seven one four two eight five seven one four") and human process ("greatgranma Ma grew how do you do blooming thanks and you drooping thanks and you withered thanks and you forgotten thanks"). This is a drama of consciousness awaking from dark to light. What these voices do, singing what Beckett calls in his Addenda a "threne," is initiate a process of thought at the same time that they express the futility of thought, the fact that the process will go nowhere, except in an endless enumeration of decimals or generations. The threnodic quality of the song is derived from its speaking of no goals achieved, nothing finally encountered, only a round of bloom and decay. The comedy of the song, expressed in its repetitive and singsong quality, lies in its contradictory nature: *because* you seek you shall not find. This is the contradiction in enumerating the decimals of a surd, in approaching the irrational rationally. The choir of voices Watt hears rouses him from the ditch, disturbing his silence, setting him in motion, at the same time that it detains him there, briefly. The song expresses his dilemma, his necessity to seek what he cannot find in the seeking: a refuge from thought. Watt travels in order that he may rest at last. The sense of the irrational initiates a rational attempt to come to terms with it. In the ditch we hear the nightsong of being gradually become a song of seeking.

One problem that Beckett has with Watt as protagonist (and with

Murphy before him) is that Watt is inarticulate. Beckett seems more ill at ease with the authority of his third-person voice in *Watt* than in *Murphy*. There are no sustained monologues in *Murphy*, but *Watt* has several, and the finest of these is Arsene's speech to Watt after Watt arrives at Knott's house, a speech in which Beckett creates, for the first time, the sardonic voice that will become the voice of the Trilogy and the "Texts for Nothing." In *Watt*, as we shall later discover, Beckett sets up a third-person narrative, only to undermine its authority entirely.

Arsene's "short statement" (!) prepares us for Watt's experience in Knott's house, and puts into clearer perspective some of the paradoxes I have been describing. The first part of his speech is about change (39–45). Arsene berates Watt for sitting in Knott's kitchen, waiting for the dawn:

> The man arrives! The dark ways all behind, all within, the long dark ways, in his head, in his side, in his hands and feet, and he sits in the red gloom, picking his nose, waiting for the dawn to break. The dawn! The sun! The light! Haw! . . . Then at night rest in the quiet house, there are no roads, no streets any more, you lie down by a window opening on refuge, the little sounds come that demand nothing, ordain nothing, explain nothing, propound nothing . . . the secret places never the same, but always simple and indifferent, always mere places, sites of a stirring beyond coming and going, of a being so light and free that it is as the being of nothing. (39)

In this marvelous and tonally complex passage, the dark lyricism of the description of Watt's quest is salted with Arsene's ironical interpolations about its futility. Arsene laughs at Watt's thinking he is proceeding from darkness to light, toward refuge. The "dark ways" are described as Christ's wounds, suggesting that Watt's suffering is spiritual, or at least a-temporal, that what Watt seeks at Knott's house is a kind of redemption from mortal life, "all the soil and fear and weakness offered, to be sponged away and forgiven" (40). What Arsene is commenting on here, and laughing at, is that redemption from life's dark ways is a loss of life —not, as Christians have traditionally imagined it, a life free of the physical in the abode of the eternal. According to Arsene, and he should know, having had his stay at Knott's, Watt wishes for process to continue (the dawns to break, the sounds to occur, the roads and gardens to remain) but to mean "nothing." The idea of going on, of bearing the burden of consciousness, will, to Watt, no longer be necessary at Knott's, it will be sponged away. At Knott's Watt hopes to exist beyond all that.

But what Arsene has come to realize is that this hope of redemption is impossible: "How I feel it again, after so long. . . . All forgiven and healed. For ever. In a moment. To-morrow. Six, five, four hours still, of the old dark, the old burden, lightening, lightening. For one has come, to stay. Haw!" (39–40). It is impossible because we live in change, and cannot live outside it. Arsene goes on to a more abstract example, still using as his subject "the man," including thereby Watt and all who seek redemption. The man has arrived at Knott's house: "He is well pleased. For he knows he is in the right place at last . . . he being what he has become, and the place being what it was made, the fit is perfect. And he knows this. No. Let us remain calm. He feels it. The sensations, the premonitions of harmony are irrefragable, of imminent harmony, when all outside him will be he . . ." (40–1). He is redeemed, and at one with his world, like Crispin at one with his soil, like the rabbit in Stevens' gently satiric "The Rabbit as King of the Ghosts," who feels at night that "everything is meant for [him] / And nothing need be explained." "What a feeling of security!" says Arsene, "nature is so exceedingly accommodating, on the one hand, and man, on the other" (41). The life of forms is imagined behind him: "Having oscillated all his life between the torments of a superficial loitering and the horrors of disinterested endeavour, he finds himself at last in a situation where to do nothing exclusively would be an act of the highest value, and significance" (41). Having described this state with some relish, Arsene brings his point home: "The fool! He has learnt nothing. Nothing" (42). The man learns this in two senses, in the sense of not having learned anything, and in the sense of having learned nothingness. Because change occurs, as it must occur. The dark will become light, the light dark, turn and turn about.

To describe the change that inevitably occurs, Arsene switches to a personal incident. He was once in Knott's yard, peacefully regarding the light on the wall:

I felt my breast swell, like a pelican's I think it is. For joy? Well, no, perhaps not exactly for joy. For the change of which I speak had not yet taken place. Hymeneal still it lay, the thing so soon to be changed, between me and all the forgotten horrors of joy. . . . The change. In what did it consist? It is hard to say. Something slipped. There I was, warm and bright, smoking my tobacco-pipe, watching the warm bright wall, when suddenly somewhere some little thing slipped, some tiny little thing. Gliss—iss—iss—STOP! . . . I felt, that Tuesday afternoon, millions of little things moving all together out of their old place, into a new one nearby. . . . (42–3)

Arsene's is a radical sense of atomistic process, Susanne Langer's "pure sense of life." It is only when change occurs (or when it is perceived) that one feels the "joy" of what one had, for joy—and despair—are concomitant with change. The "only true Paradise," says Beckett in *Proust*, "is the Paradise that has been lost" (*Proust,* 14). Arsene elaborates on this idea when he says,

> But in what did the change *consist*? What was changed, and how? What was changed, if my information is correct, was a sentiment that a change, other than a change of degree, had taken place. . . . This I am happy to inform you is the reversed metamorphosis. The Laurel into Daphne. The old thing where it always was, back again. As when a man, having found at last what he sought, a woman, for example, or a friend, loses it, or realises what it is. (44)

To lose it *is* to realize what it is. Only in this sense does the phrase "horrors of joy" seem anything but merely perverse. In Beckett's world joy and horror, hope and despair, are aspects of the same realization, that only in process of change can you realize at once the joy of what you had and the pain of losing it. Watt will only be able to experience Knott in the process of failing to find refuge with him.

Arsene describes the feeling that he had *prior to* the change, the feeling of harmony, as being "so sensuous that in comparison the impressions of a man buried alive in Lisbon on Lisbon's great day seems a frigid and artificial construction of the imagination" (43). The comparison is telling, for to feel this static harmony, the harmony Arsene sought and Watt will seek at Knott's, is to experience "nothing," to be "transported . . . to some quite different yard, and to some quite different season, in an unfamiliar country" (44). It is what Murphy thinks that he realizes about what Mr. Endon experiences: the annihilation of consciousness, as of one buried in an earthquake or autistically unaware of the outside world. It cannot be *known* (recall Arsene's emphasis on feeling instead of knowing); in this state, the voices have ceased, language has yielded to silence. Such a state does not, strictly speaking, exist, for change is constant; rather, it is the "presence of what did not exist," not an "illusion" (45). And we seek it, we desire it, "it is useless not to seek, not to want, for when you cease to seek you start to find, and when you cease to want, then life begins to ram her fish and chips down your gullet until you puke . . ." (44). The experience of "the being of nothing" occurs, then, between the seeking and the finding of it, since one only finds it when one has lost it. It is a presence. To say that it is an instant is to falsify it, for it is timeless. Its analogy, in mathematics, would be a surd: we can extend the decimals of, say, $2/7$ (as the voices do in their threne), but we cannot, through these decimals, obtain the surd, because it *does not exist* in the domain of rational decimals.

Thus Watt's situation is paradoxical. He seeks Knott, or Naught, a refuge from change. If he did *not* seek him, then life as Habit would absorb him. Yet if he seeks Knott, he cannot find him in the seeking—for to seek is to engage oneself in the coming and going. As Richard Coe states, in Beckett "the condition of man is a kind of Purgatory . . . the ultimate realisation of the Self in a *Néant* beyond space and time, void united with void; yet to desire such a Paradise is to be aware of a self desiring, and a Self desiring is not a void, and therefore cannot enter."[26] Watt comes, seeking, and he will eventually have to go, as Arsene is going: "And then another night fall and another man come and Watt go, Watt who is now come, for the coming is in the shadow the going and the going is in the shadow of the coming, that is the annoying part about it" (57), says Arsene. Watt will seek the "light"—that is, Knott, redemption—which is to seek nought, nothing, an impossible end. There is only the seeking, in change. There is no final light, nor final dark, only a movement from one to the other.

Changelessness can be perceived only in change, the irrational only by means of the rational, silence only in words. In the world of process, life and death, purpose and purposelessness, are one. In the following passage, Arsene touches on these paradoxes; he has just spoken of the servants coming and going around Knott, who neither comes nor goes but "seems able to abide in his place":

> Or is there a coming that is not a coming to, a going that is not a going from, a shadow that is not the shadow of purpose, or not? For what is the shadow of the going in which we come, this shadow of the coming in which we go, this shadow of the coming and the going in which we wait, if not the shadow of purpose, of the purpose that budding withers, that withering buds, whose blooming is a budding withering? . . . And what is this coming that is not our coming and this being that is not our being and this going that will not be our going but the coming and being and going in purposelessness? (58)

Process is both purposeful and purposeless. To return to the paradox that Beckett describes in his essay on Joyce, if one is an individual coming and being and going, one has purpose; if one is a part of a universal coming and being and going ("this coming that is not our coming," etc.), then one is purposeless. Watt is both an individual and a term in a series of servants revolving around Knott. Arsene continues, "And though in purposelessness I may seem to go now, yet I do not, any more than in purposelessness then I came, for I go now with my purpose as with it then I came, the only difference being this, that then it was living and now it is dead, which is what you might call what I think the English call six of one and half a dozen of the other, do they not, might you not?" (58). The distinction between being alive and being dead with purpose is the distinction between being complete and whole (six of one) and being part of a series (half a dozen of the other). Watt is Watt, and Watt is a servant ousting Arsene and moving Erskine upstairs, who is soon to be moved upstairs by Arthur, who in turn has ousted Erskine and will be moved upstairs by Micks, who in turn will oust Watt, and so on, "for ever about Mr Knott in tireless assiduity turning" (61). It is dizzying to read the long passages in *Watt* in which these series are worked out. "For Vincent and Walter were not the first, ho no, but before them were Vincent and another whose name I forget, and before them that other whose name I forget and another whose name I also forget, and before them that other whose name I also forget ..." (57). These passages are sudden bogs that trap the reader in their relentless logic, making him painfully aware of the medium of language. They are parodies of rational discourse, language extended to fulfill its suddenly distorted utility, which is to analyze, to follow through to conclusions. The language both fulfills and undermines itself, and in that contradiction is the source of the comedy.

The drift of Arsene's speech is a subtle and intellectual development of the basic premise that the universe is as Heraclitus saw it, changeless change. In the first place, to realize truly that we live in change is to realize that change subverts all concepts of meaning and direction. Thus Arsene laughs—"Haw!"—at Watt's search, which was, and still is, his own. Second, to realize truly that we live in change is to be aware of the essential formalism of change. Motion always tends to pattern, what we might here call Form (to distinguish it from forms, or what Beckett calls in *Proust* "the haze of conception—preconception"), and pattern leads us, drives us to conceive of a Content, an essential meaning: God, Godot, whatever. The recurring patterns of existence are manifestations of a principle of order; they suggest a design and with that, a designer. And so we are back where we started, seeking changelessness in change, a final light or a final dark, mounting or descending the ladder, in a world that dawns and dies continuously.

In this context, Arsene's intrusive explanation of his rude laugh becomes more clear, and helps us to relate his Heraclitean vision to comedy. Arsene speaks of three laughs: the bitter, the hollow and the mirthless:

> The bitter laugh laughs at that which is not good, it is the ethical laugh. The hollow laugh laughs at that which is not true, it is the in-

tellectual laugh. . . . But the mirthless laugh is the dianoetic laugh, down the snout—Haw!—so. It is the laugh of laughs, the *risus purus,* the laugh laughing at the laugh, the beholding, the saluting of the highest joke, in a word the laugh that laughs—silence please—at that which is unhappy. (48)

This final laugh is the greatest, the highest, the finest, the most inner and the most *formal* of the three. *Dianoetic* means relating to the thought process, particularly that of logical thought. Arsene's dianoetic laugh is, ultimately, a laugh at the human condition ("the highest joke"), a condition involving him as well as Watt. It is beyond the laughter of a man detached from the futile pursuit of meaning. It is laughter which includes as its target both subject and object. It is the laughter of a man who realizes that his own thought is an inextricable part of the process he is laughing at, the laugh of the Cretan who has just observed that all Cretans are liars. It is laughter that comes from the realization that, as Richard Coe remarks in reference to Arsene's entire speech, "man can *never* escape his own rationality."[27] The dianoetic laugh is both ironic and accepting; its acceptance is dependent on the operation of its irony, at the same time that it sets the irony in motion. It is the laughter of Darl on the way to Jackson, the laughter of the comedy of language. It debunks matter and relegates itself to form, is intimately connected to what Beckett calls the "Idea" in *Proust,* the essence of things revealed when all conceptions and preconceptions have been cleared away—in this case, by the action of a scornful irony.

Arsene's laugh derives from the consciousness of consciousness, the impossible situation of commenting, with one's mind (one cannot avoid it) on the futility of the mind's operations. Arsene's speech is a superb strategy for establishing the heightened narrative perspective on Watt which is to follow in the relation of Watt's adventures.

Watt's desire is to experience Naught, to come to rest. Arsene says, "And yet there is one who neither comes nor goes, I refer I need hardly say to my late employer, but seems to abide in his place . . ." (57). The dilemma is that what does not change (Knott) can only be experienced in change, and so Watt will take his place in the servant rotation, the inexorable coming and going. For Knott/Naught is, literally, Nothing, a void. As a haven and a refuge from change, he exists only as Idea. Knott may be described, as Sam will describe him later in the novel, as that which a circle encloses, a void which can only be described by the line that moves around it in dynamic directionlessness (relative to linearity). Knott is, then, both Form and Idea.

Before Arsene's speech, as Watt is sitting in the kitchen, the following image occurs:

> Watt saw, in the grate, of the range, the ashes grey. But they turned pale red, when he covered the lamp, with his hat. The range was almost out, but not quite . . . So Watt busied himself a little while, covering the lamp, less and less, more and more, with his hat, watching the ashes greyen, redden, greyen, redden, in the grate, of the range. (37–8)

This is an image of Watt's mind, fading into rest and stirring from rest. Near the end of his speech Arsene says that he thinks he has said enough to light a fire in Watt's mind that can only be snuffed with difficulty, just as Vincent did for him, and so on (62). He has, then, at once dimmed and fanned Watt's desires with his laughter. After Arsene leaves, Watt can't be sure if the day has yet dawned or not, despite his holding his hat before the lamp (63–4). The certainties of day and night are gone. The first section of *Watt* ends with a premonition of dawn:

> For if it was really day again already, in some low distant quarter of the sky, it was not yet day again already in the kitchen. But that would come, Watt knew that would come, with patience it would come, little by little, whether he liked it or not, over the yard wall, and through the window, first the grey, then the brighter colours one by one, until getting on to nine a.m. all the gold and white and blue would fill the kitchen, all the unsoiled light of the new day, of the new day at last, the day without precedent at last. (64)

This passage is delicately poised between joy at the dawn of an entirely new day, the unprecedented nature of which fires the quest growing within Watt, the individual—and irony at the day's being only one day in a series, and Watt only one servant in a series, extending to infinity. It is a passage poised between Watt's nostalgia and Arsene's "Haw!". Although Arsene's speech has its effect on our experience of this coming dawn, Beckett allows Watt the lyricism of waiting, the strength of his desire. Watt knows the day will come because (1) it always *does* come, in a universal round, and because (2) the fire within him wills it, or so he feels. It is a fine and typical moment of Beckettian comedy, the beauty of the passage deriving from the very irony that calls it into question. The dawn is both Watt's hope and his despair—that is to say, it is neither one, and both. As Arsene says, "Erskine is here still, sleeping and dreaming what the new day holds in store, I mean premonition and a new face and the end in sight. But another evening shall come and the light die away out of the sky and the colour from the earth—. . . haw!" (56–7). This too is inevitable, and this too is not final. Watt yearns for the light, and will see it fade to darkness; he will yearn for darkness, and see it fade into light. There are no ends in sight in this comic round.

Watt enters Mr. Knott's service. Knott's establishment is a peculiar mixture of the real and unreal, like Kafka's castle.[28] Some aspects of it, like Knott's confidence-man disguises, are impossible; some aspects, like Knott's eating habits and the servant arrangement, are bizarre; and some, like the phone and the postman and the occasional callers, are commonplace. These outside "acknowledgements" of Knott's establishment keep it going (69). The inner world of Knott's depends on the outer; as Arsene says, Knott is "quite incapable of looking after himself" (58). What is considered by the mind to be beyond the mind exists by the mind's good graces. Unless words enclose it, nothingness cannot exist, and, enclosed by words, it becomes something. It is not only Knott's house that is kept going by the outer world, but Watt as well. The incident of the Galls makes this clear, and introduces the subject of language to some of Arsene's ideas.

Two men, one old and one middle-aged, knock at Knott's door and announce they have come to tune the piano, after introducing themselves as the Galls. After tuning it, they mysteriously pronounce to one another as "doomed" the piano, the piano-tuner, and the pianist. Then they leave. This incident is the first of many that Watt experiences at Knott's, in that it is "of great formal beauty and indeterminable purport." It continues to "unfold" in his head, over and over again, passing from light to shadow and back, sound to silence and back, in "the irrevocable caprice of its taking place." It "gradually lost, in the nice processes of its light, its sound, its impacts and its rhythm, all meaning, even the most literal" (72–3). In the outer world Watt had been content with the outer meaning of events. He would have said, before entering Knott's, that the Galls came, pronounced as doomed the piano, etc., and left. "That is what happened then" (73). But at Knott's the event becomes unintelligible, and "this fragility of the outer meaning had a bad effect on Watt, for it caused him to seek for another, for some meaning of what had passed, in the image of how it had passed" (73). Watt cannot accept that the incident has broken up into "the farce of its properties" (74), into a Bergsonian shimmer of vibrations, movements, changes. He runs the incident again and again through his mind, brooding on its properties, pursuing its meaning so that he can put it out of his mind, for "to explain had always been to exorcize, for Watt" (78). He is like Bergson's Intellect, brooding on what eludes it, forced to confront that "nothing had happened, that a thing that was nothing had happened, with the utmost formal distinctness" (76). In its clarity it *seems* to mean, and that seeming is the fuel for Watt's logical machine.

Watt has no choice, he is "forced to submit" to the pursuit of meaning; "to elicit something from nothing" is his inheritance. The more meaning dissolves, the more he seeks it, so that he may "extract" something "in self-defence" from the suffering of having a radically unique event elude his Habit of thought (79). There are no words to describe or explain an event in which nothing occurs, yet Watt desires words to be applied to his situation, to Mr. Knott, and "in a general way to the conditions of being in which he found himself" (81). Although he seeks rest from the outer world, he still needs "semantic succour" (83), is compelled to suffer the pain of going on in his mind, as if his mind were a motor that could not stop. Though occasionally satisfied by his "dereliction" from the outer world, he "often found himself longing for a voice, for Erskine's, since he was alone with Erskine, to speak of the little world of Mr Knott's establishment, with the old words, the old credentials" (84–5). This is his comic dilemma. He is Hugh Kenner's "The Man of Sense as Buster Keaton,"[29] processing a chaos of new information with archaic habits of mind, trapped by mechanism. Or, to make another comic analogy, when Watt undergoes at Knott's the painful experience of not quite being able to *name* things, such as a pot (81), he is like Lewis Carroll's Alice stepping into the wood of no names: "Well, at any rate its a great comfort . . . after being so hot, to get into the—into the—into *what?*"[30] she says, driven by questions as the familiar is left behind.

The comedy of Watt's stay at Knott's derives from the unnerving contradiction between what Watt experiences and what he can say about it (since, as we later learn, he is relating his story to someone else). He is the servant of two masters: of his desire to escape meaning and of his need to search for it, if only in self-defence. The comedy of his situation is cogently expressed in the phrase, "to elicit something from nothing requires a certain skill" (77), and in this hilarious passage: "For the only way one can speak of nothing is to speak of it as though it were something, just as the only way one can speak of God is to speak of him as though he were a man, which to be sure he was, in a sense, for a time, and as the only way one can speak of man, even our anthropologists have realised that, is to speak of him as though he were a termite" (77). More than any other modern writer, Beckett is aware of how mysterious and unspeakable the subjects of our discourse are, and with what comical confidence we marshal our language units to express them.

The Galls incident allows Beckett to meditate on the theory of the problem. But that incident is only prelude to the other problems that absorb Watt, problems that will elicit from his mental processes the wild strings of reasoning that are Beckett's comic hallmarks. The problem of disposing of the food that Knott does not eat results in Beckett's first extended use of "the comedy of an exhaustive enumeration" (*Proust,* 71). The problem occurs, given Mr. Knott's garbage, and given the idea that a dog is to come and dispose of it when and if there is any, in determining by what means the dog and the food were to be brought together (93). This banal problem had already been solved long before Watt arrived, but he considers it in a parody of ratiocination. "But was there any guarantee that the messenger would indeed give the food to the dog, or dogs, in accordance with his instructions? What was to prevent the messenger from eating the food himself, or from selling all or part of the food to some other party, or from giving it away, or from emptying it away into the nearest ditch or hole, to save time, and trouble?" (95–6). Examples of this reasoning proliferate. In its attempt to make sense of what is, after all, "irrevocable caprice," language takes on a comic life of its own, floating free from whatever reality it was meant to explain. As Watt seeks to cover every logical possibility, his language comes to seem, after pages, *ir*rational. We are reminded, as we laugh, of how much normal reasoning takes for granted, how much it operates only in habitual channels. As Watt reasons, we enter a world of Rube Goldbergian logic, extending itself to what we fear is infinity, madly pursuing its own processes, operating from the principle that the world itself is a machine, and so making us realize how much the world is *not* a machine. In exposing the mechanisms of language, the comedy implies what lies beyond language.

Watt's thinking is continually undermined. In detailing the makeup of the Lynch family (the "disease" of mankind breeding itself on and on) Watt concludes, at one point, "Five generations, twenty-eight souls, nine hundred and eighty years, such was the proud record of the Lynch family, when Watt entered Mr Knott's service," to which a footnote is appended: "The figures given here are incorrect. The consequent calculations are therefore doubly erroneous" (103–4, & n). This blow is immediately followed by this paragraph: "Then a moment passed and all was changed. Not that there was death, for there was not. Not that there was birth, for there was not either. But puff puff breath again they breathed, in and out, the twenty-eight, and all was changed" (104). The mechanism involved in a rational grasp of things is defeated by change. When Kate Lynch is mentioned as a "bleeder," this footnote appears: "Haemophilia is, like enlargment of the prostate, an exclusively male disorder. But not in this work" (102n). This work is a lie, an invention, a fiction, something spun out of the mind. When considering the bell that sounds in the night from Erskine's room, Watt, in his mania for exploring every possibility in an attempt to account for the event, even entertains the notion that he himself might have rung the bell: "And if he had got up and gone down, to where the bell was, and he did not know where the bell was, and pressed it there, could he have got back into his room, and into his bed, and sometimes even fallen into a light sleep, in time to hear, from where he lay, in his bed, the bell sound?" (121). The very syntax of this is funny, and the comedy is as much a function of the familiarity of the reasoning as it is of its absurdity. Sense dissolves into nonsense; nonsense is expressed sensically.

It is not as if Watt could say, I know nothing, and rest in that knowledge. Nor can he be content, like the people in the outer world, that he does know something. Watt simply (Haw!) can't be sure, and is driven by that uncertainty. The "old words" don't work at Knott's, and those are all he has. In reference to the dog-feeding:

> Not that for a moment Watt supposed that he had penetrated the forces at play, in this particular instance, or even perceived the forms that they upheaved, or obtained the least useful information concerning himself, or Mr Knott, for he did not. But he had turned, little by little, a disturbance into words, he had made a pillow of old words, for a head. Little by little, and not without labour. Kate eating from her dish, for example, with the dwarfs standing by, how he had laboured to know what that was, to know which the doer, and what the doer, and what the doing, and which the sufferer, and what the sufferer, and what the suffering, and what those shapes, that were not rooted to the ground, like the veronica, but melted away, into the dark, after a while. (117)

The melting shapes recall Faulkner's disembodied imagery in *As I Lay Dying;* the "pillow of old words," our mean comfort in the face of reality, is a phrase that Addie Bundren would have appreciated. The "veronica" is both a rooted shrub and a "true" image (*verus* + *iconicus*)—more specifically, the image of a Godhead: Jesus, and by extension, Knott. Veronica, beholding her bloody handkerchief, *knew* what the sufferer and what the suffering, the image she beheld was both essential and presentational. Watt, on the other hand, is only presented with shapes that never take form, about which he can know nothing. Perhaps the most interesting thing about the above passage is that its rhythm and movement defeat its point: the inherited words *are* a pillow of sorts, a momentary contentment, an illusion of stasis and order. But the passage does not end with the image of the pillow. It picks up again, "Little by little . . . ," and continues its rumination, ending in futility. Words are at once a comfort and a burden.

"Saying is inventing," says Molloy, and then, "Wrong, very rightly wrong. You invent nothing, you think you are inventing, you think you are escaping, and all you do is stammer out your lesson, the remnants of a pensum . . ." (Trilogy, 32). His first pronouncement is that words are false, the critique that follows is that words are assumed. We are not even privileged to lie in any pure sense. The very word "inventing" implies both truth and falsehood. "Saying is inventing" is a vicious-circle paradox, hence "wrong, very rightly wrong." The epistemological problem must be reflexive; we can't know that we can't know. This extends to the narrator, whom we later learn is Sam: "And so always, when the impossibility of my knowing, of Watt's having known, what I know, what Watt knew, seems absolute, and insurmountable, and undeniable, and incoercible, it could be shown that I know, because Watt told me, and that Watt knew, because someone told him, or because he found out for himself" (127–8). At this point, truth and falsehood clearly merge, and we perceive this not just as Watt's problem, but as Sam's and ours—we who so blithely confront words on a page and think *them* a fiction.

Seeking to solve the mystery of the bell, Watt rather magically enters Erskine's locked room and beholds there a picture of a circle, broken at its lowest point, and a dot, outside the circle and seemingly on a different and shifting plane of perspective (128–9). Watt considers the possibilities of what the picture might mean, and concludes with "the thought that it was perhaps this, a circle and a centre not its centre in search of a centre and a circle respectively, in boundless space, in endless time. . . . Watt's eyes filled with tears that he could not stem . . ." (129). Watt's crying leads us to consider that perhaps the meaning of the picture is this: that Watt (the dot) is unable to attain the same plane as, much less enter into, the circle that surrounds the nothingness that is Knott. Watt wishes the dot to slip into the circle from below, "home at last" (130). To achieve "home," Watt has gotten off the tram and come to Knott's house. But he does not think he has entered the circle, because he does not *know* Knott, has not achieved rest or refuge. Words are still with him. Yet if that which is Not cannot be known, it can at least be formally defined, delimited in some way. Hence the circle, the defining circumference, and its damnable breach, leading Watt "on." The circumference of the circle is an image, specifically, of the revolving of the servants around the fixity of Knott, as well as an image, generally, of the coming and going around an essential nothingness, which could not be experienced or sensed except by the coming and going. The nothing which is contained in the circumference is made something by that circumference, even though it remains nothing. Form is all. About to depart from the ground floor, Watt considers, "What had he learnt? Nothing. What did he know of Mr Knott? Nothing. Of his anxiety to prove, of his anxiety to understand, of his anxiety to get well, what remained? Nothing. But was not that something?" (148). The circle is an image of, among other things, the labor of consciousness, endlessly revolving, achieving nothing but the perfection of its own shape. And yet it achieves nothing by making the "presence" of nothingness felt. Thus in the futility of Watt's words is his strange success.

If the circle were completely self-contained and whole, then Watt could despair, but the circle is broken, and at best Watt can only cry and achieve a temporary refreshment in crying. The breach keeps Watt hoping, going on. Yet is this representation a mere fiction? Watt considers whether the picture is indeed a stable part of Knott's or, like him and Erskine, a "term in a series" (131). Watt concludes that it is such a term, and nothing is resolved.

Two passages near the end of section II establish Mr. Knott as a Godhead of sorts. The first is a liturgical, the second a Biblical allusion:

> Watt had more and more the impression, as time passed, that nothing could be added to Mr Knott's establishment, and from it nothing taken away, but that as it was now, so it had been in the beginning, and so it would remain to the end, in all essential respects. . . . (131)

> Add to this that the few glimpses caught of Mr Knott, by Watt, were not clearly caught, but as it were in a glass, a plain glass, an eastern window at morning, a western window at evening. (147)

That is, Watt sees Knott through a glass darkly. But not only that. Watt also glimpses Knott in the sunrise and sunset, as the "significant presence" (131) behind process. Mr. Knott is a "harbour" and a "haven" from change (135), yet can only be glimpsed in and through change. Knott represents a principle that is alive, yet beyond the world of forms. As such he is an Idea of God, or the shape of an Idea of God. Like a circle, he is a perfect form, not one to be found in nature. Molloy says that the experience of hearing "pure sounds, free of all meaning" is analogous to seeing something "inordinately formal" (Trilogy, 50). "Inordinately" I take to mean in excess of the forms we normally experience—that is, presentational forms. All Knott's presentational forms, the costumes he wears about the house, are disguises. From Knott's voice "nothing was to be learnt," the words of his low, rapid songs "were either without meaning, or derived from an idiom with which Watt, a fair linguist, had no acquaintance" (208). Knott's voice, like the voices murmuring in Watt's head, is a kind of pre-verbal chatter, sounds that are not yet words, suggesting both words and silence. Knott is the principle that makes one embark on the impossible task of attaining silence in words. There is no other way; we can't go "home" again. Near the end of section II, Watt remembers a quiet and lovely and brief pastoral experience he had with Knott in the garden:

> So there for a short time they stood together, the master and the servant, the bowed heads almost touching . . . until the worm was gone and only the flower remained. One day the flower would be gone and only the worm remain, but on this particular day it was the flower that remained, and the worm that went. And then Watt, looking up, saw that Mr Knott's eyes were closed, and heard his breathing soft and shallow, like the breathing of a child asleep.(146)

This is a brief moment of stillness, the worm of process momentarily arrested, the Garden returned to. The sleeping child sound takes us back to the lost Paradise of the womb, the silence before words. In the next section, we behold the disintegration of Watt's language.

Section III seems to be, chronologically, the last one of Watt's story (on the novel's structure, more later). As such, it takes place at "the end of the line" (244), the point to which Watt buys his ticket after leaving Knott's house. Since the "line" in Beckett describes the Habit of living in both a personal and historical sense, then the "mansions" and their grounds and pavilions in section III would seem to be a kind of afterlife. It is common in the criticism of *Watt* to refer to the strange setting of III as a mental asylum,[31] a viewpoint which limits the resonance of this section. The word "mansions" suggests a heaven-haven: "Let not your heart be troubled: yet believe in God, believe also in me. In my Father's house are many mansions; if it were not so, I would have told you: I go and prepare a place for you" (A.V. John 14:1–2). As the section unfolds we come to see this setting—the distant and imperious mansions, the little gardens, the barbed wire, the windy and lucid weather—both as a real and a mock Paradise.

Certainly there are suggestions of a mental asylum, what with the institutional overtones: attendants, cells, loud patients playing at ball, "rescuers" ready to help out should someone cut himself on the barbed wire. But these make up Beckett's reticent joke rather than the salient reality of the scene; they convey the hope of heaven as a hope of ultimate "asylum," of being *cared for*. It is as ironic a vision of Paradise as Arsene's

(42–5). Watt and the narrator ("me" becomes "Sam," addressed as a third person) remain, most of the time, in their separate mansions, "in our windowlessness, in our bloodheat, in our hush" or "in a vacuum" or "in deepest night": isolate and wordless. But section III is a record of their rare conversations in the gardens when the weather suited both of them. They find holes in the barbed wire, they touch, they talk. It is the most intensely darkly lyrical part of the novel, the least ironically described vision of human communication.

Knott was not a haven or a refuge for Watt, and neither are the mansions. Although one can be "in his separate soundless unlit warmth" (152), there is nothing Paradisical in this womb-like silence. Rather, Watt and Sam are "peers in peace" only in their infrequent meetings, although "the disappointment of one of us at least was almost certain, and the regret, the bitter regret, at ever having left his mansion at all, and the vow, the hollow vow, never to leave his mansion again, on any account" (151–2). The painful burden of consciousness is shouldered again, the "ancient labour" of communicating meaning, of seeking to understand, is begun once more. There is no rest, no death: Watt, like the protagonists of the Trilogy, must go on.

This further passage from the Gospel of John illuminates the relationship between Watt and Sam: "I go and prepare a place for you. And if I go and prepare a place for you, I will come again, and receive you unto myself, that where I am, there ye may be also. And whither I go ye know, and the way ye know. Thomas saith unto him, Lord, we know not whither thou goest: and how can we know the way? Jesus saith unto him, I am the Way, the Truth, and the Life: no man cometh unto the Father but by me" (A.V. John 14:2–6). Watt and Sam are related much as are Molloy and Moran. The former in each case has lived off the track, or apart from the Organization (the life of forms), and the latter sees himself mirrored in the former and seeks to recount what he has experienced. Moran discovers the Molloy within himself; Sam embraces Watt symbiotically, and tries to catch his rapidly murmured, Knott-like speech concerning his tenure at Knott's. Watt comes from Knott. That he is a Christ figure in this respect is made clear when Sam first sees him advancing backwards, falling in the briars, then resting on the barbed wire and turning to face Sam:

> His face was bloody, his hands also, and the thorns were in his scalp. (His resemblance, at that moment, to the Christ believed by Bosch, then hanging in Trafalgar Square, was so striking, that I remarked it.) And at the same instant suddenly I felt as though I were standing

before a great mirror, in which my garden was reflected, and my
fence, and I, and the very birds tossing in the wind, so that I looked at
my hands, and felt my face, and glossy skull, with an anxiety as real
as unfounded. (159)

Sam sees himself in Watt. Their symbiosis is expressed in their embrace
across the bridge and in their strange walks along the "couloir" between
their respective barbed-wire fences: Sam forwards, Watt backwards,
together, simultaneously coming and going, as a unit.

What can or does Sam learn from this suffering servant? The Way, the
Truth, and the Life? In the first place, we can't know. Sam's information
is, to put it mildly, unreliable: "Of this impetuous murmur much fell in
vain upon my imperfect hearing and understanding, and much by the
rushing wind was carried away, and lost forever" (156). And it takes time
for Sam to adapt to each stage of the successive inversions of Watt's discourse, and so much is not understood by him. Nor could Watt understand Sam. And Sam's hearing begins to fail him. And so on. As an
instance of human communication, their dialogue is farcical. And yet, the
much quoted and much translated examples of Watt's discourse (164–9)
are, as Michael Robinson says, "the nonsense of a rational mind. It is not
pure irrationality but the inversion of words or letters according to an in-
flexible logic that adopts its own consistent form of expression rather
than the equally arbitrary common form."[32] Watt's discourse *means*. It
can be translated into common English—though to do so is to falsify its
import. Watt's languages exist as languages in their own right to the extent that they can be pronounced and have some sort of logical structure,
however inverted or inconsistent. Sam says that with Watt "euphony was
a preoccupation" (164), and so it is: Watt's discourse is always musical
and rhythmical. Language approaches music, approaches the purely
formal, as did the voices that sang to Watt in the ditch: "Lit yad mac, ot
og. Ton taw, ton tonk. Ton dob, ton trips. Ton vila, ton deda," etc. The
world of forms has, for Watt, collapsed (he cannot understand Sam, for
example), all his former habits have been unlearned or inverted. And yet
something lives on, something touches, talks, however strangely, something goes on, bringing Watt out of his solipsism. A euphony, a communication—as Stevens would say, "a queer assertion of humanity"—is
established. Sam says, "To be together again, after so long, who love the
sunny wind, the windy sun, in the sun, in the wind, that is perhaps something, perhaps something" (163). It is the "something" that has come
out of the "nothing" at Knott's, something that lives in the very music of
that passage, the lyrical rhythms of its word-dance. Watt experienced

Naught, in ineffable sadness and resignation, and this *is* a Way, a Truth, and a Life, though it has nothing to do with the Habit of living.

Watt, like Christ, is of two worlds. The "divine" world in *Watt* is as complex as the idea of the kingdom of God in the Gospels. In the first place, "the kingdom of God is within you" (Luke 17:21). Watt is never seen as a functioning part of the "outer" world, even before journeying to Knott's. He is something different, as is clearly established in the opening scene. He reminds us of something ancient, something in our fathers and in ourselves, what Molloy represented to Moran. "Or was it not perhaps something that was not Watt, nor of Watt, but behind Watt, or beside Watt, or before Watt, or beneath Watt, or above Watt, or about Watt, a shade uncast, a light unshed, or the grey air aswirl with vain entelechies" (220). It is this "something" that Fitzwein sees in Mr. Nackybal, as we shall see. Whatever it is, it has nothing to do with the world of reason, direction, meaning, purpose. It makes Watt seem strangely more than human.

The kingdom of God is more realized in Knott's house, where Watt journeys in order that he might fulfill what is inside him, and be cleansed of all else. He fails because of his humanity, his *need to know*, when Knott cannot be known. And so he journeys to the end of the line, disappearing in what must be considered, in the light of the setting of section III, a kind of death, though ultimately a temporary one. In III, we discover Watt in another metaphor of the kingdom of God, the mansions in which one can abide, like Knott in his room, "in empty hush, in airless gloom" (200). But Watt can't and does not wish to abide there. He continues, rather, to crucify himself on the cross of his humanity by painfully journeying to the gardens to keep alive his verbal quest. Watt is Kierkegaard's subjective thinker, who strives for the infinite because it moves within him, yet is not "able to discover it through anything appearing outwardly," and so involves himself in the self-contradiction that Kierkegaard felt to be "the true form of the comic."[33] Watt is a comic Christ.

"The only Paradise is the Paradise that is lost." So Watt never frees himself of the burden of his human consciousness. But he is not a parody of Christ; if that were true, *Watt* would be only ironic, and there would be little need for nightsongs, and meetings in the gardens, and Knott's child's breathing—all the dark lyricism in the novel, the small joys. Watt represents a Way, a Truth, a Life, even if he does not embody or fulfill them—just as Christ was both a fulfillment of prophecies and a sign that fulfillment would come: "Truly, truly, I say to you, the hour is coming, and now is, when the dead will hear the voice of the Son of God, and those who hear will live" (R.S.V. John 5:25).

Sam offers the following words as a bridge between the examples of Watt's own discourse and the substance of what Watt told him: "To these conversations we are indebted for the following information" (169). But the narrative that follows—absurdly rational, as we shall see—could not possibly have been conveyed in the inverted simplicities of Watt's discourse. Within a paragraph the word *obnubilated* turns up. It would seem that Sam had "translated" Watt's conversation into his own style. But such a translation would have to be, for the most part, invention. Is it Watt who is still laboring at the ancient labor? The previous examples of his speech—fragmented, sensory, simple, passive—indicate that he is not. So is it *Sam* who is endeavouring to make rational sense of what Watt says? Where does Watt leave off and Sam begin? The answer can only be, in Watt's language, "Ton wonk."

This casts a new light on the third-person narrative of the first two sections, which seem to be a reflection of Watt's thoughts (and indeed, for purposes of convenience, I have so identified them in my discussion of these sections). Watt never speaks within the narrative, so we identify the voice of the narrative with his voice. Yet it remains a third-person narrative, with occasional intrusions of a first person (115, 119). Whose voice, then, is it? The problem becomes more pronounced and complex in the first-person narratives of the Trilogy and the "Texts for Nothing." In the fourth of the "Texts," the first person, railing at his creator, says, "He protests he doesn't reason and does nothing but reason, crooked, as if that could improve matters. He thinks words fail him, he thinks that because words fail him he's on his way to my speechlessness, to being speechless with my speechlessness . . ." (*Stories*, 91–2). This illuminates Beckett's narrative technique in *Watt*. Beckett makes rational discourse out of Watt's irrational adventures. Beckett makes words out of words failing Watt. Beckett yearns for speechlessness and so invents an almost speechless protagonist and then talks about him. Wordlessness is contained within words, but of course it can't be, and so a comedy of language results.

The narrative paradox is made clearer with the introduction of Sam in section III. Beckett invents himself as a fictional character, throwing the whole narrative into question. In the main text of III—Sam's story of Watt's story of Arthur's story of Ernest Louit, Mr. Nackybal, and the Grants Committee—rational discourse is, again, reduced to a comic absurdity. In the only direct record of Watt's speech, Watt seems to be approaching speechlessness, though he fails. Then we read the product of his and Sam's conversations, expressed by Sam in the same voice of much of the first two sections, and we note the distinction between Watt's experience and the record of it. It becomes clear that reason, in its innate and hectic absurdity, is the product, not only of an individual sensibility, but of words themselves, of the whole idea of *telling a story.* Using words, one becomes a term in a universal series, each term using the same language, laboring at the ancient and futile labor.

John Mood has demonstrated that out of thirty-seven combinations, permutations, series and lists in *Watt,* twelve have errors. He concludes from this that an inner and personal system of certainty, founded on reason, is as "hopelessly flawed" a project as "the quest for the reality of meaning of whatever structure or significance . . . is out there."[34] Reason only creates an *illusion* of order. In Arthur's story, told to Mr. Graves, we experience the linguistic manifestations of a rationalist mentality creating a vision of chaos. For example,

> So Mr Magershon turns to Mr O'Meldon, to find Mr O'Meldon looking, not at him, as he had hoped (for if he had not hoped to find Mr O'Meldon looking at him when he turned to look at Mr O'Meldon, then he would not have turned to look at Mr O'Meldon, but would have craned forward, or perhaps backward, to look at Mr MacStern, or perhaps at Mr de Baker, but more likely the former, as one less lately looked at than the latter), but at Mr Mac-Stern, in the hope of finding Mr MacStern looking at him. (177)

As Poe might put it, such language does not hold "the solemn sea / To the sands upon the shore." It is only an extension, however, of "Dick and Jane saw the wet grass and decided it had rained." In the recounting of the actions and divagations of the Grants Committee, the strictures on language that reason imposes are carried to absurd lengths, and we experience the obverse of reason. We simply find it difficult to figure things out. It is said that five members of the Committee looked at one another, and a kind of time-lapse occurs as Arthur attempts to convey rationally such an action in its entirety. The result, rather than being analytically clear, is a kind of hallucination. As in time-lapse photography, one experiences a radical and unreal sense of *change,* beautiful perhaps in its own right but hardly comforting in its vision of order.

Reasoning things through leads, not to order or fixity, but to a chaos of detail. Arthur says, "If I tell you all this in such detail, Mr Graves, the reason is, believe me, that I cannot, much as I should like, and for reasons that I shall not go into, do otherwise" (181). One simply goes on, laboring, helpless to stop. Reason cannot produce a reason for its own being, except that it is an involuntary escape from nothingness. "Watt learned later, from Arthur, that the telling of this story, while it lasted, before

Arthur grew tired, had transported Arthur far from Mr Knott's premises, of which, of the mysteries of which, of the fixity of which, Arthur had sometimes more, than he could bear" (198). The story, in its incomplete form, does not accomplish its original intention—that is, to illustrate how the aphrodisiac Bando has to be smuggled into England. We learn, as a kind of afterthought, that had Arthur finished his story, we would have discovered that Mr. Louit wound up running Bando *after* his academic demise (198). But Arthur's intention is not really to reach that point, but to work out, in a rationalist fantasy, a story to transport himself from Knott's. But one tires of the words, too. Watt says that although he understood the story with more clarity than anything else at Knott's —being himself a rationalist *par excellence*—and that he enjoyed it, he grew tired of it, as did Arthur. And why? Because Arthur desired to leave Louit and *return* to the mysteries and fixity of Knott's, "For he had been absent longer from them, than he could bear" (199). So the circle continues, in change.

There is a counterpoint to the rational craziness of Arthur's story which leads us into the last part of section III, the part concerning Knott himself. It first occurs when Arthur interrupts his story to remark to Mr. Graves how much he despises details, and yet is compelled to relate them. He says that when Mr. Graves sows his vegetables he doesn't do so "with punctilio," but quickly opens a rough trench line and absently and fatalistically lets the seeds fall (181–2). Mr. Graves, whose occupation brings him close to natural process, is passive and casual and humble before Chance. Arthur says that as a younger man Mr. Graves no doubt "used a line, a measure, a plumb, a level" to place his vegetables in careful order, and wonders at what age Mr. Graves ceased to use these "mechanical aids" and arrived at his present freedom, when all he needs "is earth, excrement, water and a stick . . ." (182). In his tediously detailed wondering about all this, Arthur makes us glad for the simplicity of these elemental words, with which he ends his long sentences. In this way, the brooding about punctiliousness and freedom is made relevant to the use of language, to Arthur's very narrative. The point of this brief address to Mr. Graves, in the context of the entire story of Louit, is to counterpoint the idea of freedom from reason's tedium in a kind of surrender to natural process, over and against the rational, manic disorder of Louit's and Nackybal's confrontation with the Grants Committee.

Beyond the formal atmosphere of the Grants Committee and their and Louit's obsession with cubes and cube roots (along with their clear avoidance of surds such as the cube root of three, with the exception of O'Meldon's alarming introduction of a false cube, 190–1)—beyond these lies the Formality of natural process, diurnal change. Some examples of this counterpoint, inserted as brief interludes in the ongoing chaos, are the following:

> Soon the room, empty now, was grey with shadows, of the evening. A porter came, turned on all the lights, straightened the chairs, saw that all was well and went away. Then the vast room was dark, for night had fallen, again. (189)

> When the demonstration was over, then it was question-time. Through the western windows of the vast hall shone the low red winter sun, stirring the air, the chambered air, with its angry farewell shining, whilst via the opposite or oriental apertures or lights the murmur rose, appeasing, of the myriad faint clarions of night. It was question-time. (191)

The western and eastern windows recall the times when Watt glimpsed Knott through a dark glass. Here are glimpses of what Stevens would call reality, changing to no purpose except to change, seen in a sudden change of focus from the hectic structures and speculations of the world of forms, parodically represented by the Grants Committee.

One member of the Committee, Mr. Fitzwein, seems to glimpse this world, not out the windows, but in the face of Mr. Nackybal, and it unnerves him. Fitzwein, Chairman of the Committee, is immediately struck by Nackybal's face: "Mr Nackybal now, to the general surprise, transferred, from the sky, his eyes, docile, stupid, liquid, staring eyes, towards Mr Fitzwein, who after a moment exclaimed, to the further general surprise, A gazelle! A sheep! An old sheep!" (183). As the Committee goes about its business of ascertaining information about the old man, Fitzwein interrupts again with "A goat! An old quinch!" and "His eyes coil into my very soul" (184). The Chairman claims that Nackybal's face is familiar, and from then on is not able effectively to chair the questioning, which duty is taken over by others. Fitzwein, obviously obsessed with the face, only obstructs the Committee's questioning with irritating remarks that reveal he has not been paying attention to the proceedings. He has been transported. Finally, Fitzwein becomes impatient with the proceedings and begins to speak of going home to bed. "Raise your point for the love of God, said Mr Fitzwein, and let me get home to my wife. He added, And children." (194). Again he says, "Where have I seen that face before" (195). What Fitzwein sees in this bony hairy old Caliban, who scratches his crotch and falls asleep during the proceedings, and whose "mental existence" is supposedly "exhausted by the bare knowledge,

emerging from a complete innocence of the rudiments, of what is necessary for his survival" (174), is the face of Primal Man, the Form behind
forms, the archetypal, pre-knowledge, pre-rational, free man. We survive, "every man his own fertiliser" (174), we excrete, we plod, gross
masses towards our graves in the ending light. It doesn't matter that
Mr. Nackybal is a hoax, that "his real name was Tisler and he lived in a
room on the canal" (198). That fact only underscores the archetypal
quality of his face; like Molloy, he lurks in all of us. It is what the face of
Watt is to Mr. Hackett: passive, docile, and above all, free. And yet, and
yet, the original sin of ratiocination is there: Nackybal has been taught to
cube root easy figures.

Just so, Watt attempts to come to terms rationally with Knott. The rest
of section III is taken up with Watt's random speculations about Knott.
We move from the analytical chaos of Arthur's story to the mysterious
"ataraxy" of Knott's world.

> Of the nature of Mr Knott himself Watt remained in particular ig-
> norance.
> Of the many excellent reasons for this, two seemed to Watt to
> merit attention: on the one hand the exiguity of the material pro-
> pounded to the senses, and on the other the decay of these. (199)

Watt (and Sam and we) are in ignorance because our mode of thought is
designed to grasp something, and Knott is Nothing. He is both a "fixity"
and a continually changing presence, wearing various clothes, appearing
in various guises, murmuring meaningless songs. Watt attempts, of
course, to enumerate these changes, but only confronts the mystery of
Knott's presence: "For there was no place, but only there where
Mr Knott was" (199). Knott is the constant presence, the unifying key,
like Stevens' *noued vital*.[35]

In the midst of Watt's ratiocination there appears, abruptly, a sort of
interlude paragraph, which brings into focus what Arthur spoke of as
"freedom." It is worth quoting in full:

> To think, when one is no longer young, when one is not yet old, that
> one is no longer young, that one is not yet old, that is perhaps
> something. To pause, towards the close of one's three hour day, and
> consider: the darkening ease, the brightening trouble; the pleasure
> pleasure because it was, the pain pain because it shall be; the glad
> acts grown proud, the proud acts growing stubborn; the panting the
> trembling towards a being gone, a being to come; and the true true
> no longer, and the false true not yet. And to decide not to smile after

all, sitting in the shade, hearing the cicadas, wishing it were night, wishing it were morning, saying, No, it is not the heart, no, it is not the liver, no, it is not the prostate, no, it is not the ovaries, no, it is muscular, it is nervous. Then the gnashing ends, or it goes on, and one is in the pit, in the hollow, the longing for longing gone, the horror of horror, and one is in the hollow, at the foot of all the hills at last, the ways down, the ways up, and free, free at last, for an instant free at last, nothing at last. (201–2)

In this freedom, desire is gone, direction is gone. One exists at once in change and out of change, as Arsene did looking at the light on the wall. One lives an instant in its integrity, in its lack of duration, in its nothingness. And yet that instant is in a series, and the series involves change. There is, in this moment of freedom, no cause and effect, no hope or despair. Antinomies disappear. One exists in the momentarily calm heart of Zeno's paradoxes. This paragraph bears no relation to the paragraphs surrounding it, it is interpolated, a sudden rest from thinking. In the next paragraph Watt returns to ruminating on Knott, but in the instant of this interlude we come as close to *experiencing* Knott/Naught as we can. Then we go on, because it is a muscular, a nervous, an involuntary impulse to do so. At the end of III we see, as Sam sees, Watt departing "over the deep threshing shadows backwards stumbling, towards his habitation," until we see him no more, "but only the aspens" (213). Shadows and wind and quaking aspens, these are expressive of the formal beauty of change, seen with a kind of painful nostalgia. "And from the hidden pavilions, his and mine, where by this time dinner was preparing, the issuing smokes by the wind were blown, now far apart, but now together, mingled to vanish" (213). Watt and Sam have come together and parted, like the smoke, in the wind of change, irrevocably a part of the endless round of change. This is the last we and Sam see of Watt, but it is not the end of his story, or, rather, the telling of his story.

"As Watt came, so he went, in the night" (215). He came as dawn was about to break, and he leaves Knott's premises at night, and in his coming was his going, and as he goes Micks comes and Arthur mounts to the first floor, "and through the open door the light, from darkness slowly brightening, to darkness slowly darkening . . ." (216). Circles, series. Watt, with an expression of such "vacancy" that Micks is astonished, and with an air about him "aswirl with vain entelechies," begins his journey to the railway station and thence to "the further end" of the line—a line that will end, presumably, at the mansions.

Watt has been changed by his experience at Knott's. He seems to be not so much concerned with the meaning of things as with their form. Micks, waiting in the kitchen to take Watt's place, delivers a speech about himself and "Watt listened for a time, for the voice was far from unmelodious. The fricatives in particular were pleasing. But as from the proscript an encountered nightsong, so it faded, the voice of Micks, the pleasant voice of poor Micks, in the soundless tumult of the inner lamentation" (216–7). What matters to Watt is not the substance of what Micks relates, but that all words are the music of a lamentation, a lament, perhaps, to the loss of silence, a lament to futile labors. And so he makes no helpful parting speech to Micks, or so he realizes after finding himself on the road. And having arrived at the station, and perceived an apparently human figure advancing at a distance, Watt at first ruminates on what the figure might be, but then realizes that it is not necessary to be precise about this. "For Watt's concern . . . was not after all with what the figure was, in reality, but with what the figure appeared to be, in reality. For since when were Watt's concerns with what things were, in reality? But he was forever falling into this error, this error of the old days when, lacerated with curiosity, in the midst of substance shadowy he stumbled" (227). The old error is the error of reason, of trying to name what a thing is (a woman, a priest, a nun, an "inverted chamberpot"). Though "logic was on his side" (219), logic is not knowledge, or a road to knowledge, of reality. Watt assumes the figure is approaching, and waits for it, in order to know it, but the figure turns out, comically, to be moving away, and finally grows fainter and disappears. Indeed, it might have been an "hallucination" (228). With his curiosity, with his logic, Watt comes to know nothing. Logic operates in a world of forms, not "entelechies." And yet, ignoring substance and listening to the music of forms, to the formal changes of light and sound in appearances, one can sense the Nothingness of Being, the silence that words enclose, the form-giving cause rather than the existing forms. Once having been admitted to the station waiting-room, Watt "lay on a seat, without thought or sensation, except for a slight feeling of chill in one foot. In his skull the voices whispering their canon were like a patter of mice . . ." (232). He hears, once again, the music of pre-thought, proto-words, the nightsong soon to become the day labor.

The sensations and perceptions that Watt experiences in the waiting-room, as dawn slowly comes, are those of thought emerging from pre-thought, as the influence of Knott's wears off. The room, uniformly gray and white, is an image of Watt's skull, smells and sounds and light gradually entering, objects (the chair, the colored print) gradually outlined, defined and named, studied in detail. The process of coming into the world, expelled from refuge, begins once again: a "merry whistling" sounds far off and then, abruptly and violently, Mr. Nolan the signal-man unlocks the door and kicks it open, knocking Watt to the floor. "Now I am at liberty, said Watt, I am free to come and go, as I please" (238), just as Mr. Nolan told him earlier he would be. The irony is savage. The "freedom" of the outside world, with its insistence on coming and going as meaningful and purposive movement, is well symbolized by the violent blow, like the blow infants receive as an introduction and awakening to the world of forms. From the moment of Watt's being knocked to the floor unconscious, the outside world takes over the novel, and we are treated, in the last pages, to its comical inanity, cruelty, vitality, and obsession with time ("The five fifty-five will be upon us").

Eventually Watt goes on: gets up, buys a ticket to the end of the line and, characteristically, disappears. The train entering "did not take up a single passenger" (245); as in the first scene of the novel, Watt seems to vanish. In that first scene he is last glimpsed "faintly outlined against the last wisps of day" (18). At the end Watt rises from the floor just as the sun rises (243), and as he disappears, our attention is shifted from him to a goat rising from a ditch and moving away down the road, to the trembling sea and the quivering leaves (245). Watt, presumably, vanishes to the "mansions" of section III, but it is not so much an apotheosis as it is a going on, in the eternity of process, fading and reappearing like a shadow slipping through the world of forms.

Confronted with the exhilarating dawn of a summer day and forgetting the recent trouble with Watt, Mr. Gorman the station-master is moved to exclaim, "All the same . . . life isn't such a bad old bugger. He raised high his hands and spread them out, in a gesture of worship. He then replaced them in the pockets of his trousers. When all is said and done . . ." (245–6). This is at once ironic and true. It is ironic because the outside world's idea of "life" is unthinking Habit. Mr. Gorman is worshipping himself. But it is also true because life isn't so bad "when all is said and done," when the silence is reached and labor completed, if that is possible, when life is Life: pure process, "nothing at last." In the balance of Beckett's irony and lyricism, here expressed in the reviving of a cliché, is Beckett's comedy.

I have discussed Beckett's comedy as involving a constant clash between the labors of rational consciousness and the "nightsong" of lyrical rest: how each gives rise to the other, in a sinking to silence and a rising to speech, a darkening and brightening of the mind as a language-maker. It is appropriate to conclude with a brief discussion of the structure of *Watt*, since confusion over it has resulted from a failure to see it as a comic structure, full of contradiction.

Michael Robinson discusses it as some length, mentioning, among other things, that the entire book is Sam's narration, though this fact is only revealed in section III; that while III takes place *after* IV in terms of the chronology of the narration, the story that is narrated in III (Watt's stay on the first floor) fits right in chronologically, between Watt's stay on the ground floor (II) and his leaving Knott's (IV); that the shift in narrative time "adds force to the ironic ending" and results in a sandwich-like structure, "the two outside parts describing Watt's arrival and departure" creating "a satisfying unit," a closed circuit.[36] A few holes begin to appear in this rational formulation. How can Watt be said to have related to Sam the very opening and closing scenes, in which he is not present? Sam is not present either, unless we identify Sam as Hackett, which is a clever play on sounds but gets us nowhere (Hackett does not know Watt, but Sam and Watt appear to have known each other for some time). Did Sam make up the opening scene, or the very last scene, after Watt vanishes? Putting the question of the Addenda aside (who wrote those? and the footnotes?), it can be assumed that the novel follows this basic chronology: (I) Watt leaves the tram, sees Nixon, goes to the railway terminus, travels to Knott's house; (II) Watt is Knott's servant on the ground floor; (III) Watt is Knott's servant on the first floor; (IV) Watt leaves Knott's, travels to the railway station, buys a ticket and vanishes. And it can be concluded that the placing of III at the end of the novel would disrupt this chronology while satisfying another, as well as depriving the novel of a certain circularity. But what about the opening sentences of section IV, in which Sam addresses himself to the problem of the narrative, and which Robinson avoids mentioning? "As Watt told the beginning of his story, not first, but second, so not fourth, but third, now he told its end. Two, one, four, three, that was the order in which Watt told his story. Heroic quatrains are not otherwise elaborated" (215). The "four, three" order is clear, but what are we to make of "two, one"? Section II clearly comes after I, in a conventional narrative sequence. But that's Sam's sequence (presumably), and not Watt's. The more one tries to puzzle this out, the more one's thoughts take on the cast of Watt's own, and that, it seems to me, is the major and comic point.

The narrative is, rationally speaking, a bog. Section III indicates a radical distinction between the narrative *as story* (which seems to be chronologically sequential) and the narrative *as a story told* (which is certainly not chronological and, given the opening and closing scenes, not even clear). Section III accomplishes this by undermining our complacency about third-person narrations. Between event and rumination about event, there is no clear relation. Watt's reaction to the Galls incident is instructive. What we encounter, on reading this novel, is a sequence of events taking place with "formal distinctness," but the "purport" of the events has been filtered through untrustworthy minds (Watt's, Sam's, Arthur's, Beckett's) until—to paraphrase a passage on the Galls—the incident of Watt's journey ceased so rapidly to have even the paltry significance of one man, coming to serve at Knott's, serving a time, then going, that it seemed rather to belong to some story heard long before, an instant in the life of another, ill-told, ill-heard, and more than half-forgotten (74).

In other words, the formality of the story breaks down in the process of being told, and yields to a greater Formality, that of existence itself, the essential existence of men and smoke and aspens and goats and pots and stones—ancient and arresting, like the face of Mr. Nackybal. "I seem to have known him [Watt] all my life," says Mr. Nixon. Our experience of *Watt* is not an experience of a rationally sequential narration, but an experience of light and sound and change, the music of words like a night-song in our heads, heard in a ceaselessly darkening and brightening light: Hackett crying as night comes, Watt in the kitchen as dawn comes, Arthur appearing "on a morning white and soft . . . the earth . . . dressed for the grave," Watt disappearing as Case, Nolan and Gorman stand "in the early morning light" with "the sky falling to the hills, and the hills falling to the plain," ready to begin "a day's march."

It does not matter so much that someone has come and gone, or that someone has organized words to tell about it, but rather that we have sensed through these events and words the changelessness and silence in which we cannot abide. Just as Watt, on leaving Knott's, appears to be vacant of expression and touched with something not-Watt, with "entelechies" perhaps—yet these "entelechies" are "vain," and inside the passive vacancy Watt's mind is "busy, busy wondering. . . ." The comedy establishes and undercuts both the rationalism and the something that exists beyond it, the world of forms and the unknowable energy that informs it—expresses them in a dynamic relationship, as the terms of a circular paradox. In so doing, Beckett's comedy of language discovers both the absurdity and the necessity of what keeps man going on, *through* the absurdity and the necessity of his language: "But he had hardly felt the absurdity of those things, on the one hand, and the necessity of those others, on the other (for it is rare that the feeling of absurdity is not followed by the feeling of necessity), when he felt the absurdity of those things of which he had just felt the necessity (for it is rare that the feeling of necessity is not followed by the feeling of absurdity" (133).

Afterword

The quotation from Beckett with which I concluded the previous chapter can be considered a *locus classicus* for understanding the comedy of language. Watt's mental life, and the "constructions" of logic and language that issue naturally from it, are absurd in the light of an uncertain reality. For example, in the context in which this passage appears, the possibility that the length of service on Knott's ground and first floors might depend on the servants employed, on their individual and unknowable natures, exposes as absurd the "monstrous" assumptions from which Watt's mind proceeds in its determination to know. The suggestion of the "arbitrary" dispells all habits of measure and sorting. The unspeakable "being" of the world has the force of the necessary. The feeling of the absurdity of the mind's constructions brings us to a sense of the necessity of the reality that eludes them. But the very fact that the irony of exposing the constructions as illusory reveals to us something that has the strength and force of reality precludes the finality of the irony. No conclusion is reached, no resting point from which a satire on the mind and its language could be devised. Rather, only one half of the arc has been described; the arc will continue and describe the circular, paradoxical vision of the comedy of language. For Watt's mind will continue in its uncertainty. The nature of reality, which had seemed so necessary, is felt as absurd, and the mind's constructions are felt as necessary. Just as reality continues in the flux of its coming and being and going, so Watt's mind continues to contrive more arguments, to devise more assumptions in the necessity of its will to know—only to feel these constructions are absurd, and so on, *ad infinitum*. As Stevens said, "It can never be satisfied, the mind, never" (CP, 190), and *this,* its "never-resting" quality, is what puts it in touch with a reality that must continually frustrate its desire for form. In this full and ongoing movement, in which doubt and certainty are only relative, is comic joy, inextricable with comic irony.

We behold this comedy in the very language of Beckett's passage. For in the balance of the sentence lies its beauty, and in that beauty lies its peculiar impotence. When we hear the sentence it is comically pleasing in its exquisite balance of sense and nonsense. In fulfilling its circular logic, in turning back on itself, it has both sealed itself off from any realization of the world and realized the world in its infinitely repetitive, directionless flux. The full range and vital life of the metaphysic is expressed in its comedy. The contradictory heart of that comedy is what beats in Joyce's and Faulkner's and Stevens' and Beckett's sense that in the emptiness and absurdity of our attempts to make language of the world, something endures and gives life as the world does, necessarily and pointlessly and ineluctably.

In all the works I have discussed there flows "the full stream of the world," to use Shakespeare's Rosalind's words (*As You Like It*, III.iii.410–11). Her phrase specifically refers to human society in all its crazy inconstancy; she says she drove a suitor to foreswear it for the monastic life. By describing human society in such an image, she relates it to the natural world and its changeableness. It becomes, then, what Bergson simply called "the living," an imagining of the social as a realm of natural value. For the writers we have studied, "the full stream of the world" would have a metaphysical meaning. The imagination of ontological flux is in Joyce's "stream of life," Faulkner's "myriad original motion," Stevens' "River of Rivers," and Beckett's "coming and being and going," the "unintelligible succession of changes." By its very "unintelligible" nature it is beyond conception and valuation. It flows through the minds of the comic protagonists like a nightsong or dayvision, and gives their comic adventures a peculiar gravity or gaiety, as the case may be. It appears as a "floating opera" in John Barth's novel of that name, and helps the protagonist to understand that a vision of pure relativity need not be a vision of despair, since despair is conclusive. It can be heard in the train whistles and window-banging and the tapping of night watchmen in Chekhov's comic plays. It is the ineffably strange country in which K. in Kafka's *The Castle* finds himself, where nothing is certain, and in which he must vow to himself that, "however difficult the way and however doubtful even the prospect of his being able to get back, he would not cease from going on."[1]

What drives the protagonists "on" in this reality is their attempt to conceive of it, and so to find a home in it, and this is the source of the comedy. It is this drive that makes them, in Chekhov's funny phrase, "stumble even on a smooth road."[2] For their attempts to conceive of this reality in language will make them stumble indeed, even when there are no natural obstacles, but merely the mysterious otherness of the world. Nevertheless, in their going on, their search to make forms of the formless, they imitate in an expressive way the reality that frustrates them. Their continuous failure pulls them fully into the world of change, the life of things.

The stress and effect that this vision of reality has on language has been my constant subject. An intense light is turned on its operations, a light that exposes its inadequacies and illuminates its beauty. If the modern need is for language to express the inexpressible, fix what cannot be fixed, that need cannot be satisfied with language's failure; it must make of its failure a celebration. The mechanisms of language, revealed in puns, wordplay, nonsense, rhetorical inflation, and so on—the sudden revelations of how *incumbent* language is on the world we presumed to perceive through it—are, of course, the great source of all verbal comedy. But in modern comedy that assumes the reality of change I have described, language becomes all that we have, because reality cannot declare itself.

The comedians of language want to make us aware of the wrongness of language, its comically stumbling attempts to contain the flow of reality, and at the same time make us aware of the ability of language, through the acknowledgement of its wrongness, to achieve an expression of reality that could not otherwise be achieved. This balance between failure and success can only be struck through a constant comic tension and interplay. This is Humbert Humbert's description, in Nabokov's *Lolita*, of the comic artist: "We all admire the spangled acrobat with classical grace meticulously walking his tight rope in the talcum light; but how much rarer art there is in the sagging rope expert wearing scarecrow clothes and impersonating a grotesque drunk!"[3] Nabokov speaks of his own art here, and it is one way of describing the art of the comic writers I've discussed. They have no interest in the illusion of ease, in the art that conceals art. Their skill is revealed in a comedy that throws skill into question. They make us aware of the mechanisms of skill (failure, recovery from failure, and so on) so that we never forget the depths that lie below the thread of our language.

Notes

The Comedy of Language

1. James Joyce, *Ulysses* (New York: The Modern Library, 1961), p. 684.
2. Samuel Beckett, *Three Novels: Molloy, Malone Dies, The Unnamable* (New York: Grove Press, 1965), p. 249. Hereafter abbreviated in text as Trilogy.
3. Wallace Stevens, *The Collected Poems* (New York: Knopf, 1967), p. 75.
4. Donald Barthelme, "A Shower of Gold," *Come Back, Dr. Caligari* (Garden City, N.Y.: Doubleday, 1964), p. 138.
5. Vladimir Nabokov, *Lolita* (New York: Fawcett, 1959), p. 32.
6. Wylie Sypher, "The Meanings of Comedy," Appendix to *Comedy* (Garden City, N.Y.: Doubleday, 1956), p. 193
7. Henri Bergson, "Laughter," in Sypher, *Comedy*, p. 65. Quotations from text hereafter cited in parentheses.
8. Sigmund Freud, *Jokes and Their Relation to the Unconscious*, trans. James Strachey (New York: Norton, 1963), p. 149. It is worth noting in this context that Freud's analysis of laughter appears in a chapter entitled "Jokes as a Social Process."
9. Henri Bergson, "On the Nature of the Soul," Lecture 2 in *Les Etudes Bergsoniennes*, VII (1966).
10. Henri Bergson, *An Introduction to Metaphysics*, trans. T. E. Hulme, 2nd ed. (Indianapolis: Bobbs-Merrill, 1955), p. 44.
11. Bergson, *Metaphysics*, p. 53.
12. Bergson, *Metaphysics*, pp. 48–9, 51.
13. See pp. 49–53, from which all the quotations in this paragraph are taken.
14. Albert Cook, *The Dark Voyage and the Golden Mean: A Philosophy of Comedy* (Cambridge, Mass.: Harvard University Press, 1949), pp. 3–28. Quotations from text hereafter cited in parentheses.
15. Miguel de Cervantes Saavedra, *The Adventures of Don Quixote*, trans. J. M. Cohen (Baltimore, Penguin Books, 1950), p. 940.
16. Jorge Luis Borges, "Partial Magic in the Quixote," trans. James E. Irby, in *Labyrinths*, ed. Donald A. Yates and James E. Irby (New York: New Directions, 1964), p. 194.

17. Morris Kline, *Mathematics in Western Culture* (New York: Oxford University Press, 1953) p. 377. See also chapters XXIII and XIV.
18. Robert Corrigan, ed., *Comedy: Meaning and Form* (San Francisco: Chandler, 1965). Hereafter cited as Corrigan, *Comedy*.
19. Corrigan, "Introduction" to *Comedy*, p. 3.
20. Corrigan, *Comedy*, p. 6.
21. Benjamin Lehmann, "Comedy and Laughter," in Corrigan, *Comedy*, p. 166.
22. L. J. Potts, "The Subject Matter of Comedy," in Corrigan, *Comedy*, p. 207.
23. Harold Watts, "The Sense of Regain: A Theory of Comedy," in Corrigan, *Comedy*, pp. 195–6.
24. Northrop Frye, *Anatomy of Criticism: Four Essays* (Princeton, N.J.: Princeton University Press, 1957), p. 43. See also pp. 163–86.
25. William F. Lynch, S.J., *Christ and Apollo: The Dimensions of the Literary Imagination* (New York: Sheed and Ward, 1960), p. 110. Quotations from text hereafter cited in parentheses.
26. Friedrich Duerrenmatt, "Problems of the Theatre," in *The Context and Craft of Drama*, ed. Robert Corrigan and James Rosenberg (San Francisco: Chandler, 1964), p. 266. First published in *Tulane Drama Review*, 3, no. 1 (1958), 3–26, trans. Gerhard Nellhaus.
27. Arthur Koestler, *The Act of Creation* (New York: Dell, 1964). Quotations from text hereafter cited in parentheses.
28. R. W. B. Lewis, "The Aspiring Clown," in *Learners and Discerners: A Newer Criticism*, ed. Robert Scholes (Charlottesville, Va.: University Press of Virginia, 1964), p. 70.
29. Lewis, p. 108.
30. Albert Camus, *The Myth of Sisyphus and Other Essays*, trans. Justin O'Brien (New York: Vintage Books, 1955), see pp. 37–8. Quotations from text hereafter cited in parentheses.
31. See pp. 88–91. All of the quotations in the following paragraph are taken from these pages.
32. Loren Eisely, *The Immense Journey* (New York: Vintage Books, 1957), p. 182.
33. Allen Wheelis, *The End of the Modern Age* (New York: Harper and Row, 1971), p. 64. Emphasis mine.
34. Susanne K. Langer, *Philosophy in a New Key* (New York: New American Library, 1951), p. 78. Ms. Langer is commenting on Carnap's *The Logical Syntax of Language*.
35. Langer, see particularly pp. 45–9.
36. Henri Bergson, *Creative Evolution* (New York: The Modern Library, 1944), p. 173. All quotations from the following paragraph can be found on pp. 173–6, 354.
37. Beckett, *Three Novels*, p. 88.
38. Samuel Beckett, *Watt* (New York: Grove Press, 1959), p. 133.
39. Beckett, *Watt*, p. 83.
40. Beckett, *Watt*, p. 117.
41. Martin Heidegger, *Existence and Being*, Introduction and analysis by Werner Brock (Chicago: Henry Regnery, 1949), p. 266. Quotations from text hereafter cited in parentheses.
42. Implicit in the passage just quoted is a near contempt for the "ordinary" idea that words are "empty." The poet is said to "descend" to the phrase, "Foolish is my speech." In comedies of language (and Holderlin is not a comic poet, I repeat), the idea of language as an empty illusion is of equal significance to the idea of language as

joyous. Heidegger's tone in both his essays on Holderlin is more affirmative and elegiac than it is skeptical. Its keynote is the power of poetry. This places it, tonally, at a great remove from, say, Samuel Beckett's comic and acerbic "Three Dialogues," but the ideas are still strikingly similar.

43. Susanne K. Langer, *Feeling and Form* (New York: Scribner's, 1953), pp. 326–50.
44. Langer, *Philosophy in a New Key*, p. 47.
45. See Langer, *Feeling and Form*, p. 331.
46. Heidegger, p. 185.
47. Frank Kermode, *The Sense of an Ending* (London: Oxford University Press, 1967), p. 45.
48. Duerrenmatt, p. 265.

Joyce: *Ulysses*

1. Ezra Pound, "James Joyce: to His Memory," a 1941 broadcast, in *Pound/Joyce: The Letters of Ezra Pound to James Joyce, with Pound's Essays on Joyce*, ed. Forrest Read (London: Faber & Faber, 1967), p. 271.
2. Frank Budgen, *James Joyce and the Making of "Ulysses"* (Bloomington, Ind.: Indiana University Press, 1961), pp. 71–2.
3. S. L. Goldberg, in his *James Joyce* (New York: Grove Press, 1962), calls *Ulysses* a comedy, but does not discuss it as such beyond mentioning that Joyce affirms a "deeper, more joyful, more inclusive mode of living," or a "spirit of life which is manifest not merely in traditional myths but also in the very creation of myths." See pp. 69, 78, 98–9.
4. *The Critical Writings of James Joyce*, ed. Ellsworth Mason and Richard Ellmann (London: Faber & Faber, 1959), p. 144.
5. Ibid., p. 144.
6. Harry Levin, *James Joyce: A Critical Introduction* (Norfolk, Conn.: New Directions, 1960), p. 130. All following passages are quoted from pp. 129–35.
7. Budgen, p. 90.
8. L. A. Murillo, *The Cyclical Night: Irony in James Joyce and Jorge Luis Borges* (Cambridge, Mass.: Harvard University Press, 1968), pp. 50–1. All following passages are quoted from pp. 38–51.
9. A. Walton Litz, *James Joyce* (New York: Twayne Publishers, 1966), p. 93.
10. Litz, pp. 81, 95.
11. Arnold Goldman, *The Joyce Paradox: Form and Freedom in his Fiction* (Evanston, Ill.: Northwestern University Press, 1966), p. 83.
12. James Joyce, *Ulysses* (New York: The Modern Library, 1961), p. 3. Quotations from text hereafter cited in parentheses.
13. Budgen is especially good on "Proteus." See pp. 48–50.
14. Budgen, p. 258.
15. Levin, p. 122.
16. William B. Warner, "The Play of Fictions and Succession of Styles in *Ulysses*," *James Joyce Quarterly*, XV, 1 (Fall 1977), p. 33.
17. Warner, p. 33. See also Budgen, p. 257.
18. Stanley Sultan, *The Argument of "Ulysses"* (Columbus, Ohio, 1964), p. 382. Quoted in Richard K. Cross, *Flaubert and Joyce: The Rite of Fiction* (Princeton, N.J.: Princeton University Press, 1971), p. 158.

19. Donald Barthelme, an acknowledged Joycean, has more than any other modern writer explored the comic possibilities of catechism. See, for example, "The Catechist," in *Sadness* (New York: Bantam Books, 1974).

20. Quoted in Hélène Cixous, *The Exile of James Joyce*, trans. Sally A. J. Purcell (London: John Calder, 1976), p. 733.

21. William F. Lynch, S.J., *Christ and Apollo: The Dimensions of the Literary Imagination* (New York: Sheed & Ward, 1960), p. 136.

22. Richard Martin Adams, *Surface and Symbol: The Consistency of James Joyce's "Ulysses"* (New York: Oxford University Press, 1962), p. 82.

23. Elizabeth Sewell, *The Field of Nonsense* (London: Chatto & Windus, 1952), see pp. 82, 100–1.

24. Budgen, p. 262.

25. Adams, p. 255.

26. Warner, p. 34.

27. His exact words, in a letter of October 7, 1921, were "The 'Ithaca' episode is in reality the end as *Penelope* has no beginning, middle or end." Quoted in Goldman, p. 110.

Faulkner: *As I Lay Dying*

1. Alfred Kazin, *Bright Book of Life: American Novelists and Storytellers from Hemingway to Mailer* (Boston: Atlantic/Little, Brown, 1973), p. 33.

2. Olga Vickery, "*As I Lay Dying*," *Perspective*, 3 (Autumn, 1950), 179–91, reprinted in *The Novels of William Faulkner: A Critical Interpretation* (Baton Rouge: Louisiana State University Press, 1959, rev. ed. 1964); Jack Gordon Goellner, "A Closer Look at *As I Lay Dying*," *Perspective*, 7 (Spring, 1954), 42–54; Joseph L. Blotner, "*As I Lay Dying*: Christian Lore and Irony," *Twentieth Century Literature*, 3 (April, 1957), 14–9; Hyatt H. Waggoner, *William Faulkner: From Jefferson to the World* (Lexington: University of Kentucky Press, 1959); Cleanth Brooks, *William Faulkner: The Yoknapatawpha Country* (New Haven, Ct.: Yale University Press, 1963); J. M. Mellard, "Faulkner's Philosophical Novel: Ontological Themes in *As I Lay Dying*," The *Personalist*, 48 (Autumn, 1967), 509–23; Calvin Bedient, "Pride and Nakedness: *As I Lay Dying*," *MLQ*, 29 (March, 1968), 61–76.

3. Roma King, Jr., "The Janus Symbol in *As I Lay Dying*," *The University of Kansas City Review*, 21 (Summer, 1955), 287–90; Edward Wasiolek, "*As I Lay Dying*: Distortion in the Slow Eddy of Current Opinion," *Critique*, 3 (Spring-Fall, 1959), 15–23; Edmond L. Volpe, *A Reader's Guide to William Faulkner* (New York: Noonday Press, 1964).

4. Irving Howe, *William Faulkner: A Critical Study* (New York: Vintage Books, 1962), p. 189.

5. William Faulkner, *As I Lay Dying* (New York: Vintage Books, 1957), p. 26. Quotations from text hereafter cited in parentheses when they cannot be located from context.

6. Richard P. Adams, *Faulkner: Myth and Motion* (Princeton, N.J.: Princeton University Press, 1968), p. 72.

7. Lawrence LeShan, "Human Survival of Biological Death," *Main Currents in Modern Thought*, 26, no. 2 (Nov.-Dec., 1969), 35–45.

8. See Karl E. Zink, "Flux and the Frozen Moment: The Imagery of Stasis in Faulkner's Prose," *PMLA*, 71 (June, 1956), 285–301.

9. Hugh Kenner, *Flaubert, Joyce and Beckett: The Stoic Comedians* (Boston: Beacon Press, 1962), p. 48.
10. Samuel Beckett, *Proust* (New York: Grove Press, 1931), p. 8.
11. Hugh Kenner, *The Counterfeiters: An Historical Comedy* (Garden City, N.Y.: Doubleday, 1973), pp. 31–55.
12. Vickery, p. 240.
13. Panthea Reid Broughton, *William Faulkner: The Abstract and the Actual* (Baton Rouge: Louisiana State University Press, 1974), p. 192.
14. Bedient, p. 71.

Wallace Stevens: The Poet as Comedian

1. Wallace Stevens, *The Collected Poems* (New York: Alfred Knopf, 1967), p. 154. Hereafter abbreviated CP and cited in parentheses in the text.
2. Wallace Stevens, *Opus Posthumous,* ed. Samuel French Morse (New York: Alfred Knopf, 1957), p. 158. Hereafter abbreviated OP and cited in parentheses in the text.
3. Wallace Stevens, *The Necessary Angel: Essays on Reality and the Imagination* (New York: Random House, 1951), p. 14. Hereafter abbreviated NA and cited in parentheses in the text. The Bergson quotation is from *Creative Evolution* (New York: The Modern Library, 1944) p. 4.
4. *Letters of Wallace Stevens*, ed. Holly Stevens (New York: Alfred Knopf, 1977), p. 294.
5. Frank Doggett, *Stevens' Poetry of Thought* (Baltimore: Johns Hopkins Press, 1966), p. 22.
6. See Eugene Paul Nassar, *Wallace Stevens: An Anatomy of Configuration* (Philadelphia: University of Pennsylvania Press, 1965), pp. 64–7, 141. Without benefit of Shakespeare, he comes to similar conclusions.
7. Doggett, p. 25.
8. Joseph N. Riddel, *The Clairvoyant Eye: The Poetry and Poetics of Wallace Stevens* (Baton Rouge: Louisiana State University Press, 1956) p. 89.
9. See Stevens, NA, pp. 13–27.
10. James Baird, *The Dome and the Rock: Structure in the Poetry of Wallace Stevens* (Baltimore: Johns Hopkins Press, 1968), p. 102.
11. See R. W. B. Lewis, "The Aspiring Clown" in *Learners and Discerners: A Newer Criticism,* ed. Robert Scholes (Charlottesville, Va.: University Press of Virginia, 1964), p. 97.
12. William F. Lynch, S.J., *Christ and Apollo: The Dimensions of the Literary Imagination* (New York: Sheed and Ward, 1960), p. 91.
13. See Wallace Stevens, *Mattino Domenicale ed altre poesie,* trans. Renato Poggioli (Torino: Giulio Einaudi, 1954), p. 179.
14. Riddel, p. 98.
15. Helen H. Vendler, *On Extended Wings: Wallace Stevens' Longer Poems* (Cambridge, Mass.: Harvard University Press, 1969), p. 43.
16. Vendler, p. 43.
17. See in particular Hi Simons, " 'The Comedian as the Letter C': Its Sense and Significance," in *The Achievement of Wallace Stevens,* ed. Ashley Brown and Robert S. Haller (Philadelphia: University of Pennsylvania Press, 1962), pp. 97–113.
18. Daniel Fuchs, *The Comic Spirit of Wallace Stevens* (Durham, N.C.: Duke University Press, 1963), p. 55.

19. *Letters*, pp. 351–2.
20. *Letters*, p. 352.
21. Henri Bergson, *An Introduction to Metaphysics*, 2nd ed., trans. T. E. Hulme (Indianapolis: Bobbs-Merrill, 1955), p. 28.
22. Hugh Kenner, *Flaubert, Joyce and Beckett: The Stoic Comedians* (Boston: Beacon Press, 1962), p. 106.
23. In "Wallace Stevens, Bergson, Pater," in *The Act of the Mind: Essays on the Poetry of Wallace Stevens*, ed. Roy Harvey Pearce and J. Hillis Miller (Baltimore: Johns Hopkins Press, 1965), pp. 58–91.
24. Fuchs, pp. 23–4.
25. Vendler, pp. 38–9.
26. Baird, p. 194.
27. See Samuel French Morse, OP, p. xxiii.
28. Baird, p. 194.
29. See Lewis for an exegesis of Hart Crane's poem, "Chaplinesque," from which this line is quoted.
30. Bergson, *Creative Evolution*, pp. 175–6.
31. Bergson, *An Introduction to Metaphysics*, pp. 27–8.

Samuel Beckett: *Watt*

1. Samuel Beckett, *Stories and Texts for Nothing* (New York: Grove Press, 1967), p. 70. Hereafter cited in parentheses in the text, and abbreviated *Stories*.
2. Wallace Stevens, *The Collected Poems* (New York: Alfred Knopf, 1967), pp. 525–6.
3. Samuel Beckett, *Three Novels: Molloy, Malone Dies, The Unnamable* (New York: Grove Press, 1958), p. 291. Hereafter cited in parentheses in the text, and abbreviated Trilogy.
4. J. D. O'Hara, "About Structure in *Malone Dies*," in *Twentieth Century Interpretations of Molloy, Malone Dies, The Unnamable*, ed. J. D. O'Hara (Englewood Cliffs, N.J.: Prentice-Hall, 1970), p. 67.
5. Quoted in J. P. Lebel, *Buster Keaton*, trans. P. D. Stovin (London: A. Zwemmer Ltd., 1967), p. 156.
6. Samuel Beckett, *Watt* (New York: Grove Press, 1970), p. 74. Hereafter cited in parentheses in the text, without title.
7. Eugene Fink, "The Oasis of Happiness: Toward an Ontology of Play," trans. Ute and Thomas Saine, in *Game, Play, Literature*, ed. Jacques Ehrmann (Boston: Beacon Press, 1968), p. 21.
8. Fink, p. 21.
9. Quoted in Lebel, p. 156.
10. Samuel Beckett, *Proust* (New York: Grove Press, 1931), p. 14. Hereafter cited in parentheses in the text.
11. Richard N. Coe, *Samuel Beckett* (New York: Grove Press, 1964), p. 77.
12. Samuel Beckett, *Murphy* (New York: Grove Press, 1957), p. 14. Hereafter cited in parentheses in the text.
13. In *Transition*, 16–7 (June, 1929), 244.
14. Coe, p. 52.
15. Coe, p. 2.
16. In *Samuel Beckett: A Collection of Critical Essays*, ed. Martin Esslin (Englewood Cliffs, N.J.: Prentice-Hall, 1965), pp. 16–22.

17. Samuel Beckett, "Three Dialogues," in Esslin, ed., p. 20.

18. "Three Dialogues," in Esslin, ed., p. 21.

19. Northrop Frye, "The Nightmare Life in Death," *The Hudson Review*, 13 (Autumn, 1960), 449.

20. Hugh Kenner, *Samuel Beckett: A Critical Study*, new ed. (Berkeley: University of California Press, 1968), p. 109.

21. Kenner, *Samuel Beckett*, p. 99.

22. William F. Fry, *Sweet Madness: A Study of Humor* (Palo Alto, Calif.: Pacific Books, 1963). See chapters VII and VIII. The theologian Harvey Cox, in his chapter, "Christ the Harlequin" from *The Feast of Fools* (Cambridge, Mass.: Harvard University Press, 1969), also discusses how both Christ and the spirit of "play" involve the bringing together of "disparate spheres" (155) in a paradoxical relation. Christ as both human and divine and hence a paradoxically comic character is an idea that will be taken up later in my own exegesis of *Watt*.

23. Fry, p. 147.

24. Sigmund Freud, *Jokes and Their Relation to the Unconscious*, trans. James Strachey (New York: W. W. Norton, 1963), pp. 130–1.

25. Jacqueline Hoefer, "*Watt*," in Esslin, ed., p. 75.

26. Coe, p. 5.

27. Coe, p. 46.

28. See Ruby Cohn, "*Watt* in the Light of *The Castle*," *Comparative Literature*, 13 (Spring, 1961), 154–66.

29. Hugh Kenner, *The Counterfeiters: An Historical Comedy* (Garden City, N.Y.: Doubleday, 1973), pp. 31–55.

30. This adventure occurs at the end of chapter III ("Looking-Glass Insects") of *Through the Looking-Glass*.

31. See Michael Robinson, *The Long Sonata of the Dead: A Study of Samuel Beckett* (New York: Grove Press, 1969), p. 102*ff* for an intelligent discussion of this; and Raymond Federman, *Journey to Chaos: Samuel Beckett's Early Fiction* (Berkeley: University of California Press, 1965), p. 100*ff* for an unintelligent discussion of it.

32. Robinson, p. 127.

33. Sören Kierkegaard, *Concluding Unscientific Postscript*, trans. David F. Swenson and Walter Lowrie (Princeton, N.J.: Princeton University Press, 1971), p. 84.

34. John J. Mood, " 'The Personal System'—Samuel Beckett's Watt," *PMLA*, 86, no. 2 (March, 1971), 264, 256.

35. Wallace Stevens, *The Necessary Angel: Essays on Reality and the Imagination* (New York: Random House, 1951), pp. 44, 49.

36. Robinson, pp. 101–3.

Afterword

1. Franz Kafka, *The Castle*, trans. Willa and Edwin Muir (Middlesex, England: Penguin Books, 1966), p. 34.

2. Anton Chekhov, *Ward Six and Other Stories*, trans. Ann Dunnigan (New York: New American Library, 1965), p. 159.

3. Vladimir Nabokov, *Lolita* (Greenwich, Conn.: Fawcett Publications, 1959), p. 227.

Index

227297

Library of Congress Cataloging in Publication Data
Robinson, Fred Miller, 1942–
The comedy of language.
Bibliography: p.
Includes index.
1.American literature—20th century—History and
criticism.   2.Comic, The.   3.English fiction—
Irish authors—History and Criticism.   4.English
fiction—20th century—History and criticism.
1.Title.
PS228.C59R6   820'.9'17   80–125
ISBN 0–87023–297–5